THE MOJO HANDBOOK

The Mojo Handbook: Theory to Praxis offers a detailed and engaging crash course on how to use mobile tools to create powerful journalistic stories.

Drawing on both theoretical underpinnings and practical techniques, the book outlines the fundamentals of mobile journalism methods, by placing mobile storytelling within a wider context of current affairs, documentary filmmaking and public relations. The book offers expert advice for how to use storytelling skills to transform mobile content into engaging and purposeful user-generated stories for audiences. Topics covered include tips for recording dynamic video and clean audio, conducting interviews on your phone and editing and post-production processes, as well as advice on how to handle copyright issues and a primer on journalistic ethics. The book also includes a comprehensive glossary of terms to help students navigate the video production and mobile journalism world.

The Mojo Handbook is a valuable resource for aspiring multimedia professionals in journalism, strategic and corporate communication, community and education, as well as anyone looking to incorporate mobile into their visual storytelling tool kit.

Ivo Burum, PhD, lectures in media industries, mobile and digital journalism and television at La Trobe University in Melbourne. A journalist and award-winning television executive producer and director, he is a self-shot pioneer who has worked extensively across genres including frontline international current affairs. He runs Burum Media, a mojo and web TV consultancy that provides mojo training for journalists, students and remote marginalised communities. This is his fourth book on mobile journalism.

"Whether you're a beginner MOJO learner or a leading expert, you'll find *The Mojo Handbook* an inspiration."

–**Rana Sabbagh**, MENA Editor at the Organized Crime and Corruption Reporting Project (OCCRP)

"Ivo Burum is the Mojo Master. Few people on the planet know as much as he does about mobile journalism. He combines practical video experience and global context with high intelligence and precise technical skills."

–**Stephen Quinn**, PhD, professor of mobile journalism at Kristiania University in Norway

"Ivo Burum has the rare ability of working in the sweet spot between practical journalism and the academic world, combining technical skills with professional storytelling."

–**Geir Ruud**, Norwegian National News Agency

THE MOJO HANDBOOK

Theory to Praxis

IVO BURUM

Routledge
Taylor & Francis Group
NEW YORK AND LONDON

First published 2021
by Routledge
52 Vanderbilt Avenue, New York, NY 10017

and by Routledge
2 Park Square, Milton Park, Abingdon, Oxon, OX14 4RN

Routledge is an imprint of the Taylor & Francis Group, an informa business

Library of Congress Cataloging-in-Publication Data
Names: Burum, Ivo, author.
Title: The MOJO handbook : theory to praxis / Ivo Burum.
Other titles: Mobile journalist handbook
Description: New York : Routledge, 2020. | Includes bibliographical references and index.
Identifiers: LCCN 2020012127 | ISBN 9780367332624 (paperback) | ISBN 9780367332617 (hardback) | ISBN 9780429318924 (ebook)
Subjects: LCSH: Online journalism—Handbooks, manuals, etc. | Citizen journalism—Handbooks, manuals, etc. | Digital storytelling—Handbooks, manuals, etc. | Broadcast journalism—Handbooks, manuals, etc.
Classification: LCC PN4784.O62 B85 2020 | DDC 070.4—dc23
LC record available at https://lccn.loc.gov/2020012127

ISBN: 9780367332617 (hbk)
ISBN: 9780367332624 (pbk)
ISBN: 9780429318924 (ebk)

Typeset in Akzidenz-Grotesk and Franklin Gothic
by codeMantra

To all the people who have trusted me to let me into their lives to tell their yarns over more than 30 years of global storytelling, thank you. To the teachers who over those years helped steer me through journalism's and television's difficult balancing act—the battle between the budget, being creative, staying sane and meeting deadlines—thank you. To Tony, Steven and Stephen, Peter, Harley, Drew, Roger, Geir, Rana, Erik, Ili, Aiden, Philip, Mark, Justine, Jo, Magne and Dave—to all of you and the many others—the continued development of this work is testament to your support—thank you.

CONTENTS

P XVI **LIST OF FIGURES AND TABLES**

P XXII **FOREWORD**

P XXVI **PREFACE**

P 2 **CHAPTER 1**
INTRODUCTION

The history of journalism is tied to the evolution of technology. The advent of TV meant that by the 1950s broadcast TV news was challenging newspapers for supremacy. Just as TV became a watershed for news publication, so too would digital. The lure of the digital revolution and cheaper, more streamlined technology led to a slew of new hybrid forms. One of those was a self-shot form called video journalism. From 1995, the Internet enabled even more citizens to bypass network gatekeepers and publish their own content. This relatively free and limitless publication platform and the eventual proliferation of affordable mobile devices, with an already rampant voyeuristic TV culture, increased the level of self-shot production. Mobile journalism (mojo) is a storytelling form using a smartphone or hybrid forms to create and edit video and audio into complete stories for publication on radio, TV, social media and various other platforms. In global conflict situations including revolution (Arab Spring) and pandemics (COVID-19) the mobile enables communication, story and program production to continue. This chapter establishes the mojo timeline and

introduces the concept of mobile journalism before introducing convergence and the current impact of mobile on the news business.

P 14 **CHAPTER 2**
MOJO TOOLS

Three billion smartphone users use more than 6 million apps to upload more than 500 hours of user-generated content (UGC) every minute. Journalist Charles Feldman (2008) called this 24/7 convergent clickstream an "information tsunami." I see it as an opportunity to teach a common digital language (CDL) to enable cross-genre mobile storytelling and a more effective use of a growing list of mobile tools. In this chapter we learn how to choose a mobile phone for doing mobile journalism (mojo), which mobile apps are essential, and about the microphones and other peripheral hardware mojos use to create user-generated stories (UGS).

P 50 **CHAPTER 3**
DEVELOPING MOJO STORIES

This chapter introduces concepts of mobile video story development, audience and angle. Transforming user-generated content (UGC) into user-generated stories (UGS) and user-generated programs (UGP) at source can create a greater level of diversity. To enable this to occur we introduce the SCRAP story tool with a focus on story, character and structure. We discuss the value of knowing your audience, choosing the correct style and having a strong story focus. The chapter introduces an investigative approach and discusses Mark Lee Hunter's tool kit, before suggesting the need for a common digital language across the mobile content creation sphere.

P 70 **CHAPTER 4**
RECORDING MOJO STORIES

Shooting video can be a time-consuming task fraught with variables like changing light, noisy locations and talent that won't play ball. It's the same whether you use a big expensive camera or a smartphone. Video stories require pictures. How we plan and shoot these is discussed in this chapter. The multi-award-winning cameraman, former executive producer of *Foreign Correspondent* and producer at ABC investigative series *Four Corners*, Wayne Harley, provides a Break-out Box of tips, as does talented RTÉ mobile journalist Philip Bromwell.

P 96 **CHAPTER 5**
RECORDING AUDIO ON A SMARTPHONE

Recording audio on a smartphone is not unlike recording audio for video, except mojos will generally not work with a sound recordist. This chapter explores recording audio situations including actuality and interviews, recording narration, hardware and software, and includes recording tips and developing an audio strategy. In particular, we look at how to record a location interview and we explore the various microphones used to record mojo audio. Award-winning sound recordist Roger Van Wensveen provides expert opinion and a Break-out Box.

P 116 **CHAPTER 6**

RECORDING AN INTERVIEW

We live in an interview age where everyone with a mobile is a potential interviewer. In this chapter we define interview styles, explore interview questions, learn how to prepare and record a video interview and consider ethical aspects. Former foreign correspondent and Australia's leading interviewer, Walkley Award-winning journalist and broadcaster Tony Jones provides specialist comment and a Break-out Box of tips.

P 132 **CHAPTER 7**

WRITING MOJO STORIES

Aristotle said, when story dies we are left with decadence. The responsibility of the press, recognised by its Fourth Estate role as advocate and political watchdog, is to investigate the facts and write and report the story. In a convergent ecosphere where video is critical to driving traffic across screens and platforms, writing is still a key binding agent. Mojos write video and audio scripts, pieces to camera, and narration to segue between grabs and bridge story moments. They write headlines and introductory paragraphs for online stories. These skills enable mojos to write in and out of pictures and sound bites. This chapter introduces these skills and provides Break-out Boxes of tips by eminent radio and video journalists, including award-winning RTÉ mojo Philip Bromwell.

P 200 **CHAPTER 10**

MOJO IN THE AGE OF SOCIAL MEDIA

The emergence of network societies has ushered in a new global communications sphere defined by mobile, instant messaging and social media. Accordingly, the notion of a public sphere defined by a nation-state has shifted to one increasingly built around social platforms and global communications. An effective public sphere enables citizens to have a voice, something social media and new technologies potentially facilitate, especially in marginalised communities. In this chapter we use a social media event to explore trends in social interaction and content creation and introduce strategies mojos might use to help their stories get heard above the online noise.

P 228 **CHAPTER 11**

MOBILE STREAMING

This chapter explores the amazingly visceral world of mobile streaming to social media and proprietary sites. A theoretical and a practical approach describes the nuts and bolts of streaming from your smartphone—everything from planning your live stream, streaming tips, platform options, streaming apps, gear and understanding codecs. Streaming expert, renowned radio producer and reporter, Peter Stewart, author of *The Live Streaming Handbook*, provides expert advice and a Break-out Box of streaming tips.

FIGURES AND TABLES

FIGURES

TABLES

FOREWORD

by Rana Sabbagh

Whether you're a beginner and slow mojo learner like me, or a top expert, you'll find *The Mojo Handbook: Theory to Praxis* as inspirational as Ivo.

He blends his professional expertise with academic theory and research and passion to pass on vital knowledge. Knowledge that teaches a common digital language (CDL) to enable cross-genre mobile storytelling and how to use a growing list of mobile tools and applications to help create user-generated stories.

Each of the 14 chapters in this must-have book works with theory and its application, followed with tips from international award-winning mojo experts who have a demonstrated ability to convert their mentees into mojo disciples.

Ivo works globally, and in the MENA region he has shaped the professional lives of hundreds of brave Arab investigative reporters trained by him on basic and advanced mojo along with impactful storytelling. Ivo's training has been a blessing in disguise to Arab journalists, performing one of the riskiest jobs in the world's most dangerous area, a region where a camera crew filming in public with no permission can be arrested or attacked. Over 500 Arab journalists who have worked with support from Arab Reporters for Investigative Journalism (ARIJ), promoting the hitherto unknown culture of "accountability journalism," have been through his specialised workshops. Others have attended his guerrilla mojo trainings at the annual ARIJ Forum, the only such gathering for Arab investigative journalists and editors in the region.

In the past five years, several of the "Ivo Disciples," as many beneficiaries of his training like to refer to themselves, have used his avant-garde training and story-telling techniques to engage in compelling stories and produce award-winning investigations in the largely autocratic region. They include Osama Al-Deeb in Egypt, Mohamed Adnen Chaouachi of Tunisia, and Ruba Anebtawi in Jerusalem. So inspired by Ivo, Osama worked hard on developing his skill set to become a certified mojo and new media trainer at the prestigious American University of Cairo (AUC). Tunisian journalist and TV producer Mohamed Adnen Chaouachi, also one of Ivo's trainees, is now trainer at the pan-Arab Al-Jazeera Media Center, training hundreds of Arab journalists on mobile journalism every year. And investigative reporter Anebtawi is using her mobile to film, edit and broadcast on her website short documentaries promoting environmentally friendly practices.

In all our trainings over the years, Ivo always got the highest rankings in evaluations by those he trained. What they love about him most is his ability to combine and pass on his expertise as journalist, TV producer, author of several mojo books, TV executive and lecturer at La Trobe University in a very simple and innovative manner. They have enjoyed the Ivo minting process. His new book includes lessons learned during those and the hundreds of other training workshops he's run in more than 40 countries.

His name will go down in history as mojo magician, guru trainer and innovator in mobile journalism and new media.

Rana Sabbagh 2020

Rana Sabbagh is MENA editor at the Sarajevo-based Organized Crime and Corruption Reporting Project (OCCRP), working with Arab journalists to produce high-quality, ambitious, cross-border investigations under difficult conditions. She is also co-founder of the award-winning Arab Reporters for Investigative Journalism (ARIJ), launched in 2005. She ran the ARIJ network for 14 years until the end of 2019, promoting free speech, human rights and gender equality. As the former chief editor of the *Jordan Times*, she became the first Arab woman journalist to run a political daily in the history of the Levant. Before that, she was a correspondent for Reuters. She holds a Master's in Positive Leadership and Strategy from the IE University in Madrid.

PREFACE

Figure 0.1 Ivo Burum using Beastgrip Pro.

Ivo Burum

Mobile journalism (mojo) is a digital storytelling form using a smartphone to create and edit video and audio into complete stories for publication on radio, TV, social media and various other platforms. Mojo's story-centric and audience focus means that hybrid workflows can include DSLRs and/or laptops.

The mojo described in *The Mojo Handbook: Theory to Praxis* was developed over more than 30 years of television production and journalism experience across a variety of factual genres: documentary, magazine, current affairs, history, gardening, motoring, reality, news, docudrama and self-shot formats. It's a skill base that's relevant to the current and next and third stage of mojo development—multi-story series and user-generated programs (UGP) created by professionals, community and students.

The book outlines a set of cross-genre development tools that work in any mojo story or program context. Whether trying to decide on a story-defining shot, racing the clock on nightly turn-around production, or making a movie of your dear old mum, the mojo skills discussed in this book help you stay ahead of your deadline and stand out from the social media pack.

The Mojo Handbook: Theory to Praxis provides a complete easy-to-follow road map to more purposeful and politicised forms of content creation, which I call user-generated stories (UGS). Linked thematically, UGS can become UGPs that are included behind subscription paywalls and on Web TV and television.

The book will have a broad appeal:

- **Among media companies and journalists from print, radio and television**
- **In communities trying to promote their local voice**
- **In education where it will be important in propagating mojo and video curriculum design**
- **With NGOs who are realising the value of mojo to create more visceral field reporting**
- **In the conflict world where revolutions such as the Arab Spring can benefit from a more purposeful mobile information flow**
- **In countries like Myanmar where a slow exodus from military rule and a mobile-first approach provide a contemporary mediated frame within which to explore mojo potential**

The mojo skills described in this book have been taught to investigative journalists, citizens and journalism students from more than 40 countries including Australia, Timor, China, Myanmar, Jordan, Syria, Egypt, Yemen, Qatar, Iraq, Canada, the UK, Denmark, Norway and Sweden.

The insight gained from working for decades with citizens and professionals to help tell their own extraordinary self-shot stories for prime-time TV set the foundations for this book and helped develop a sensible common mobile language. The real potential of this book is that it describes a theoretical approach and praxis that's based on a common digital language (CDL) that aims to disrupt a techno-determinist view about mobile production. Each chapter of *The Mojo Handbook: Theory to Praxis* is introduced through a theoretical lens that contextualises the praxis by framing it around a market-driven context:

- ***Introduction:*** **Sets up the mojo ecosphere and defines a more complete form where mojo is both a smartphone workflow and a hybrid form of video storytelling.**
- ***Mojo Tools*****: I'm often asked to what extent does gear make the mojo? We know that in the Middle East and other conflict regions smaller is better. In the EU and the UK the opposite is often true. This chapter discusses mojo equipment from a cultural, social and political perspective.**
- ***Developing Mojo Stories:*** **The mojo story development process includes creating synopses and describes story literacy tools like SCRAP and the impact of a neo-journalistic philosophy. It introduces a variety of forms and the various workflows. Mark Lee Hunter, investigative journalist and research fellow at INSEAD, provides tips.**
- ***Recording Mojo Stories:*** **Includes the various steps for recording strong mojo stories: how to assess and work on location, what to shoot first, who to interview first, and how and when to capture B roll, record narration and interviews. I consider the application and implication of hybrid mojo. Wayne Harley, a multi-award-winning ABC news, current affairs and documentary cameraman, producer and video journalist provides a Break-out Box, as does award-winning RTÉ mojo, Philip Bromwell.**
- ***Recording Audio on a Smartphone:*** **This chapter explores basic, intermediate and advanced audio strategy with associated hardware and software. In particular I look at radio mic and multi-track options. Award-winning sound recordist, Roger Van Wensveen, provides tips and a Break-out Box.**

- *Recording an Interview:* I have produced interviews with everyone from kings to IRA killers. In this chapter I reveal the various styles I use. I discuss the various types of interview situations and techniques and microphones. Tony Jones, Australia's leading broadcast interviewer, provides specialist tips and a Break-out Box.
- *Writing Mojo Stories:* When does the process begin and how do you write in and out of pictures? I worked for *Foreign Correspondent*, where writing to pictures is regarded as a producer's and journalist's key skill. Here I reveal the tips that make stories great and enable fast dynamic editing. Former radio journalist Dr Nasya Bahfen and RTÉ mobile journalist Philip Bromwell provide specialist Break-out Boxes.
- *Editing Video Stories:* The edit process is a way of seeing various states of immediate and fluid possibilities and constructing local contexts and diversity at source. Editing skills filter and make sense of the relationship between these unsettled realties. This chapter introduces a theoretical perspective on editing around which we wrap skills and mobile technology. I discuss workflows and hybrid variants, edit apps, when to begin the edit, how much can be done on a smartphone, how I use narration and more. Multi-award-winning cross-genre editor Steve Robinson provides specialist tips and a Break-out Box.
- *Post-production*: This chapter answers questions about mojo cross-genre, cross-screen and cross-platform workflows, multi-track audio editing, and asks how much tech and polish is enough? We discuss hybrid options and when mojos might consider these. Drew McPherson, grader and post-production guru, provides specialist tips and a Break-out Box.
- *Mojo in the Age of Social Media*: This chapter unpacks the various aspects of the relationship between social platforms and the mobile form. How do we immerse ourselves into what's been called a content tsunami and retain objectivity and ethical standards? To what extent is mojo a perpetrator of fake news and to what degree is it a method of combatting it.
- *Mobile Streaming*: Explores the various streaming possibilities for mojo-related work and takes a pure and hybrid approach and asks when do we stream and why? Mobile streaming expert Peter Stewart provides tips and the Break-out Box.
- *Ethical Mojo*: With social media content spreading like wildfire across platforms, working ethically has never been more important. In this chapter I explore how mojos can be ethical in their dealings with the public and their representation

of information. I introduce a set of checks for ethical journalism and speak with Aidan White, the founder and president of the Ethical Journalism Network, who provides a Break-out Box.

- ***Defamation and Copyright*: This chapter includes an overview of basic copyright and defamation. Check the laws in your country.**
- ***Training: A Common Pedagogical Bridge:* This pedagogical perspective, particularly relevant for teachers and trainers, describes the various milestones confronted by mojo trainers, including an evaluation scaffold and exercises.**

As convergence continues to impact communications and specifically journalism, I hope this book provides a set of skills with which to embark on mojo praxis in a clickstream that's been described as a tsunami of content creation. *The Mojo Handbook: Theory to Praxis* provides a theoretical underpinning for formulating an aesthetic and a personal view about a visceral form of storytelling, especially when, to extend the metaphor, the seas become creatively overwhelming.

Go mojo …

CHAPTER 1

INTRODUCTION

SUMMARY

The history of journalism is tied to the evolution of technology. The advent of TV meant that by the 1950s broadcast TV news was challenging newspapers for supremacy. Just as TV became a watershed for news publication, so too would digital. The lure of the digital revolution and cheaper, more streamlined technology led to a slew of new hybrid forms. One of those was a self-shot form called video journalism. From 1995, the Internet enabled even more citizens to bypass network gatekeepers and publish their own content. This relatively free and limitless publication platform and the eventual proliferation of affordable mobile devices, with an already rampant voyeuristic TV culture, increased the level of self-shot production. Mobile journalism (mojo) is a storytelling form using a smartphone or hybrid forms to create and edit video and audio into complete stories for publication on radio, TV, social media and various other platforms. In global conflict situations including revolution (Arab Spring) and pandemics (COVID-19) the mobile enables communication, story and program production to continue. This chapter establishes the mojo timeline and introduces the concept of mobile journalism before introducing convergence and the current impact of mobile on the news business.

Figure 1.1 **Ivo Burum recording piece to camera.**

Ivo Burum

The history of journalism is tied closely to the development of technology. Around 1440, Johann Gutenberg invented the first printing press and gave rise to mass daily publication. In 1610, the first weekly newspaper appeared in Vienna and by the 1830s newspaper editors were using homing pigeons to deliver the news. In 1880 the first photograph appeared in a newspaper. In 1920, the first radio news broadcast occurred in Pittsburgh in the USA and in 1939 NBC and CBC, two US TV networks, began broadcasting television. By the 1950s, broadcast news was big business and television news networks began to challenge newspapers for dominance.

The media business was always interested in new, more dynamic and lucrative ways to tell and sell stories. As far back as the 1960s storytellers like Academy Award-winning documentary maker and news cameraman, the late D. A. Pennebaker, were experimenting with less expensive, more mobile ways to tell stories. After shooting with a digital video (DV) camera, Pennebaker, arguably the father of modern-day untethered location-based filming, said "I would be surprised if I did any [shooting on] film ... ever again" (Stubbs 2002: 51). Moreover, his documentary partner, Chris Hegedus, summed up the importance of digital when she observed that DV transferred filmmaking into the hands of the masses (ibid). In Yuendumu, a remote central-Australian Indigenous community, this is exactly what happened in the early 1980s. People began experimenting with video and participatory journalism so that they could control publication of their own stories (Michaels 1986).

From 1985, in Australia we were all plugging in to a digital revolution including the advent of satellite television. The proliferation of cheaper, smaller DV cameras provided a milieu within which astute storytellers (in news, radio and television) could experiment with story creation. Affordable digital edit suites with onboard image manipulation technology (DVEs) and inbuilt audio-mixing systems completed the turnkey desktop production chain. Convergence and the reduced cost of technologies meant "sizzle reels" (short promotional video tapes) produced using inexpensive DV cameras and laptop edit suites could be produced cheaply to sell innovative concepts. At about this time we developed a self-shot form of TV that enabled citizens to participate in the digital storytelling process (Burum 2018). We didn't know it then, but we were in the midst of a mini-revolution, readying our mindset and workflows for reality TV and mobile content creation forms.

The lure of the digital revolution and cheaper, more streamlined technology led to an array of new hybrid forms. This resulted in a proliferation of TV channels that changed what was programmed (Jacka 2000). In the early 1990s I began experimenting with self-shot television formats that were produced by non-professionals and mirrored the stylistic and technological development of factual television. This was a form of skills convergence where ordinary citizens (consumers) created content (became producers).

As self-shot became popular and users became proficient, the form found a home on prime-time television, particularly current affairs programs, where it was called video journalism. Popularised by video journalists (VJs) like Michael Rosenblum in the US and Mark Davis in Australia, the style involved the journalist also being cameraperson and sound recordist, and where possible the editor. The VJ style of storytelling was a little more personal, had more of a journalistic presence, and was often embraced by younger up-and-coming journalists wanting to make a name for themselves or camera people wanting to make a shift to being a journalist and/or producer. The holistic skill sets required by VJs are almost identical to the skills required to produce mojo stories.

By 1993 Tim Berners-Lee was stabilising html—the Web was born, and publishing was about to change forever. From 1995 the Internet became a public tool for communication that enabled people to bypass network gatekeepers and publish their own content. This relatively free and limitless publication platform, the eventual proliferation of affordable mobile devices, and an already rampant voyeuristic TV culture increased the level of self-shot production. By 2020, almost 500 hours of video was being uploaded to YouTube every minute. That's enough video content uploaded every 18 minutes to fill a television channel running 24/7 for a year. As technology got smaller and more powerful, DV cameras made way for smartphones. Users could now edit high-quality user-generated content (UGC) into user-generated story (UGS) and publish it from almost anywhere. Smartphones spawned a new group of citizen content creators who found the technology addictive and the lure of free publishing platforms like YouTube irresistible. Content was shared across fragmented digital network societies where participants with similar interests engaged in activities of importance to them (Meadows 2005, Castells 2008).

By 2007, communication moved from the desktop into the palms of our hands and a new, more personalised smartphone era was born. In theory the Internet created a more democratic and diverse publishing model in a potentially more robust marketplace of ideas. The assumption is that an audience with diverse content options consumes a diversity of content (Napoli 1999), which potentially promotes a diversity of views and public issues. In this essentially Marxist view of a network society, communication technologies potentially lead to greater inclusivity for participants. This can lead to greater deliberation around freedom, ethics and use value, which media critic Robert McChesney (2007) believes are "central to democratic theory and practice." In particular, news could now be produced by legacy media and social networks and published and watched from almost anywhere.

Crucial to appreciating the impact of the shift to online communication is an assumption by users that they are part of the fabric of a networked society—not merely as consumers, like those before them—but as producers:

> The people formerly known as the audience wish to inform media people of our existence, and of a shift in power that goes with the platform shift you've all heard about. … Think of passengers on your ship who got a boat of their own … viewers who picked up a camera … who with modest effort can connect with each other and gain the means to speak—to the world. … The people formerly known as the audience are simply the public made realer, less fictional, more able, less predictable.
>
> (cited in Rosen 2006)

The above trope, widely attributed to Professor Jay Rosen, is not his. It was made on his blog, *PressThink*, by one of his readers with a growing frustration with legacy media. At the Melbourne Writers Festival (2011) at the Wheeler Centre in Melbourne, Rosen told the audience that "everything that broadens your horizon is journalism." Media analyst Robert McChesney felt current opportunities for media reform were so profound that in years to come we "will speak of this time as either a glorious new chapter in our communication history—where we democratized societies and revolutionized economies, or as a measure of something lost, or, for some, an opportunity they never had" (McChesney 2007). How will educators and trainers embrace these possibilities, and new horizons in communication?

A conduit in the home, work and play continuum, the mobile is our new digital pen and we never leave home without it. All we need to know is how to write with it. Not just single words, but cursively, where individual words (pictures and video) are joined into sentences (edited sequences) and stories. To achieve this, we need to democratise relevant skills to enable journalists and citizens to use digital and mobile tools to create politicised stories. As renowned filmmaker Ken Burns observes, "we love the new technology and the accessibility to everybody, that democratization of the process. But at the same time, we see, particularly with regard to the Internet and video, the way in which the technological tail is now beginning to wag the dog. I think we've lost touch with story" (cited in Stubbs 2002). The ever-expanding reach of the media gives us the opportunity to send stories beyond borders to billions. But is the speed of the clickstream eroding the overall quality of storytelling?

MOJO: The Mobile Journalism Handbook (2015) describes a form of mobile storytelling that I called user-generated story (UGS). UGS involves using a mobile to record and edit real events, strong narrative and gritty actuality into powerful story and to know how to employ hybrid recording forms when mobile is not enough. Complete UGS can drive grass-roots diversity by promoting more relevant content that encourages development of the user's own counter-discourses, identities and deliberations within a wider public sphere (Meadows 2005, Burum 2018).

A lack of training diminishes a potential for more diverse local media representation. Andrew Keen believes the Internet is full of online "gossip" produced by groups of "untrained amateur monkeys" (Burum 2018); however, Archer (2007) doesn't see the "digital noise" as all bad. Her analytical dualistic approach posits that without people and their noise, there would be no structure. Hence, she argues, internal conversations in whatever form, noise or otherwise, generate important patterns of social mobility. In other words, the effects of associations (like those created online) will depend on how they are interpreted and how individuals relate them to their own subjectively defined concerns.

While technology can provide a vehicle for a global forum, diversity only comes from balanced and reflective representation (Rheingold 2012). Hence, what's required is a media sphere that's conceived as a politically active voice, based on ideologies and supported by digital communication skills. Once people are trained to use portable mobile technologies, they potentially become local change agents. The type of training required depends on the environment. Erik Sonstelie, Editor-in-Chief of *Oppland Arbeiderblad* (*OA*), an online newspaper in Gjovik in Norway, has continued mojo training we began many years ago. After training his staff to mojo, Erik began training local citizens to deliver their own cultural, sport and political content for *OA*'s online site. Unlike the Arab Spring, which trumpeted the potential of mojo (see p xx), Gjovik citizens are producing work across specific genres and for a specific site and pages.

Ilicco Elia, a mobile pioneer and now Head of Mobile at DeLoitte, believes the key to any shared community strategy or advantage, whether social, educational or business, is digital, and more specifically, mobile. "Social media is nothing without mobile. If you had to wait to get to your computer to talk to people, they wouldn't do it, or if they did, it wouldn't be as intimate a relationship as you now have using mobile." Elia believes mobile provides a revolutionary modern-day campfire-extended storytelling experience because "it enables you to take people on an anytime anywhere cross-platform journey that creates the social in social media" (Elia 2013). While an interesting analogy, the question still remains, how do we increase mobile's use value?

I understand Elia's campfire concept because it drives the reason for this book. As a child I lived in a small village where telling stories around the kitchen table was how we learned stuff. I listened trustingly as my parents told me about events and characters. In the twenty-first century the nature of storytelling and the language and modes of story delivery have shifted from an oral culture, of telling stories around the table, to an era of global communication. Where the book, newspaper and text once dominated, today's world of convergent media captures daily life and plays it back to a global audience in real time. Today's smartphones are mobile creative suites with more processing power than NASA had at its disposal when it first put a man on the moon. With around 80% of Facebook revenue coming from mobile, the smartphone is key to new revenue streams. Its utilitarian form is one reason people are willing to pay for news again. The question is, what are we doing with all this potential? Access to powerful mobile technologies made us one of the "smart mobs" (Rheingold 2002). However, a decade later, after the proliferation of user-generated content (UGC), in particular in the mobile-aided Arab Spring (see p xx), Rheingold's view shifted from a techno-determinist position, to one of social realism. To benefit from the revolutionary opportunities afforded by convergence and mobile, to gain "techno-agency," we needed to get "net smart" (Rheingold 2012).

What sets our smartphones apart from any phone or computer that came before them is their ability to run third-party apps that transform them into hand-held computers. More than 6 million apps are available, generating an expected annual turnover of US$190 billion in 2020. It's a brave new world that mobile pioneer Ilicco Elia says is changing the way we run our lives: "When we look for a restaurant on a computer we want to book, when we do it on a mobile, we want to eat" (Elia 2013). With millions of apps available, we are doing a lot more with our mobiles than booking food, especially in crisis times like wars, floods, revolutions or pandemics.

Initially, journalists used smartphones for calling, collecting email and texting; then smartphone cameras became part of the content creation workflow. Because many of the editors running digital were ex-print journalists, their view about what smartphones "could be in news" was restricted by their own experience. This very flat representation generally involved nothing more than a still, a raw interview or the odd shot of a riot used to color an online print story. In a sense we weren't yet ready to use the technology to its fullest potential. In 2011, only months after the Arab Spring uprisings, the director of the Global Editors Network (GEN) said that he would include mojo at their conference if I could prove that mobile would play a significant and continuing role in news. It is.

Change research tells us that how we define a technology at the outset of its use determines its use for generations (Boczkowski 2004). It has taken a great deal of effort to change the techno-determinist mindset of journalists, communities and education about the potential use value of mobile. At one level, the disruptive shift we need is learning to create proper mobile video stories that are more than radio with pictures. There's also a greater cultural disruption that's required in many news rooms, as editors struggle with mobile-first concepts (Hill and Bradshaw 2018). One view is that change must begin at the digital front page where stories are still referred to as articles. It's a psychological battle says Massimo Grillo, former executive producer with ebTV, in Denmark. "There is a big difference about making TV first and not thinking we need to make the article first and then stick the pictures around it" (cited in Burum 2018). This need for a mindset shift can still exist and cause tension when a Web TV story or program, which has taken a day to produce, is relegated lower down the online news site's front page due to a lack of news currency. Hence, finding the right publishing models to capitalise on mojo possibilities, which can include alternative community and school-based media, is key to growing revenues.

In 2000, Professor Stuart Cunningham, from Queensland University of Technology (QUT), wrote that television provides a prime platform for public life, largely displacing the newspaper as a trusted source of news for the majority of the population. In 2018 that beachhead was shifting as citizens moved online looking for more diverse and immediate sources of information. Even in its function as a type of glue that held together "a sense of us—of who we are," television is being replaced by online alternatives. One of these is Red Border, *Time* magazine's online production company, designed to deliver fully funded documentaries for the Web. The *New York Times* and the *Wall Street Journal*'s online video slates contain examples of stories 3–12 minutes long. The *Chicago Tribune* sacked their photographers, choosing instead to teach journalists how to use smartphones to shoot pictures and video, and hire photographers as and when required. At *Ekstra Bladet* in Denmark, all 110 print journalists were taught to mojo, to supply stories for their online, pay-wall and ebTV platforms. At the *Dili Weekly* in Timor-Leste all journalists have learned to mojo, and at seven of

Myanmar's leading media, mojo is a video production toolkit. In Norway, 30 of the country's leading news media have been training journalists to mojo for the past six years. And in the Middle East, smartphones are being used to gain difficult access and create award-winning investigative journalism. And these are only the groups that I have trained. The increased use of smartphones in news production makes it difficult to ignore the convergence that's taking place in digital mobile story construction. Being mobile first means thinking outside the 16:9 rectangle, even the digital square, but it doesn't mean throwing the digital baby out with the social bathwater. Whether you are producing portrait for Instagram or landscape for Web TV, story is the glue that sprinkles media moments with agency.

In closing, convergence has created an ability to publish anytime from almost anywhere and has changed the speed with which we communicate. We've moved from what was regarded as the sublime era of mobile to a less techno-determinist view more focused on story and outcome. As we transition through the third phase of the development of the mobile ecosphere—user-generated programs (UGP), specifically created for mobile screens—our focus on skills and revenue-model development is even more essential.

Moreover, convergence has created paradigm shifts in the way we access media, in particular the newspaper business. Almost 2 billion people log onto Facebook daily using their mobiles. More than 70% of Americans get their news on a mobile device. Once seen as the big threat to traditional news operations, mobile's always-on characteristic, which enables access to news anytime anywhere, is now seen by some as a possible savior of the industry (Newman, Fletcher et al. 2018).

As Peter Sellers put it, we all loved to "watch." And as media converged into a 24/7 click-stream, we did that more and more. Even though we upload media at the rate of 500 hours every minute, the more we "watched" stories—and in 2019 we watched 5 billion videos on YouTube daily—the less time we had to "tell" them. It was not unlike the loss of our ability to write cursively. Mojo is a way of teaching us how to write with a mobile digital pen—to be storytellers again. I am a professional television person who has spent his working life immersed in all manner of storytelling across styles and genres. One over-arching passion has been to create new possibilities for citizens to participate in our media work, including using their smartphones to engage in a new digital public sphere. Convergence has opened the media floodgates and citizens are now a part of media's online workflows. There's no going back; the 2020 pandemic showed that. Mobiles enabled journalists, anchors and editors to create from home. Many TV series were only able to continue because of mobile communication and content feeds. We need to embrace this new form of communication and the storytelling possibilities, and that means training citizens to be even more involved, to be even more media savvy and productive, and providing journalists with digital skills to facilitate what will become their growing overseer role.

My old journalism professor, John Avieson, once told me that journalism cannot be learned through discussion (talking about being a journalist) or reading (newspapers, magazines and books). He said journalism is about "learning by discovery, learning by doing." He said this just before he told me to get off my bum and go and make a story. I did, and now almost 35 years later I'm hopefully helping you do the same. This time you'll be using your mobile and the skills discussed in this book to turn the smartphone into a TV network in your pocket.

Go mojo …

REFERENCES

Archer, M. (2007). *Making Our Way Through the World.* Cambridge, Cambridge University Press.
Boczkowski, P. (2004). *Digitizing the News: Innovation in Online Newspapers.* Cambridge MA, MIT Press.
Burum, I. and S. Quinn (2015). *MOJO: The Mobile Journalism Handbook, How to Make Broadcast Videos with an iPhone or iPad.* New York, Focal.
Burum, I. (2018). *Democratising Journalism Through Mobile Media.* Abingdon, Routledge.
Castells, M. (2008). "The New Public Sphere: Global Civil Society, Communication Networks, and Global Governance." *Annals of the American Academy of Political and Social Sciences* **616**(78): 78–91.
Hill, S. and P. Bradshaw (2018). *Mobile-First Journalism: Producing News for Social and Interactive Media.* Abingdon, Routledge.
Jacka, E. (2000). *Public Service TV: An Endangered Species?* Sydney, Allen & Unwin.
Elia, I. (2013). Interview with I. Burum.
McChesney, R. (2007). *Communication Revolution: Critical Junctures and New Media.* New York, The New York Press.
Meadows, M. (2005). "Journalism and the Indigenous Public Sphere." *Pacific Journalism Review* **11**(1): 36–41.

Michaels, E. (1986). "The Aboriginal Invention of Television in Central Australia 1982–1986." *Institute Report series.* Canberra, Australian Institute of Aboriginal Studies.

Napoli, P. (1999). "Deconstructing the Diversity Principle." *Journal of Communication* **49**(4): 7–34.

Newman, N. et al. (2018). "Reuters Digital News Report." Reuters.

Rheingold, H. (2002). *Smart Mobs.* Cambridge MA, Perseus Books.

Rheingold, H. (ed.) (2012). *Net Smart.* Cambridge MA, MIT Press.

Rosen, J. (2006). "The People Formerly Known as the Audience." *PressThink* http://archive.pressthink.org/2006/06/27/ppl_frmr.html.

Stubbs, L. (2002). *Documentary Filmmakers Speak: "D A Pennebaker and Chris Hegedus—Engineering Nonfiction Cinema".* New York, Allworth Press.

CHAPTER 2

MOJO TOOLS

SUMMARY

Three billion smartphone users use more than 6 million apps to upload more than 500 hours of user-generated content (UGC) every minute. Journalist Charles Feldman (2008) called this 24/7 convergent clickstream an "information tsunami." I see it as an opportunity to teach a common digital language (CDL) to enable cross-genre mobile storytelling and a more effective use of a growing list of mobile tools. In this chapter we learn how to choose a mobile phone for doing mobile journalism (mojo), which mobile apps are essential, and about the microphones and other peripheral hardware mojos use to create user-generated stories (UGS).

OVERVIEW

When I first got involved in mojo the space was dominated by technical people who came from a broadcast engineering background. It also included radio and print journalists needing to upskill in an ecosphere where video and audio were playing an increasingly important role. There weren't many TV people in the space then because we were still busy; after all, video was popular and our jobs were safe, or so we thought.

From the outset there was a very techno-determinist view about mojo praxis and a very flat, single-planar, almost radio-with-pictures feel. It was very much about what Vincent Mosco (2004) referred to as the "digital sublime," a belief that cyberspace was opening up a new world and tech was the way in.

This drove the mojo space forward and also choked it.

Between 2009 and 2013 there were numerous people and organisations playing with mojo. Mostly they were using smartphones to record video (news) or audio (radio features and news). Video editing was done primarily on desktop or laptop devices, by trained editors, and sometimes these people also shot the mojo footage.

My television skill set enabled me to see mojo development through a holistic lens during those early years. From 2010, primarily because of my TV background, I was training people

Figure 2.1 **The author with mojo gear.**

Ivo Burum

to edit complete stories on their phones. In January 2011, I published my first complete shot-and-edited-on-an-iPhone story to YouTube. It felt like TV production in a pocket.

This volatile period in media was disruptive and exciting. The first mojo workshops I ran were in Indigenous communities and then in 2012 I taught journalists and photographers at the *Sydney Morning Herald* (*SMH*), one of Australia's oldest print editions, to do the same. While the alternative community space welcomed a full style of mojo, what Prof Stephen Quinn called "complete mojo," the restrictive forces at play in the professional sphere held it back. *SMH* journalists were initially apprehensive about learning to edit complete stories on their phones, but hours later, when their photographers became converts, attitudes changed, and another six workshops were scheduled. One of the issues was that in-house digital trainers at the *SMH* were predominantly print trained and this impacted a view about what mojo could be. *SMH* Online Editor Simon Morris said he wanted his journalists to upload content as fast as possible, and if this meant it was unedited, that's what he wanted.

This was a common attitude in the early days that sometimes choked mojo. But as tools and apps developed, so did workflows, and it became obvious that a very flat radio-with-pictures style of mojo could be greatly enhanced if journalists had a few basic skills, in particular how to use multitrack video edit apps to create stories.

THEORETICAL PERSPECTIVE

Apart from the use of mojo by journalists, convergence and the proliferation of mobile technologies have resulted in unprecedented opportunities for citizens at grassroots levels, in particular those living in marginalised communities, to create and publish their own voice (Burum 2016). Essentially, the skills and technology discussed in this book potentially create a new bridge between alternative and more mainstream news creators. In the paperback edition of his book *We, the Media* (2006), author Dan Gillmor is amazed by "the growth of grassroots media," especially within media such as CNN1 and the BBC that "feature the work of citizen journalists." Gillmor is right; accessibility to computer and mobile technologies potentially creates opportunities for citizen journalists to infiltrate more mainstream media. However, two years later, journalist Charles Feldman (2008), in his book *No Time to Think*, was calling the digital content stream a "potential disaster." Feldman was alluding to fragmented user-generated content (UGC) created by citizens using smartphones and posted on social media.

The great paradox in journalism, as Hirst (2012) points out, is that news often happens when the press is absent, at least it did in an analog news environment. But because mojo is based around accessible smart technologies, almost anyone with the skill set and a smartphone is ready to record breaking news almost anywhere (Burum 2016). Technology is part of the answer, but knowing how to tell digital stories is as much a part of a mojo's tool kit as using the right technology (Burum and Quinn 2015, Burum 2016).

User research on who buys what device and why is often bound by an investigation into impact on well-being and two distinct philosophies: hedonism and eudemonism (Ryan and Deci 2001 in Burum 2016). Hedonism reflects a view that "well-being consists of pleasure or happiness," whereas eudemonism posits that it lies in the "actualisation of human potential" (Ryan and Deci 2001). These two concepts intersect when technologies like smartphones, which deliver a high degree of hedonistic pleasure, are used to achieve eudemonic outcomes. The basic premise here is that perceived ease of use and usefulness combines to influence behavioral intention, which in turn affects how the system is used. So buying the right tools will help you learn and teach others. My contention is that once beyond the subjective hedonic phase of seeing mojo tools as things that provide immediate pleasure, newly acquired skills are used for commercial gain or to enter a new moral, or eudemonic, civic mindfulness.

One method of assessing the relationship between technology and the user experience—whether you bought the right technology—especially when developing training, is to use a model developed by Hassenzahl (2003). His framework, described below, is based on the assumption that product character can be described and chosen on the basis of its pragmatic and hedonic relevance, and measured against intended function and stimulation. The major components of the framework as they apply to mobile technologies are:

- ***Product features*: Smartphones' functionality, creating a user friendliness to enable practical and theoretical components of training to be tuned specifically for each training/workshop environment.**
- ***Pragmatic attributes*: A smartphone's level and ease of connectivity between platforms (cellular and WiFi), spheres of communication and training to deliver real-world skill sets that lead to job opportunities.**
- ***Hedonic attributes*:**
    - ***Stimulation*: Positive user responses to the style and brand of technology and its usability to achieve desired training and production functions, to where it begins to empower personal growth and development of skills, which lead to job-ready expectation and increased self-esteem.**
    - ***Identification*: As a result of the expression of self and a growing value to their community through artifact use (in this case technology) and skill application, the user has a social value.**
    - ***Evocation*: The smart device's ability to provoke memories and inspire people to talk about important past events, relationships, ideas or stories.**
- ***Consequence*: An ethical judgment, holding that the value of the device, and hence the act performed, lies in its capacity to produce positive outcomes—that is, benefits to the mojo and the community:**
    - ***Emotional*: Self-esteem, pride in achievement, in being a useful community member, and being able to personalise content ideas into a broadly accessible form.**
    - ***Personal*: Growing confidence, desire to embark on further training and engagement, and enhanced job prospects.**

- *Communal*: **Immediate and purposeful role in the community (local, work or extended) as message maker, mobile journalist and sustainable role as teacher as skills are retaught to others in a local community, media or education sectors.**

The premise is that any truth or meaning imbued in technology and training "comes into existence in and out of our engagement with the realities in our world" (Crotty 2003) or through a community of practice. User experience can be viewed as a consequence of interaction impacting the user's internal state (lore, predispositions, expectations, corporate needs, community or job motivation, mood, digital literacy and so on), the characteristics of the designed system (e.g. complexity, purpose, usability, functionality and design), the social and cultural context within which the interaction occurs, and feedback from that and external environments.

The aim of any teacher/trainer/workshop is to create an environment in which participants are encouraged to describe and understand their emotional responses during interaction with technology. Referred to as the thinking-aloud method (Mahlke 2008), this reflection on successes and failures when using technology is an essential first step to understanding the value of the technology. Moreover, understanding the user experience helps shape pedagogical development and outcomes by helping define the style of use of technological tools—the type of hardware and the praxis—to determine the practical and hedonic nature of any training program. The length of training, the type of equipment and outcomes can all be impacted by the way the user perceives the experience at its outset. When planning technology, consider the following four stages of user experience:

- **Innovation—the technology or delivery**
- **Communication—the structure of the workshops**
- **Time—taken for the innovation to be adopted**
- **Communities—translation across three distinct user groups (community, media and education)**

User experience plays a pivotal role in developing mobile training strategies across the translation phase, which investigates the effectiveness of any tool, pedagogy or program (Burum 2016). Expressed in his book *Understanding Media: The Extensions of Man*, Marshall McLuhan calls this relationship the *techne* (1964). McLuhan believes "the personal and social consequences of any medium, that is any extension of ourselves, results from the new scale that is introduced into our affairs by each extension of our selves, or by any new technology." Irrespective of the type of mojo you do, or whether the workflow is smartphone only or a hybrid approach, there's no denying that mobile tools are playing a greater role in all forms of communication. Understanding which is the right technology to use is an important first step to realising its benefits. Below is a guide to the various technologies mojos might use.

Should I Buy a New Phone?

One of the first questions I am asked during my training workshops by students and journalists is "Can I do mojo on my phone?"

"Not if there is no memory." A lack of memory slows phones down and means you can't save your pictures and video.

"My phone is an Android."

"Great … does it have lots of memory?"

"It's not a new phone, maybe I need a new one?"

"Sure, get a new one with lots of memory."

"Okay, which phone do I buy?"

In 2020 there are more than 3.5 billion smartphone users worldwide. With this figure predicted to rise to 3.9 billion in 2021, we're asking the "which" question more often than ever. A reduction in iPhone sales to a paltry 217 million in 2018 and further 30% drop in Q1 2019, shows that even iOS zealots are shopping around and waiting for the future device rumor mill to settle.

There are basically two platforms that work best for mojo work: Android is like a coalition winning the race on numbers, while iOS is still a closed shop going it alone and running second. So, is there a big difference between expensive Androids and iOS phones? Some.

Figure 2.2 **iPhone 5s—old and comparatively slow but still does the job and some say still the perfect size.**

Ivo Burum

Are the cheaper Android phones any good? Absolutely. Is my old phone okay and, if not, which phone should I buy if I upgrade? The simple answer is that if you can't use your smartphone to produce your mojo story—shoot in low light, run good camera and multi-layered video apps, and your phone has lots of memory—then you need a new phone for mojo. If your phone has enough mojo to produce a story—to do the above—save your money, you're good to go.

Tip: Don't throw that old phone away. Learn to use all its capabilities and then trade it in, or keep it. Yes, keep it—see why below.

Platform—Android vs iOS?

At the outset of the mojo movement there was a big difference in what phones could do. iOS was a clear winner because of its workflow, lack of viruses, lots of third-party peripherals such as microphones and cradles, and there were more iOS mojo apps. iOS phones are still pretty much virus free, but mojo peripherals are now available for most platforms.

Google's Android operating system (AOS) is an open platform which means anyone can use the AOS to develop apps for Android devices. While Android benefits from Google's algorithmic power, there is an ongoing battle between the handset manufacturers and the AOS developer. Each manufacturer creates a different look and feel across Android phones. Android app developers say that this can make it difficult for them to scale apps across multiple manufacturers.

Hence, one aspect that can be an issue on Android is a lack of high-end mojo-type apps, in particular easy-to-use audio apps that offer *Ferrite* (iOS)[1] functionality and ease of use across all types of Android devices. Another issue can be updates that need to be effective across dozens of phones from a large number of developers and which can take time to prepare. While the top range of phones get their updates fast, app developer Matthew Feinberg, from *Alight Motion*, says it can take time for them to arrive on all Android devices, which can lead to security risks.

Tip: You need to be mindful in countries like China where Google Play store is not available and where OEM (manufacturer) app stores don't always hold a complete range.

What Phone Features Do I Need?

Effective mojo begins by deciding on story that informs process and technology. Having said that, having the right phone is important. When choosing a phone consider the following:

- **Look for an easy-to-use phone that suits your technical level. If it's difficult to use, you won't use it.**
- **Choose a phone with a fast, multi-core chip set that spreads load to increase app speed and reduce power consumption.**
- **Integration with all manner of apps, formats, workflows and peripherals is essential.**
- **Choose a phone that runs high-end apps to enable broadcast functionality.**
- **Decide if you'll be editing on your phone, tablet or your laptop.**
- **Do you need to access SD card video from a DSLR?**

- **Do you need to input and export content to laptops via transfer devices like iXpand or Airstash?**
- **Even though power banks are readily available, buy a phone with a long-lasting battery.**

Tip: Make sure your phone has lots of memory, can shoot in low light and run good camera and multi-layered video apps.

Replacing microphones is not cheap, so phone connectivity is key. My favorite phone is still my old iPhone 6s Plus. It scored 81% in a recent review by Australia's *Choice* magazine, while the top-rated phone scored only slightly higher at 84%. It shoots up to 4k (I almost always shoot in 1920 × 1080 resolution) and it has a mini-jack microphone input that matches my microphones. If you use a phone with a lightning microphone input, you'll need a mini-jack-to-lightning cable or a mini-jack-to-lightning adapter from Apple. If you use the adapter workflow you might also need a TRS-to-TRRS adapter.

Figure 2.3 **TRS and TRRS adapters.**

Ivo Burum

I buy the phone with the most storage (not an issue with many Android phones that use SD card slots) and try to leave that phone primarily for mojo use.

Tip: If you are thinking of upgrading your phone, ask whether you'll have to change your cradles, adapters and microphones. One reason I use the Beastgrip cradle system is that it works across all phone types. Essential in mixed-platform training.

One Lens or Three?

One of the very first smartphones to use a dual-lens camera was launched by HTC back in 2011. It used two lenses to capture three-dimensional photos that could be viewed on a 3D television or on the phone's own 3D display. These were 2-megapixel low-resolution images that lacked detail, essentially a gimmick and difficult to view outside the phone.

In 2016, LG hopped onto dual cameras, and in 2017 iPhone 7 Plus offered two independent cameras (12 megs each), the second featuring a 2× optical zoom. The second camera automatically takes over when you optically zoom into your subject for a close-up view so you don't lose image quality. A digital zoom, on the other hand, degrades image quality by zooming and cropping the edges of the photo and increasing the pixel size to simulate an optical zoom, which is a hardware solution rather than a software fix. Hence, picture quality is maintained. The downside is that most smartphones only offer 2× optical zoom. The latest news is that Chinese manufacturers OPPO and Huawei are planning a 10× periscopic zoom lens on their cameras. This will enable better sports, wildlife and other coverage where a long lens is required and where a DSLR hybrid approach may be necessary. Now depending on the glass and focal length, that might be worth the wait.

The newest iPhone, the 11 Pro, has four lenses—three on the back and a 12mp selfie lens on the front. This smartphone is potentially a game changer. Apart from the specs, which are excellent and include being able to switch between lenses during recording, when used with the *FiLMiC Pro* app, the user can record two of the four lenses simultaneously. However, as of writing, there are still issues between phone and app around lens matching and not being able to set exposure on the selfie lens and numerous other issues. Am I going to buy the 11 Pro? Yes, because I can use the extra-wide lens to get closer to the source for better sound quality.

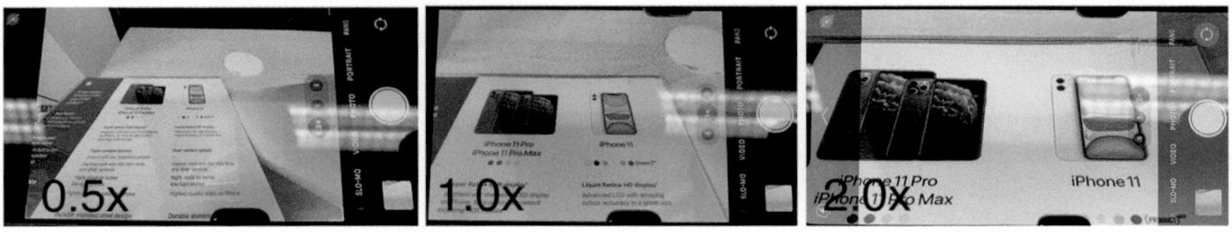

Figure 2.4 **iPhone 11 Pro showing on-board back lens's focal length.**

Ivo Burum

Aperture and Lens Speed

Another important factor is the speed of your smartphone lens. You should look for the widest (fastest) possible aperture. For example, my new iPhone Xs has a lens with an f1.8 aperture on the wide end and f2.4 on the telephoto side. The aperture, or f-stop, denotes how wide the lens will open in low light conditions. The wider the aperture (lower f-stop number) the more light a lens can capture in low light conditions, and the more expensive the lens.

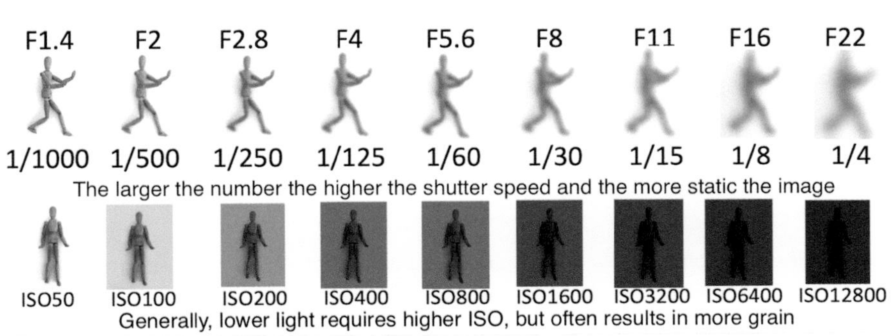

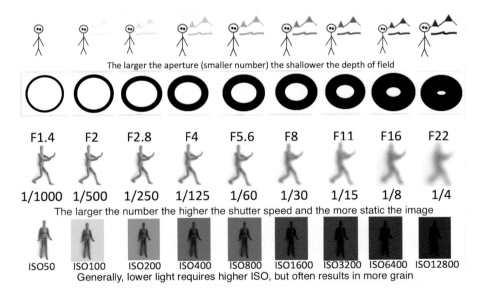

Figure 2.5 **The relationship between f-stop, shutter, and ISO.**

Ivo Burum

Figure 2.6 **Creating bokeh depth of field on a smartphone using f-stop.**

Ivo Burum

The picture in Figure 2.6 was taken using the iPhone Xs and shows the camera's ability to alter bokeh (depth of field focus) after the shot is taken. The shot on the left is dialed up to f16 and has a large depth of field, while the other shot, dialed to f1.4, has a shallow depth of field. In good light conditions use a smaller aperture (higher number) to get greater depth of field.

The Truth About Pixels

More is not always best. Pixels are square red, blue and green representations of trapped light on an electronic sensor. The sensor is a digital camera's version of film. It contains pixels that capture light that enters through the lens. The electronic sensor transmits the light-filled pixels onto an SD card to form a picture. A pixel has been described like a bucket for trapping water. The larger the bucket (pixel), the more water (light) it collects.

The truth about pixels is that more is not always best. The former Apple engineer responsible for camera technology, Nikhil Bhogal (https://twitter.com/nikbhogal), explains that when it comes to smartphone cameras, pixel quality matters more than the actual number of pixels in a camera sensor. What he means is that generally the larger the sensor size, the larger, more light-sensitive the pixels, and the better they work in low light.

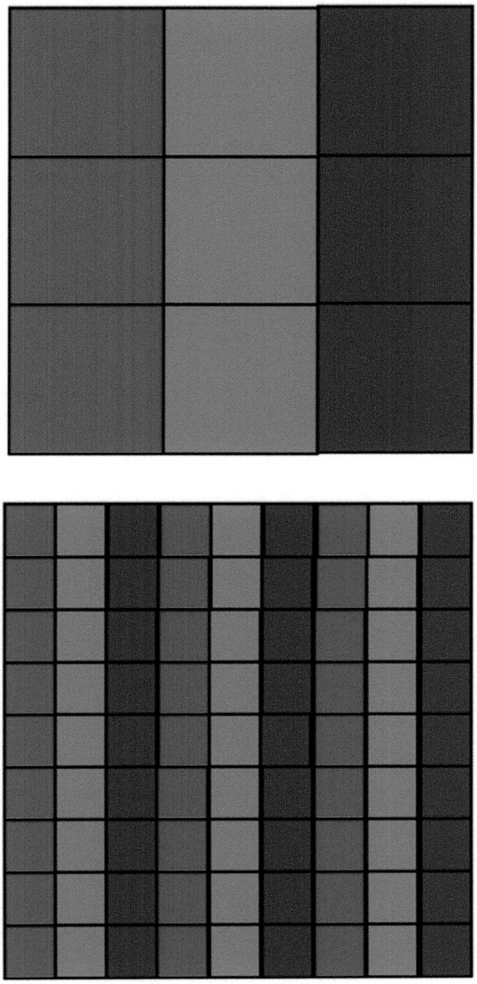

Figure 2.7 **If the same sensor size, fewer pixels are better at capturing low light.**

Ivo Burum

Let's say we have a 1-inch, 12-megapixel sensor and another 1-inch sensor with 24 megapixels. The pixels on the 12-megapixel sensor are going to be twice as big as those on the sensor with 24 megapixels and should be better at capturing light in low light conditions.

Tip: When might 24 megapixels be better? When the sensor doubles in size. If you have a terrible camera with a terrible lens with more pixels, you will end up with more terrible-quality pixels. The sharper the original picture (exposure, focus, speed) the better the photo. Skill still trumps technology, even in the mobile world.

Phone Summary

Only buy a phone when you can identify the extra features or functionality:

1. **More pixels are effective when the chip grows in size. Adding more pixels without increasing sensor size (the light collecting element) means pixels are actually smaller and less efficient in low light.**
2. **Buy a phone with at least a 12-megapixel camera.**
3. **If you want to do mobile journalism, it's essential to buy a phone with a fast processor.**
4. **Buy a phone that has access to cradles, lenses, lights, microphones and free mojo apps.**

Tip: If money is an issue, you can purchase a powerful Android smartphone that will run all the mojo apps you need for as little as US$160.

MICROPHONES FOR MOJO WORK

Figure 2.8 **Author using mojo kit—Beastgrip Pro, VideoMic NTG and Lumimuse 8 light.**

Ivo Burum

MTV taught us that we will watch wobbly shots but won't listen to low-quality audio. If you are close enough to your subject, with little or no background noise, the microphone on your smart device, or the one on your headset, will do the job (see Chapter 5).

However, my advice is get a third-party microphone. One of the following microphones can dramatically enhance your audio quality:

1. **Shotgun microphones are essential for all hand-held close-quarter filming, which is the bulk of mojo work. For general recording, especially when roving hand-held, these shotgun microphones have a cardioid pattern that predominantly records sound in front of the microphone (see Chapter 5):**

Figure 2.9 **Sennheiser MKE 400m, Rode Video Micro, Rode Video Mic NTG, Sennheiser MKE 200.**

Ivo Burum

Rode VideoMic NTG (US$250) has attenuation (variable) especially good for recording loud sounds, inbuilt rechargeable battery (30 hours), self-detecting selector (TRS, TRRS).

Sennheiser MKE 400 Shotgun Microphone (US$200) is an all-metal shotgun mic with attenuation and 300 hours' battery life. I have been using this mic for five years and the only thing mine needs is a dead cat over the foam cover.

Rode VideoMicro (US$50) and an SC4 adapter for iOS devices (US$10). This microphone connects via a cold shoe attached to your handle or cradle (see p xx) and comes with a mini-jack connector.

Sennheiser MKE 200 (US$105) no battery, mesh wind protector, internal shock mount, ships with TRS to TRS and TRS to TRRS cables and windsock.

N.B. All the above microphones except NTG come with a dead cat wind protector.

2. Lavelier microphones are excellent for sit-down interviews and can be clipped to an interviewee's lapel, 6–8 inches from their mouth, or placed on a desk between two people (when positioned correctly). The omnidirectional pattern makes these microphones an inexpensive solution for sit-down interviews.

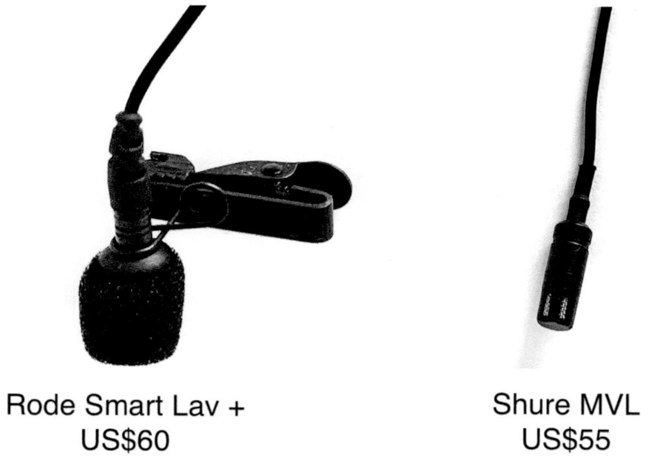

Figure 2.10 Lapel mics at price points.

Ivo Burum

Rode smartLav+ (US$55) is a cheap but very effective lapel microphone perfect for recording interviews.

Shure MVL (US$62) is an omnidirectional condenser microphone designed for smartphones and video cameras with a 65dB signal-to-noise ratio and 3.5mm mini-jack.

Tip: Choose a lapel mic with a long cable or buy a short extension so that the cable can be hidden out of shot.

3. Wireless microphones are used to record audio where the source is some distance from the smartphone and where the sound source (interviewee) might be moving in a demonstration, or in a walk-and-talk interview situation, or any interview situation where flexibility is required. In the 1960s, crystal-sync double-head recording became very popular as it freed the camera and sound from their umbilical connection. Today wireless or radio microphones which use a transmitter (on the interviewee) and a receiver (on the camera) enable clean audio to be recorded wirelessly. A new system called Memory Mic, developed by Sennheiser, imitates the early double-head recording and is able to increase distance immeasurably.

Figure 2.11 **Norwegian journalist recording a stand-up using an iPhone and Sennheiser AVX combo wireless system.**

Ivo Burum

Wireless microphones come at various price points from US$120 to thousands of dollars. My advice is, buy the best you can afford as you'll keep them for some time. Having said that, you can buy a good set from between US$170 and US$850. Here are a few I use listed according to price point.

Figure 2.12 **Rode Filmmaker wireless kit.**

Courtesy of Rode

Rode produces a Filmmaker Kit (US$399) with transmitter and receiver body packs and lapel microphone. The News-shooter Kit version (US$400) includes a hand-held microphone transmitter (Rode Reporter microphone bought separately, US$110). This well-priced system is a little larger than the two below and has built-in hard plastic casings. Range is around 100 meters, pairing is one-button simple, there are three gain levels, and it uses easy-to-replace AA batteries (excellent) that last 30 hours. Safety is via 120-bit encryption. It operates on the 2400GHz frequency. Attenuation on the transmitter is 0, +10, +20 and on the receiver 0, −10, −20—so a 60db range. My only concern is the size, which even for use with DSLRs is very bulky.

Figure 2.13 **Sony UWO-D11.**

Ivo Burum

Sony UWP-D11 (US$600) wireless microphone device operates in portions of the 617–652MHz or 663–698MHz frequencies. An excellent middle price set with smaller, metal-cased transmitter and receiver with more than 100 meters range. I have been using this set for a number of years (and a previous version for more than 20 years), including in conflict zones that are full of military radio bands, and they have never let me down. Their smaller size suits mojo work. The kit ships with a lapel microphone.

Sennheiser AVX with ME2 mic (US$850) is the most expensive of the three sets, but comes as a kit that includes a handheld microphone as well as body pack and lapel microphone. The reduced size suggests the AVX wireless system was produced with smartphone and mojo work in mind. The range is over 100 meters and you will need to choose between two versions of the lapel mic (ME2 ii or the smaller MKE2). The ME2 ii has more presence and picks up more ambient noise. The ME2 ii is US$80, the MKE2 is US$190. I use this set a lot.

Figure 2.14 Sennheiser AVX combo.

Courtesy of Sennheiser

Sennheiser XSW ENG Lav (US$450) is a more expensive digital kit, also in the 2400GHz band, that includes a compact wireless hand mic and rechargeable batteries with 5 hours' run time. This system will link with up to five systems. The included ME2–11 condenser omnidirectional lapel mic is a favorite. I have tested it to beyond the 75-meter range that Sennheiser recommends and the XSW remains clear. Excellent system that is expensive given it doesn't have attenuation.

Figure 2.15 Sennheiser XSW ENG.

Courtesy of Sennheiser

Figure 2.16 **Rode Wireless Go.**

Courtesy of Rode

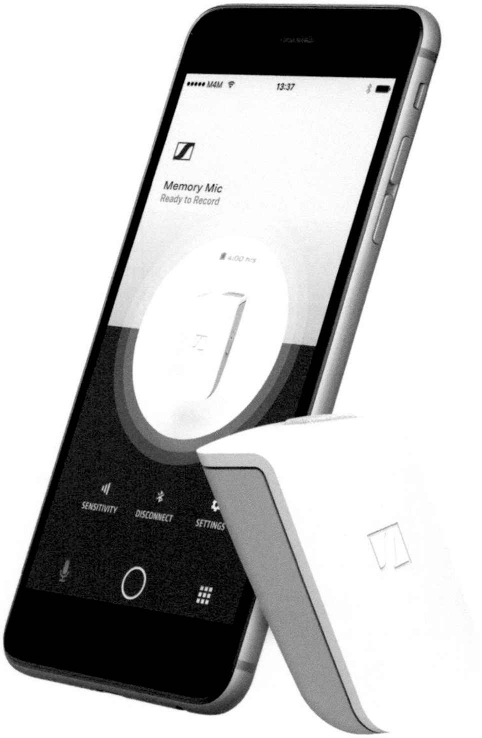

Figure 2.17 **Sennheiser Memory mic.**

Courtesy of Sennheiser

Rode Wireless Go (US$200) is a small system (10 times smaller and 6 times lighter than their Filmmaker Kit) that is purpose-built for DSLRs (ships with TRS-to-TRRS cable) and is excellent for smartphones. Rechargeable batteries; 80 meters plus line-of-sight range (41 meters with operator's back to receiver); three-step on-the-fly attenuation 0, –6, –12, but it's set up a little hotter, which makes it useful when shooting with some DSLRs (I shoot at +10db with Canon so a high setting works and you can dial it down for a Sony DSLR). It uses an onboard condenser microphone with 3.5mm input for a lavalier. The system weighs 30 grams and ships with an excellent onboard mic. Rode sell a Wireless Go lapel mic, but I use my smartLav+, or the Shure MVL and you can use any number of high-end lapel microphones. No mute function.

Sennheiser Memory Mic (US$205) is a different type of wireless microphone that takes design cues from the old film days. It stores its own recordings that are later automatically synced with the vision on the smartphone. That means that distance is not an issue. If you need to record someone in a boat, or where distances between smartphone and microphone are

beyond 150 meters, try this new microphone. I love it. Check out this video (http://smartmojo.com/2017/05/21/diy-wireless-microphone/) on how to use an old smartphone and a cheap smartLav+ to create your own version of the Memory Mic for about US$50.

Tip 1: For an interview, record within a meter of the subject and use a windsock outdoors (comes with microphone).

Tip 2: Sit your subject back to the wind to shield the lapel microphone, which is attached about 8 inches below the subject's mouth. If using a shotgun mic, flip it so that the wind hits the back of the mic (the operator's back).

Tip 3: If you buy a radio microphone, spend a bit more because it's a tool you will keep.

Here is a link to a video of the AVX: https://youtu.be/-W26-xJItAU, and an article on the first impression of the AVX system: http://smartmojo.com/2015/09/17/sennheiser-avx-combo-first-look/. And here's a link to a YouTube video with samples from each: https://youtu.be/4kZ-xaxqxGo.

CAMERA CRADLES, LENSES, TRIPODS, LIGHTS AND GIMBALS

Cradles

Cradles add structure, useability and balance when working handheld, and they provide attachment points for microphones, lights and tripods. Wide-angle lenses add stability when shooting handheld and enable you to get closer to your subject and still maintain a medium close-up interview shot. Being close to your subject and sound source improves audio quality.

Beastgrip: I use the Beastgrip Pro bundle, which includes the cradle with their Kenko Pro series 0.75 wide-angle lens (US$240) because it adapts to fit almost any size smartphone. Beastgrip also sells the Beastcage, an iPhone-specific cradle (US$139), lens converters and other peripherals. If you are teaching mobile storytelling at a school or university and need to supply equipment to students, then the original Beastgrip Pro is a strong contender.

Figure 2.18 **La Trobe mobile storytelling students using mojo kits with Beastgrip Pro.**

Figure 2.19 **Beastgrip Pro being used.**

Courtesy of Beastgrip

Moondog Labs: **make nine specific cradles/cases for iPhone and Pixel smartphones that take anamorphic lenses.**

Tip: When cradles are loaded with smartphone, light and microphone they make the mojo operator look more professional. In some cases that's great, but in situations like conflict zones, all that gear can paint you as a target. Think carefully.

Tripods

I also use a Pro Master Professional XC525C Carbon tripod (US$365). I like it because it's light and has a removable leg that transforms into a monopod. I also use a Beastgrip BT-50 (US$55). This is a very short tripod that can be used as a handle to help stabilise handheld shots when attached to a cradle. It's easy to carry and if you need extra height for a stand-up, stick it on a car roof, a wall, or on a filing cabinet. The Manfrotto Pixi is another option. Its red articulation button is still incredibly effective for changing angles.

Figure 2.20 **Beastgrip BT-50 tripod.**

Courtesy of Beastgrip

Lights

There are many different on-camera lights at various price points from US$30 to US$172. I look for the ability to choose intensity settings because interviewees can find light in their eyes distracting. I use a Manfrotto Lumimuse 8 (US$130), but in many cases a Lumimuse 3 (US$55) is enough. Both ship with color filters.

Figure 2.21 **DJI Osmo Mobile 3 gimbal.**

Ivo Burum

Gimbals

There are many on the market at the right price point and you should play with each to see which is right for you. I use the Osmo Mobile 3 (US$120) basically because it's cheap and easy to use. If you buy this gimbal you'll need a Ulanzi PT-3 cold-shoe mount (US$9) to use third-party microphones and lights.

Mojo Kits

Mojo kits can include a variety of equipment. Opposite are three kits I have and use that are designed to provide a variety of capability at different price points. You can, of course, mix and match depending on your requirements.

APPS

The app industry began in 2008 after the launch of the iPhone. Today there are more than 6 million apps for Android, iOS and other devices.

Camera Apps

I use the native camera app that ships with the iPhone, except when I need a higher level of control, in which case I use the following:

FiLMiC Pro **(US$19.99) is the most widely used advanced video camera app, with separate white balancing, light metering and focus points, variable frame rates, bit rates and real-time audio monitoring (iOS and. Android).**

Figure 2.22 **Mojo kits.**

Ivo Burum

Table 2.1 Mobile kits

Advanced mojo kit	Intermediate kit	Basic kit
iPhone XS, Beastcage (US$139), Beastgrip M series 0.6 wide-angle lens (US$129), Beastgrip BT-50 tripod (US$80), Lumimuse 8 Light (US$120), Sennheiser Clip Mic Digital (US$200), Rode VideoMic Pro + (US$240), Sennheiser AVX Combo Radio Mic (US$1000), Sandisk iXpand lightning-to-USB transfer (US$120), Bose Quiet Comfort 20 headphones (US$240)	iPhone 6s Plus, Beastgrip PRO and Kenko wide-angle lens combo (US$200), Manfrotto Pixi tripod (US$30), Manfrotto M120 light (US$30), Shure MVL mic (US$60), Rode VideoMic Pro (US$150), Rode Wireless Go radio mic (US$200)	iPhone 6s, Manfrotto Twist Grip clamp (US$60), Pixi tripod (US$30), Rode smartLav+ (US$50), Rode Video Micro (US$50), Sima light (US$20)

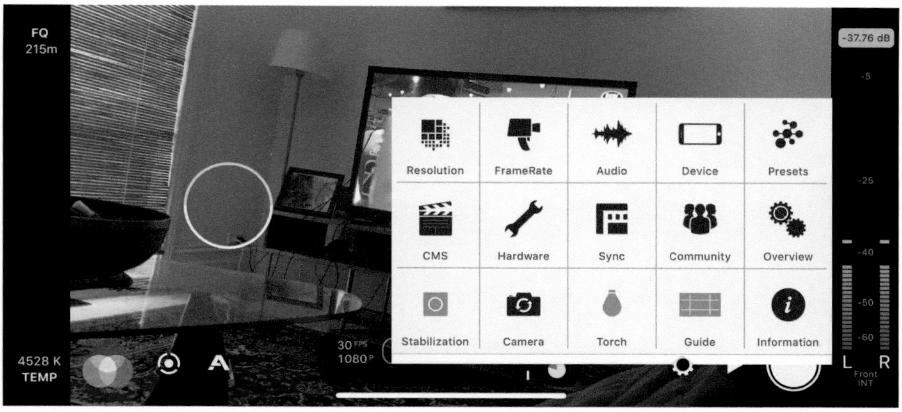

Figure 2.23 ***FiLMiC* Pro app.**

Ivo Burum

Beastcam is a new app that has many of the features of *FiLMiC Pro* but shoots stills and captures video. It's still in beta testing but look out for it (iOS).

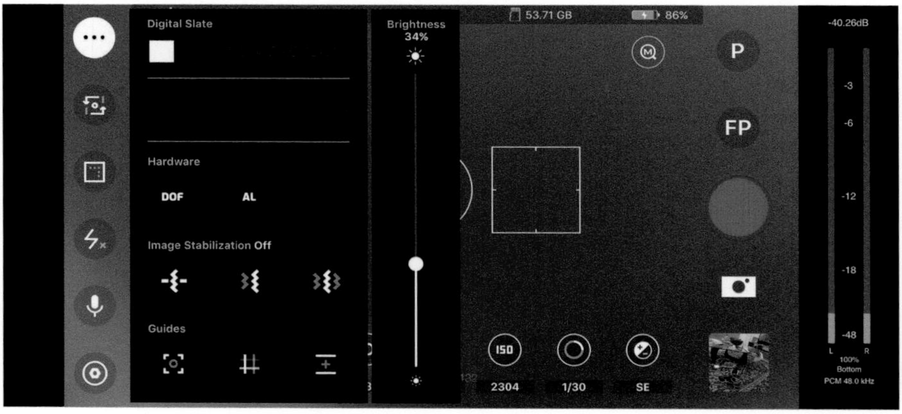

Figure 2.24 ***Beastcam* app.**

Ivo Burum

Camera+ is arguably the best stills camera app on the market, with high-level image control, stabiliser, separate exposure and focus settings, white balance, and control over brightness, color and sharpening (US$2.99).

Tip: Learn to shoot with the camera app that ships with your phone and concentrate on exposure, framing and recording shots that tell a story. Look for another app when you need more features.

Sound Apps

In the first instance, record voice-overs with video so that all media (video and audio) lives in the same spot (either in camera roll or gallery). This makes it quick to access when on a deadline and it takes no time to strip the audio from the video.

Tip: When recording a voice-over, I ask journalists to use the camera app and cover the lens so that the video track is black. That way, when viewing media in camera roll, it's obvious which is the voice-over clip—the black one.

If you need a VU meter, both *FiLMiC Pro* and *Beastcam* have one, or if you need 96kbps, lossless (ALAC/CAF), or wave formats, you might try one of these excellent audio apps:

Ferrite (iOS) is probably the best audio app I have used because it is very user friendly and the free version gives you so many features that you may never need the paid one. It has all the professional settings you will need, including

Figure 2.25 ***Ferrite* audio app.**

Ivo Burum

multi-track editing and various recording and sharing formats (includes in-app purchases).

Rode Record Le (iOS) is the updated version released since Rode acquired the *FiRe* app and has a series of filters, compression thresholds and head-room, spread of 48dB gain, 96Khz MP3 recording, markers, variable play-back speeds and a trim feature. Free with an in-app purchase to Rode Rec (US$9.99).

Rec Forge is a full-featured Android audio recording app. I find it a little complicated and so did my students.

Edit Apps

The following are the most functional edit apps on the market for advanced mojo work:

iMovie ships with the iPhone and was one of the first apps to offer two video tracks. It provides all the features you need to edit professional stories quickly, but lacks a powerful titling tool and doesn't have keyframe audio ducking. It now includes green screen (chroma) facilities. The benefit of this app is that it's easy to use (free).

LumaFusion is the new iOS kid on the block and probably the most powerful of the edit apps. It has 12 tracks (6 video/audio tracks and 6 additional audio tracks), slip-trim and anchored edit features, color correction, layered titles tool, keyframe audio, insert and overwrite edit functionality; it is optioned like a professional edit suite (US$29.99).

Figure 2.26 **Edit apps *LumaFusion* and *Kinemaster*.**

Ivo Burum

Kinemaster for iOS and Android is the first professional smartphone edit app that works across platforms. With many of the features of *LumaFusion*, it includes a chroma key tool, an easy-to-use titling tool, blur, audio manipulation and lots more. *Kinemaster* is out for iOS and Android and free with watermark. Lose the watermark and add features for an annual subscription of US$39.99.

VN the new cross platform app is free with many high end features.

Key features to look for:

- *Multitrack video*: Fast, professional smartphone editing requires an app with at least two video tracks. Cut the editorial story on video track 1, add B-roll video on video track 2 to match the words on video track 1.
- *Multitrack audio*: Look for at least three audio tracks, plus the in-video audio. Look for an edit app that enables audio to be detached from video.
- *Audio mixing*: All three apps include a mixing tool to enable audio tracks to be mixed. The least effective is *iMovie*.
- *Audio ducking*: This is an important feature that enables you to select audio key frames to lift or lower audio levels. Critical for mixing professional audioscapes. *iMovie* doesn't offer audio ducking.

Figure 2.27 **Audio ducking.**

Ivo Burum

- *Chroma key*: All three apps above include chroma key. Figure 2.28 shows an example of chroma key (green screen) on *Kinemaster*. The composite was made by shooting the journalist against a green screen then shooting a wide shot (WS) off the roof looking at the city before keying the city into the green screen.

Figure 2.28 **Journalist at the Myanmar mojo training workshop using *Kinemaster* chroma green screen feature.**

Ivo Burum

- *Titles*: A strong titles tool that's easy to use, includes a variety of fonts, and enables the creation of quick backgrounds is important. *Kinemaster* and *LumaFusion* include powerful titles tools. *iMovie* Titles is easy to use but incredibly rudimentary and when using *iMovie* I generally import the finished video into *Kinemaster* or *Vont* to do a titles pass (see chapters 8 and 9 for details on these apps).
- *Video grading*: I use *VideoGrade* (US$6), which has 14 functions for fixing underexposed or incorrectly balanced media. Correct the video before inserting it into the timeline of your edit app (see chapters 8 and 9 for details).
- *Instagram*: This story creation app is a favorite of many young people, and news agencies often create Insta news channels. Creating an *Instagram* slideshow,

where a number of pictures and or videos are linked to form aspects of a story, is quick and easy:

- **Log in**
- **Hit the plus button like you usually would to add media**
- **In the photo window look for the "select multiple" button**
- **Choose up to 10 photos or videos to share with your followers**
- **Edit the order**
- **Add text and filters to each photo/apply a filter to the whole group**

TRANSFER DEVICES, SUBTITLES, BATTERY PACKS AND DRONES

Transfer Devices

Smartphones get clogged with content, and we often delete valuable media to free up space. If you update your story months, or even years, later you may need to access the old story and its raw media. Don't delete your media—transfer it to a hard drive or computer and archive it into your very own media library.

I use transfer devices to archive media and unclutter my smartphone. There are many different brands, but two basic types. One type plugs into the phone—for example, a lightning version for iOS devices is iXpand by Sandisk. Another type that creates a local WiFi connection with your phone and works across platforms is Airstash by Maxell.

Figure 2.29 **Sandisk lightning transfer device.**

Ivo Burum

Figure 2.30 **Airstash by Maxell.**

Ivo Burum

I use the *WeTransfer* app to move content from my phone to the network editor or send to another colleague.

Tip: Do not delete media from your smart device until you have rendered your edit project into a video.

Subtitles

I often use the titles tool to create these in *Kinemaster* and *LumaFusion*. However, I also use two discreet subtitles apps:

DIY Subtitles **is a manual app that creates titles relatively easily.**
Mixcaptions **creates subtitles automatically and it works well enough that it can save a great deal of time. It offers a number of font styles and three sizes. Once the app creates the subtitles you can alter any that are incorrect.**

Battery Pack

I use the Powerstation AC at 22000mAH (US$199), which gives me between 24 and 100 extra hours of power.

One great app resource is Marc Blank Settle (@marcsettle), a BBC trainer. But avoid the trap of buying apps for apps' sake.

Drones

I use a DJI Spark (US$500)—small and affordable—for basic HD video and DJI Mavic Air (US$900)—reasonably small, longer operating distance and 4k video. I have never found that I use long pieces of drone footage, but it has always been effective if used sparingly and when it supports the story. The Spark needs the DJI controller, otherwise it can have

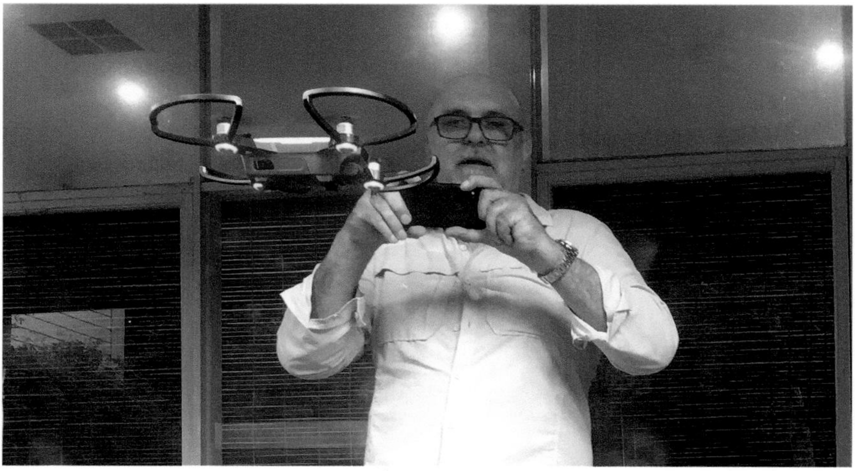

Figure 2.31 **Ivo using DJI Spark drone.**

Ivo Burum

connection issues. Audio will probably need to be recorded separately and music is often used. But low drone sound with, for example, natural sound of the rally that's being filmed mixed underneath can work well.

Tip: It's important that you check your country's drone regulations before you fly.

In closing, there are 6 million apps on the market. How do you choose? Simple. Work out what you need to do—the task—experiment, then choose the app that best does the job you need to do. Ironically, people who edit with either *VN, Power Director, LumaFusion* or *Kinemaster* apps on iOS, will still use *iMovie* for many simple tasks because it's very user friendly. *FiLMiC Pro* is an excellent camera app that mirrors many DSLR features on a smartphone. But more often than not, I still use the on-board camera app on my iPhone because it's often all I need for my mojo work. I use very few audio apps because I generally record my audio with video. You never know when you will need a picture. I detach audio from video if I need audio alone, or cover it with B roll. The trick is to learn the skills to record clean sound, shoot dynamic pictures and edit the two into powerful story. More often than not, this relies on skill and not technology. And that's what we discuss in the following chapters.

Go mojo ...

NOTE

1 *Ferrite* is a free high-end audio app.

REFERENCES

Burum, I. (2016). *Democratising Journalism Through Mobile Media*. Abingdon, Routledge.

Burum, I. and S. Quinn (2015). *MOJO: The Mobile Journalism Handbook, How to Make Broadcast Videos with an iPhone or iPad*. New York, Focal.

Crotty, M. (2003). *The Foundations of Social Research: Meaning and Perspective in the Research Process*. London, Sage Publications.

Feldman, C. (2008). *No Time To Think: The Menace of Media Speed*. New York, Continumum International Publishing.

Gillmor, D. (2006). *We the Media: Grassroots Journalism By the People, For the People*. Sebastopol CA, O'Reilly Media.

Hassenzahl, M. (2003). "The Thing and I: Understanding the Relationship Between User and Product." In M. A. Blythe, K. Overbeeke. A. F. Monk, P. C. Wright (eds.) *Funology:From Usability to Enjoyment*. Dordrecht, Springer: 31–42.

Hirst, M. (2012). *One Tweet Does Not a Revolution Make: Technological Determinism, Media and Social Change*. AcademiaEdu. www.academia.edu/1789051/One_tweet_does_not_a_revolution_make_Technological_determinism_media_and_social_change.

Mahlke, S. (2008). "User Experience of Interaction with Technical Systems." PhD dissertation, Technischen Universität Berlin: 193. https://depositonce.tu-berlin.de/bitstream/11303/2090/2/Dokument_1.pdf.

McLuhan, M. (1964). *Understanding Media: The Extension of Man*. New York, Penguin.

Mosco, V. (2004). *The Digital Sublime*. Cambridge MA, MIT Press.

Ryan, R. and E. Deci (2001). "On Happiness and Human Potentials: A Review of Research on Hedonic and Eudaimonic Well-Being." *Annual Review of Psychology* **52**: 141–166.

CHAPTER 3

DEVELOPING MOJO STORIES

SUMMARY

This chapter introduces concepts of mobile video story development, audience and angle. Transforming user-generated content (UGC) into user-generated stories (UGS) and user-generated programs (UGP) at source can create a greater level of diversity. To enable this to occur we introduce the SCRAP story tool with a focus on story, character and structure. We discuss the value of knowing your audience, choosing the correct style and having a strong story focus. The chapter introduces an investigative approach and discusses Mark Lee Hunter's tool kit, before suggesting the need for a common digital language across the mobile content creation sphere.

OVERVIEW

In 1993, while working in television, I began producing a self-shot TV series, *Home Truths*, where the audience got the opportunity to be part of the production process. Participants learned to use digital video cameras to tell their own personal stories. It wasn't cheaper TV, as some thought, and required time and patience when teaching participants about storytelling and coverage. Viewers got an insight into the unique worlds of people just like them who were now also producers of content.

In 2007, the introduction of the iPhone and apps became a game changer—a lightbulb moment that enabled stories to be shot, edited and published on the phone. Mobile technology would redefine both the way we produced content and, more importantly, who produced it.

By 2010, we were using smartphones more and more to complete the whole production process, even the all-important edit. I uploaded my first shot-edited-and-published-from-an-iPhone story to YouTube, in 2011. Being able to complete stories on the phone is an important workflow step, especially when reporting from marginalised and conflict areas. "A journalist in today's digital world will have no edge if he can't use mojo," says Rana Sabbagh, former executive director of Arab Reporters for Investigative Journalism (ARIJ), "especially journalists in the Arab world where the state, politicians and agenda-driven publishers try to muzzle media and free speech" (cited in Burum 2018).

Very quickly, the mobile space, driven by a techno-determinist view, began to focus more on story and even long-form production. More recently, acclaimed director Steven Soderbergh[1] shot his second iPhone feature, *High Flying Bird*. He angered fellow directors when he said that he'd like to shoot all his future films using a smartphone (Trenholm 2019). His reasoning, apart from technical excellence, was that it gave him the freedom to work outside the studio system. "It's a luxury to be able to take a camera and velcro it to a wall," he said. "If you want the lens on the wall, you don't have to cut a hole in the wall and put the camera behind it. It's a great tool" (Trenholm 2019).

This flexibility and the associated freedoms are also true for citizen and investigative journalists who use smartphones to tell stories. In an investigative context, Sabbagh sees these citizens and journalists, often the first on the scene, as bearing "witness to a first draft of history." She believes their mobile investigations can provide "the prima facie evidence at international criminal tribunals" (cited in Burum 2018). This potentially provides a level of editorial control that's essential to achieving transparency and accountability. Mojo students from a number of Middle East and North African countries, trained at our ARIJ mojo workshops, have created award-winning stories using their mobile phones.

Stories like *The Eastern Gateway*, by Sameh Ellaboudy, won the EU's 2017 Migration Media Award for investigation into Syrian refugee migration. Ellaboudy, an investigative journalist from ARIJ in Jordan and trained in mojo, shot much of the close-quarter documentary footage on his mobile, mixing that with video and DSLR footage. The mobile enabled him to capture intimate, difficult-to-access footage from varied points of view. Another example is Nilas Johnsen, a Norwegian Middle East correspondent for *VG*, who after training as a mojo, began reporting his international stories using his mobile.

> Hi Ivo—would like to tell you that I often think about the great lessons you taught me on making simple videos with the iPhone in the field. I am now the Middle East correspondent for *VG*. I really like doing small MoJo clips with my iPhone. That also leaves the photographer free to hunt for good pictures! And, even though *VG* have sent me professional TV equipment, for my first three weeks I have just used the iPhone.

Johnsen says the phone gives him the freedom to unobtrusively get in close to action in and around the refugee camps.

Soderbergh sees small tech as being both positive and negative for young filmmakers. "It's easier to make something that looks amazing," he said, "it's just harder to get eyeballs on it" (Trenholm 2019). In 1984, I sat in a theatre listening to the prolific film producer, Dino De Laurentius, tell us that a good story will "always get its money, and an audience." This truism might also be the answer to Soderbergh's riddle—the story is a key driver, not necessarily the technology. The use value of mobile will continue to develop beyond its ability to capture revolutionary citizen witness moments (Arab Spring), to creating more formed and politicised user-generated stories (UGS), programs and feature films.

Moreover, the focus on story that grew in the mobile space after 2015 is a cultural shift away from tech worship. In my case, this shift required a neo-journalistic[2] approach that recognised the key legacy elements of video storytelling. Simply put, it's important to embrace the possibilities that new technology brings, while not throwing the digital baby—the storytelling—out with the convergent bathwater, and that's what we discuss in this chapter.

THEORETICAL PERSPECTIVE

My first recollection of story was mum telling stories of our homeland in Croatia, over dinner. The Balkans, where I was born, has a culture of oral storytelling and mum, like her mum before her, is a great storyteller. In Indigenous Australia oral storytelling is a way of passing on cultural mores. In Macronesia, islanders choose life roles for children through a process of osmosis that involves oral storytelling.[3] Many of the stories I heard were hero journeys told as traditional folklore. These could be reinterpreted in oral storytelling to create varied versions with each iteration potentially making one person's fantasy another person's nightmare.

Ostensibly there are many types of stories, but I'd like to focus on three types:

- ***Personal*—the self-actualised journey such as the one I made on *Rule 61—A Case Against Radovan Karadzic*, or Mike Rubbo's *Waiting for Fidel.* These films about the filmmaker's journey are relevant to mojo praxis.**
- ***Traditional*—folklore, myth and instructional stories.**

- ***Created*—stories that combine aspects of both the above and use a variety of elements to construct an effective narrative. This is probably the most common story a mojo might produce.**

Irrespective of the type of story, volumes have been written about theoretical approaches to storytelling. Here are two relevant views (Miller 2011):

> **Vladimir Propp's (1928) theory states that stories have three stages: a peaceful home (Beginning), a break-up of the home often by a villain (Middle), a member of the broken home tracks down the villain, defeats him/her, and re-establishes the home (End). Propp sees characters as vessels for completing action: the villain, the donor, the helper, the princess, the dispatcher, the hero. Propp's work, which was very influential in the structuralist movement, ignores things like historical context, style and point of view (Kaas 2014).**
>
> **Joseph Campbell's (2012) theory states that a story is composed of a hero's journey through which the hero becomes self-reflexive and grows. The heroine's/hero's community needs to be fixed; the heroine/hero goes on a journey; transcends constructed archetypes to consider her/his notion of identity; obtains a sacred object to enable the fix; and returns to the community with the knowledge and revitalises it (solves the problem).**

I think both are interesting cultural perspectives. Propp, a Russian, believes story is about retribution and good conquering evil, about possible actions, and it's certainly that. Campbell, an American, sees it as a version of the American dream—we learn, then we use the knowledge to work hard and get ahead and that's great for the nation. Convergence gave rise to many forms of storytelling that may not have been conceived pre-Internet. In particular, cellular capability has driven a new genre of UGC creation that has "deeply altered notions of what it means to be literate in an increasingly global and networked society" (Wang 2013). Stories shoot across social media in milliseconds, causing a growth of fragmented kludge like UGC, online hate speech and a growing culture of misinformation. Web 2.0 has given rise to the on-camera self-shot personalised reporter and report. Internet communications made one-to-many and many-to-many interactions common, with each collaboration enabling alternative story perspectives that replace a "static and abiding notion of literacy as sustained by single literacy technology, like the printing press" (ibid). The result is millions of hours of UGC self-publishing experiences that question the very notion of literacy and authorship.

Developing stories and programs is a curious experience at the best of times. Some years ago, while working as an executive producer at ABC in Australia, I received a phone call at 10:10am on a Friday morning, followed by an email asking, "How's that series going? It's meant to be on air on Monday at 9pm." "What series?" I screamed. The blank page we had on Friday became a TV series that aired three days later. It was a new way of working, no denying that, but I often wonder, what made it possible—the technology, the skill set or a combination?

That same question has haunted me at every change I witnessed in communication—film to video, video to digital, and the inception of mobile storytelling. In 1993, when the camera department of the ABC heard I was scoping *Home Truths*,[4] a self-shot series exploring the lives of 20 Australian families, shot by the families, they went on strike. Unlike Soderberg's colleagues, who didn't want cameras velcroed to walls, our camera crews felt that giving ordinary citizens cameras and teaching them how to tell a story would lead to a downgrading of the craft and the end of their jobs. These were two of the reasons early mojo adoption was choked in broadcast TV. Even though the 2020 pandemic is changing attitudes to new ways of doing media jobs, it's possibly still one of the major reasons that mobile production is still swimming against the tide in its crawl to secure a beachhead in TV.

When Michael Moore made the documentary *Roger and Me* (1989) he was panned for creating its stylistic mish-mash and its shift in traditional concepts of documentary story. Was it a documentary, a comedy, auteur indulgence, or was it genius? Moore, who was the writer, producer, director and presenter of the film, was accused of being a polemicist, populist and that he was irreverent in the way the film treated the hollow answers from officials (Corner 1996). It was in part due to this, Moore's openness and his willingness to put himself on the spot, that the film broke all box office records. Like Nick Broomfield[5] before him, Moore popularised the reporter-on-camera character genre. In essence, Moore and Broomfield are self-reflexive modern-day mojos who insert themselves into the frame, using the medium and their own life experience and personality to tell archetypal David vs Goliath stories (see Chapter 4).

Further exploration shows that Moore has the storytelling skills to wrap around his shifting stylistic choices that ground *Roger and Me* in a compelling structure and narrative. For example, the film has a simple five-point structure: a Beginning that establishes Moore and the township of Flint; it then Develops, explaining the issue at the GM plant; in the Middle stakes increase and celebrity involvement highlights the plight of workers; in the Climax the situation gets worse so Flint tries tourism; and during the film's Resolution we see that everyone loses. Hunter et al. (2019) say, "start with a story, place it in a timeline, make a source map and build a structure as you research."

Over the past 60 years changes in factual storytelling in film, video and, more recently, digital were in part driven by technological innovation and new processes, formats and even styles of storytelling. Television gave storytelling a home and developed a series of formats and labels to help fund and schedule content (Burum 2008). Reality TV, one such construct, has ushered in a new type of field producer with little storytelling experience, a skill all factual producers traditionally needed. He/she ushers talent around while specialists pull the story together in post-production. The same occurred with mojo praxis. Accessibility to technology quickly created a new breed of producer with little experience in multi-planar video storytelling. And in some instances, specialist editors, working in the office, edited the raw content that mojos uploaded to their company sites. This is changing as mojos get more experienced at completing user-generated stories (UGS) and as networks become more adaptive to mobile workflows.

Video literacy and legacy skills can and often do work in concert with digital content production. A strong narrative and voice lie at the conceptual heart of digital storytelling (Wang 2013). Or at least it should. Goodrich (2010) provides the clever analogy of spinning thread, which can be used to describe mojo praxis and story development more specifically. He suggests that while a single fiber is weak, combining fibers results in strong thread—in our case, combining research, mojo story elements, technology, skills and publication into sequences(UGC into UGS) results in strong narrative. In the digital age, as more audience members become publishers of their own raw UGC fibers, they'll need skills to transform these into more complex UGS narratives. They will especially, as Hunter points out, need strong research.

Using these skills to transform witness UGC moments into more politicised UGS begins an important thought process about who says what to whom, when and why. Referred to as the Lasswell maxim (1948), this type of process encourages creators to think more about their content in cultural, social, political and economic terms. This level of deliberation potentially delivers politicised stories that can lay out a more meaningful agenda for public discourse in online communities.

It has been suggested that online communities revolve around a hierarchy based on meritocracy, where participants "collaborate" on unfinished artifacts. These artifacts are shaped and "improved" by the group, whose quality of work can substitute for professional content (Bruns and Schmidt 2011). The reality has proven to be quite different. Much of the online content produced and published by citizens is often no more than self-actualised moments of user life. It does not immediately replace professional work, nor is it necessarily meritocratic. However, since about 2015, aspects of mojo praxis began to shift from a techno-determinist view to one that is more story-centric, involving more holistic skill sets.

What we need, as Professor Mark Deuze identifies, are "active agents" involved in a reflexive process of meaning making (2006). Realising extended meaning online—use value, relevance and sustainability—largely depends on the degree to which education and mojo trainers embrace current opportunities to create a digitally healthy citizenry, to countervail the impact of mainstream media's online migration (see Chapter 14). Understanding how stories are created is a first step to being able to recognise misinformation and fake news online.

This is what Erik Sonstelie, the Editor-in-Chief of *Oppland Arbeiderblad*, an online newspaper in Gjovik in Norway, decided to address. He found that when he trained his journalists to mojo, they understood the mechanics and were very enthusiastic to learn new digital styles of video storytelling. "In 2017 and 2018 we had a video each day, today we have approximately one or two mojo videos a week" (Sonstelie 2020). He says the metrics in his region can play against mojo stories unless they are very specific. His audience want "breaking news, visual and sports news and user generated stories" (ibid), so Sonstelie began training his audience to mojo to create those stories. They were excited, but eventually, "I think they would rather learn how to write stories and take photos, simply because it seems easier" (ibid). It's a long-term commitment and Sonstelie has established three audience pages on his site—culture, sports and politics. The best of the best of their UGS end up on *OA*'s front page.

UGS creation trains citizens to embrace new digital technologies and storytelling in a meaningful way—something Ethan Zuckerman, the director of the Center for Civic Media at the Massachusetts Institute of Technology, believes is required if we are to transform the gossip-like nature of the current Internet (Zuckerman 2014). According to Maria Ressa (2014), CEO of Rappler, and Erik Sonstelie, this change can occur if we marry the discipline of old-school journalism with new workflows. This is the principle behind the neo-journalistic approach of mojo praxis described in this book.

PRACTICAL PERSPECTIVE

Following are some research and workflow points mojos might consider when developing stories. They are taken directly from my short- and long-form mojo courses and have been tested over many years and shown to work globally across community, education and professional media sectors.

Developing the Idea

Make sure you have an idea that you really want to make. Choose a topic and, before deciding on the story that will best convey your idea, ask:

- **Who's the audience?**
  - **Who's watching—a news, specialist (gardening), current-affairs or investigative audience?**
  - **What is the demographic?**
  - **What's the political and the cultural imperative—is the story politicised; does it want to change a cultural point of view?**
- **What's the angle?**
  - **What do you want to say? For example, how is your story on graduation different from the next reporter's—is it about whether studies prepare you for a job; who is going to which university and why? What's your angle?**

  Always ask …
  - **Have I chosen the most unique angle for this story for the intended audience?**
  - **Why is the story being told and how will I best produce it creatively and editorially for my audience?**
  - **Is it factually correct so my audience will trust the information?**
  - **Will the audience care about it? If not, should I drop this story, or find a way to make it relevant?**
  - **Can it be produced using just a smartphone or do I need a hybrid approach (see Chapter 4)?**

- **What's the style?**
  - **News (short and sharp)**
  - **Features (with exposition and character color)**
  - **Current affairs (international, political, human interest or event driven)**
  - **A long investigative exposé (documentary)**
  - **Narration and or interviewee driven**
  - **Will you appear on camera?**
  - **Does it use archive?**
- **What's the structure?**
  - **Does it have a clear simple five-part structure—Beginning, Hook, Middle, Climax (rising) and Resolution? Structure is liberating not restrictive.**

As your idea develops its story focus, complete a more specific SCRAP check. SCRAP helps answer journalism's 5 Ws—who, what, when, where and why:

- **Story: WHAT is the story, what's the focus and what type of characters does it need?**
- **Characters: WHO is in it and WHO is best to tell WHAT part of the story?**
- **Resolution: WHAT is the structure and WHY?**
- **Actuality: WHAT will be filmed, WHERE and WHY?**
- **Production: WHERE and WHEN is filming happening, WHAT are the logistics and how will the story be produced?**

Let's explore the above in more detail.

Story Focus

Robert McKee (1999) in his seminal book, *Story*, said that "Story urges the creation of work that will excite and respect audience … and does not substitute spectacle for substance." We all have stories in us and accessibility to storytelling technologies and online platforms have given many more people an opportunity to tell stories. All we need to do, as Mark Hunter from Insead suggests, is "To follow your passion." Hunter is right, but we need more than passion, we need substance and focus. A story is, as Hunter reveals, "a sequence of events in time that lead to a meaning" (Hunter and Sengers 2019), which is achieved through research that transforms raw UGC into more structured UGS.

Most mobile journalists and producers who pitched story ideas to me would begin with a character pitch, "I know this person who..." I would invariably respond by saying, "Great, but *what's the story*?" Focus and do-ability are critical factors in mojo stories. In deciding whether a story is worth the research, development and production effort, consider:

- ***Who's affected?*** **It could be about a fence dispute impacting two neighbors.**
- ***How much are they suffering?*** **What's the impact of the fence?**
- ***Can that be shown?*** **Is the fence erected, or proposed, are there plans and access to these, and what about the old fence?**
- ***Is there a journey to capture?*** **Has this dispute been going on for a while and involved council, lawyers and the tribunal? Does it involve other neighbors?**
- ***Are there bad guys and/or good guys?*** **Emotionally has one neighbor been open, or have they tried to put this through on the quiet?**
- ***Do you have access?*** **Are neighbors, council and lawyers all willing to talk and film?**

An in-depth investigative story requires even deeper investigation—we need a hypothesis. Mark Lee Hunter suggests it's imperative to ask what your thesis, or research question, will investigate. "We use stories as the cement which holds together every step of the investigative process, from conception to research, writing, quality control and publication" (Hunter et al. 2011). Figure 3.1 shows a simple example of a story statement (hypothesis) and the various investigations that might be asked around its research question. Hunter and Sengers (2019) say, ask what you want to prove, answer that, then ask another question. A hypothesis helps answer the pivotal question: Is the story worth producing?

Tip: I believe that when time permits, this level of forensic articulation is helpful on every story, irrespective of its length or genre. In fact, it occurs organically when determining a five-point structure.

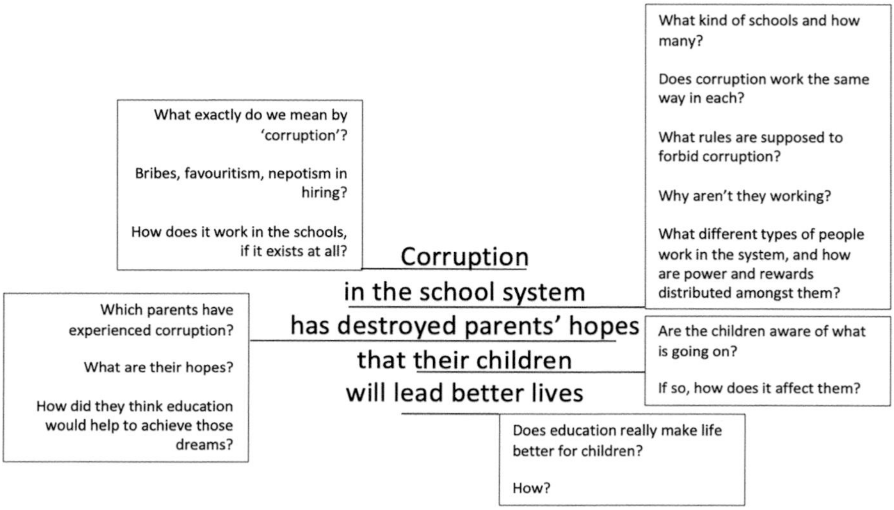

Figure 3.1 **Mark Lee Hunter's hypothesis matrix.**

A story focus insists that story dictates technology and workflow. Philip Bromwell, a video and mobile journalist from Ireland's RTÉ, says: "My job requires me to tell stories, and we have to remember the audience doesn't really care how content is created, but they will engage with a good story" (Bromwell 2017). Bromwell's focus on story, ahead of technology, is important. "Although I can film and I can edit, my primary skill is as a storyteller," he says. "I am certainly not a 'techie' and I am not as obsessed as others are with having the very latest piece of mojo gear" (ibid).

Bromwell is right. However, having the right technology can also be important. For example, shooting a story on lions in Africa may require a hybrid DSLR and long lens kit in order to shoot the required shots from a distance, so as not to get eaten. Conversely, in war-torn Aleppo, a small mojo kit can make a journalist invisible and less of a target.

Finally, to understand the relationship between your mobile story and its audience it's important to consider the following:

- ***Currency* is very important.**
- ***Significance* is impacted by *currency*.**

- ***Proximity* impacts *significance*.**
- ***Prominence* of story talent can trump *proximity*.**
- **Human interest can increase with *prominence*.**

Above all, good stories have a universality about them. A number of years ago I was producing a prime-time series for an Australian network. It was a hit in Australia, but also sold to 12 countries, demonstrating that strong story travels across borders and languages. All good stories have focus, universal themes and real characters that audiences can relate to. They also need what I call "actuality," or strong visual sequences. Bromwell (2017) points out that "It's easier to make an engaging story when it's a visually appealing subject. So, in the planning process ask what and who will I see, what will they be doing?"

Character Focus

A mojo is constantly making choices about which characters to include and in what order to use them. The order signals a character's dramatic journey through the story, which is what keeps us watching—to find out if the character will suffer or overcome their ordeal.

At the development stage I like to write a brief paragraph about each of the main characters. This includes:

- **Who (name, relationship to others in film and so on)?**
- **Why are they being interviewed?**
- **Where (where does this person fit in the story)?**
- **What (what is this character's role, what makes them interesting, important and watchable)?**
- **What is this character trying to achieve and will they overcome, or be defeated on their journey?**

Story Event

A story event (the inciting incident) creates change in a character and is expressed in terms of value (impact) and often achieved through an attempt to overcome an obstacle (conflict).

Character change occurred in every factual story I have ever produced, irrespective of genre. Risk is a test of the impact of change on a character (their journey), so I always ask: What does our character stand to lose if s/he does not get what they want?

In trying to achieve their goal, characters experience conflict with other characters: who wants what from whom, how and why? It's important to determine the primary conflicts characters have to overcome to get to their goal. Will characters express their views in conflict with each other? And how will this conflict resolve in the story?

When planning the above it's important to consider how your characters (interviewees) will work to impact audience reaction. To what extent will your storytelling choices impact your character's journey and hence, the audience's view. Will you structure your event, or inciting incident, judiciously so that the characters witness action and show emotion as a result of that (McKee 1999)? This is the job of structure, what I call resolution.

Tip: If you have the choice of a smart interviewee and an engaging one, choose the latter, if you can't have both. You can always add the factual smarts using narration and B roll.

Structural Focus

Resolution is a structural road map. Once you decide on your interviewees (your characters), re-adjust/finesse your story structure to plan around your characters' strengths, and consider the following structural story notes:

- **When will we hear from the main interviewee and will that be through actuality or interview?**
- **Which interviewee will be used to develop the story, or will you use B roll and narration?**
- **Who will I use to tell the climax and how will I create this?**
- **Who will I use and how will I close the story?**
- **Do I have B roll to introduce and cover my interviewees and key points of narration?**

You can generally work out much of the above at the research stage, pre-interviews and once you know characters and begin mapping your structure. Because real research happens on the ground where the story changes, you need to understand your options and be prepared to shift your views, characters and structure on location.

That's where a simple structural plan helps to determine where our story takes place and what happens, when and why.

Figure 3.2 describes a simple structural map that articulates the various plot points and my story bounce and acts as an on-location story and character checklist, which I adjust accordingly as I collect information during pre-production, production and post-production. It's the beginning of my edit map (plan).

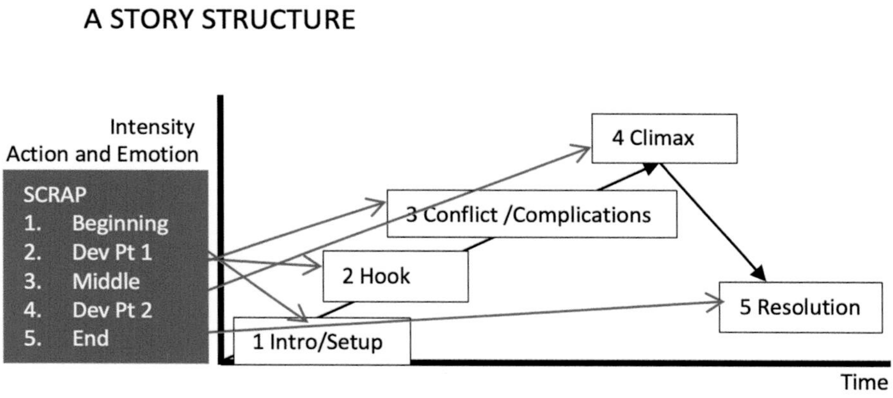

Figure 3.2 **Structural map.**

Ivo Burum

As you develop your structural map, you might find that you naturally have seven or more points, depending on the scope and length of your story. Documentaries somehow almost always have about 13 points. But these five-points are a good start:

1 **Beginning—Introduction where plot and character are revealed. Sets up the opening of your "video," so use content that grabs the audience, then information that introduces the characters and their predicament. The Beginning is an**

idea—the place to begin your story bounce, your rhythm and tempo—how long we stay in one scene, how we segue between narrator and interviewees (see Chapter 8).

2 **Rising action—Dev Point A or "Hook" broadens the story beyond your main character. How many people are affected, how often does it happen? Stakes begin to increase. The action the protagonist chooses to take becomes one of the story's driving events that leads to the climax. How you reveal crisis, action and resolve will impact the pacing, or what I call story bounce. McKee (1999) suggests it's important not to turn the tension screws too often, otherwise the audience might get exhausted and give up before the climax.**

3 **Middle—The conflict complicates plot/story as we introduce the voice of "unreason" to the counter-argument of authority. Who and why and what will happen next?**

4 **Climax—Dev Point B explores shifts in action and how stakes are further increased. If this or that doesn't happen, many more people will be affected. If I have to go to court, I'll go broke. How will we create a solution that builds to a resolution especially if after many attempts at a fix the crisis worsens?**

5 **Resolution—Is there an end in sight? Comment from protagonists on solution, or next move.**

Structure determines how your story about, for example, child soldiers in Uganda, will be different to the same story produced by *60 Minutes*: Why am I using the nun who saved the children from the LRA and how will I use her dangerous journey into the jungle to bring her girls back safe and sound? Will I begin with the nun on her knees crawling after the LRA rebels and asking them not to kill her and return the girls they stole and then step back into the story, before coming back to this horrific and brave scene? What I do and why, is my structure—in essence, it's an engagement map that works to introduce story characters to the audience.

Tip: Shooting video is more time consuming than writing a print story. A plan keeps you on schedule and is a checklist to help determine if everything is covered before wrapping location, when it forms the initial edit map.

Actuality Focus

Actuality[6] provides story currency—the rally, the race, ambulance officers working at a car accident, interview at the side of the road, formal interviews. It will form part of your primary coverage and also your B roll. Deciding what you will film is determined by your schedule, access and luck. Planning for actuality is something that I do when I decide on my characters. The structural map helps identify story-specific actuality and B roll. The earlier you decide what visuals your story needs, the sooner you'll know what's possible and what archive or graphics you'll need. As mentioned, stories need visuals and, more specifically, actuality to provide currency. In our example, an actuality focus might see my story start with the repatriation of a child, who has escaped the LRA, back to his village and family. This provides a current event or story peg. I discuss how to shoot actuality in Chapter 4.

Production Focus

Understanding production imperatives that impact story is a critical aspect of development. Creating video stories and programs requires pictures and face-to-face meetings. These take time to record, which is one of the biggest hurdles for mojos. There are a number of production aspects that impact story during the development phase:

- **availability of characters**
- **travel and accommodation**
- **permission to film on location**
- **level of narration**
- **the ability to get relevant B roll**
- **safety**
- **weather**
- **schedule**

These issues and others are discussed at length in Chapter 4.

In closing, I have outlined a series of steps and tips for developing strong stories that immerse the audience in an emotional journey. Great stories involve the audience not only as passive receivers, but as active storytelling participants. Without this buy-in, the storyteller

Mark Hunter's Break-out Box of tips for story development:

1. **Decide if the story is worth doing**
2. **Develop a hypothesis to determine story and investigation scope**
3. **Verify your research**
4. **Alter your angle to accommodate research**
5. **Find characters**
6. **Develop a timeline or structure**

is an essayist. Whether it's factual or drama, in a dynamic story the audience are active participants in the characters' lives. They relate to the ups and downs of a character's journey and are willing to explore the scene and the story through their eyes and their behaviors. Once story is developed, we need to shoot it and that's what we discuss next.

NOTES

1 Director of *Ocean's Eleven.*
2 Neo-journalism is a market-driven approach to a skill set.
3 Macronesian navigators are chosen through a process involving oral stories that begins as children.
4 *Home Truths* is a self-shot format where citizens from 20 Australian families shot their own very personal content around issues families deal with for this documentary series.
5 Nick Broomfield is a self-reflexive documentary maker, a proponent of the direct camera style.
6 Actuality is the footage that you don't need to set up, for example, emergency services working at the scene of an accident.

REFERENCES

Bromwell, P. (2017). Interview with I. Burum.

Bruns, A. and J.-H. Schmidt (2011). "Produsage: A Closer Look at Continuing Developments." *New Review of Hypermedia and Multimedia* **17**(1): 3–7.

Burum, I. (1994). "Birth & Single Parents." *Home Truths*. I. Burum. Australia, ABC TV: 26 minutes.

Burum, I. (2008). "The Missing Puzzle—Birth of a Format." *Creative Industries*. Brisbane, QUT.

Burum, I. and Quinn, S. (2015) *Mojo: The Mobile Journalism Handbook: How to Make Broadcast Videos on an iPhone or iPad*. Burlington, Focal Press.

Burum, I. (2018). "Mojo Workin': Developing and Producing on an iPhone Pt1." GIJN https://gijn.org/2018/06/04/mojo-workin-developing-and-producing-on-a-smart-phone-part-1/.

Campbell, J. (2012). *The Hero With a Thousand Faces*. Novato CA, New World Library.

Corner, J. (1996). *The Art of Record: A Critical Introduction to Documentary*. Manchester University Press.

Deuze, M. (2006). "Participation, Remediation, Bricolage: Considering Principal Components of a Digital Culture." *The Information Society* **22**(2): 63–75.

Goodrich, R. (2010). "Hide, Hiding, Hidden: Narrative as Concealment and Revelation." *Double Dialogues* **12**(Winter).

Hunter, M. et al. (2011). *Story-Based Inquiry: A Manual for Investigative Journalists*. New York, UNESCO.

Hunter, M. and L. Sengers (2019). *Story-Based Inquiry: Tools and Techniques*. Story-Based Inquiry Associates. www.storybasedinquiry.com/story-based-inquiry.

Kaas, T. (2014). "'Morphology of the Folktale' (1928) by Vladimir Propp." *The Narratologist*. www.thenarratologist.com/literary-theory/literary-theory-morphology-of-the-folktale-1928-by-vladimir-propp/.

Lasswell, H. D. (1948). *The Structure and Function of Communication in Society*. New York, Harper and Row.

McKee, R. (1999). *Story: Substance, Structure, Style, and the Principles of Screenwriting*. London, Methuen.

Miller, E. (2011). "Theories of Story and Storytelling." www.storytellingandvideoconferencing.com/67.pdf.

Moore, M. (1989). *Roger and Me*. USA, Warner Brothers.

Propp, V. (1928). *Morphology of the Folktale*. 1968 translation. Austin, University of Texas.

Ressa, M. (2014). "Challenge to a free press." Presented at East-West International Medai Conference, Yangon, Myanmar.

Sonstelie, E. (2020). Interview with I. Burum.

Trenholm, R. (2019). "iPhone Fan Steven Soderbergh: Shooting on Film is like 'Writing in Pencil'." www.cnet.com/news/iphone-loving-steven-soderbergh-shooting-on-film-is-like-writing-in-pencil/.

Wang, X. (2013). *A Genre Theory Perspective on Digital Storytelling*. PhD dissertation, Vanderbilt University.

Zuckerman, E. (2014). Keynote speech. East-West International Media Conference: Challenge to a Free Press, Yangon, Myanmar. East-West Center. www.ewcmedia.org/yangon2014/2014/03/12/ethan-zuckerman-civic-media-2/.

CHAPTER 4

RECORDING MOJO STORIES

SUMMARY

Shooting video can be a time-consuming task fraught with variables like changing light, noisy locations and talent that won't play ball. It's the same whether you use a big expensive camera or a smartphone. Video stories require pictures. How we plan and shoot these is discussed in this chapter. The multi-award-winning cameraman, former executive producer of *Foreign Correspondent* and producer at ABC investigative series *Four Corners*, Wayne Harley, provides a Break-out Box of tips, as does talented RTÉ mobile journalist Philip Bromwell.

OVERVIEW

I learned to shoot video in order to have more freedom to create sizzle reels to pitch ideas to bosses and to tell my own stories. I learned to edit so that I could finish my own stories and understand how to speak with editors. My producing is multi-planar and adapts to the stylistic media formats I work on—print and broadcast, newspapers, radio and now social media and other online platforms. The past decade has seen the diffusion of the journalist term to include, among other definitions, mojo or mobile journalist.[1]

Once the domain of video journalists, one-man-band workflows have become more common since the advent of smartphones and associated apps. The earliest example was a kit developed at Reuters in 2007 by Ilico Elia, now head of Mobile at Deloitte, UK. Elia (2012) said that Reuters journalists wanted to know whether they'd get paid more because they "were doing more." They were, in essence, being asked to do it all. Indeed, Philip Bromwell, a mojo from RTÉ in Ireland who does it all, says that his mojo approach is influenced by his previous work as a video journalist. "I shoot sequences, lots of close-ups; steady, well-composed shots, no pans, tilts or zooms" (Bromwell 2017). Bromwell, like me, has an approach to mojo that utilises relevant legacy skills My style is probably a little more hand-held and fluid, with the same reliance on strong story and characters, with relevant story-centric B roll. Philip's great work can be seen at https://vimeo.com/philipbromwell.

As mentioned previously in this book, the early days of mojo were driven in part by technical radio and print people. Their work is terribly important in mojo's development, but we needed more TV producers and VJs in the mix to map a multi-planar vision for mojo video production. I remember the focus of the incredibly important Mojocon in 2015 was more technical. It was difficult to get the conversation to shift to story. My mojo workshops are heavily story focused. Story is something journalists know a lot about and focusing on story is a way of allaying their fears about new technologies, convergence and tech-driven job loss.

The smartphone is a Swiss Army knife on steroids; in media terms, a creative suite in a pocket. Mojo kits, described in Chapter 3, varied depending on the job and the region. Rana Sabbagh (2017), a former Reuters correspondent and editor of the *Jordan Times*, says working on mobile can be an advantage because it enables press to "work and move in oppressive situations where citizens and policemen can obstruct the work of journalists and where large cameras paint them as targets." However, using a smart device properly is not easy, and it takes some practice to shoot evolving sequences dynamically, use powerful apps effectively and to understand when the mojo workflow needs to go hybrid. The approach should, of course, be dictated by story. Shooting football might require a long lens and hence a hybrid DSLR approach, as might shooting lions in Africa. No one wants to be Kimba's next meal.

The trick is to learn how to listen to mojo tech noise, because even noise can be useful. Experiment with apps and always make an informed decision based on the mojo story you need to tell. This chapter introduces a set of story-recording skills to enable mojos to focus and push through the noise to produce powerful stories on the run.

THEORETICAL PERSPECTIVE

One of the most difficult aspects of developing my mojo philosophy and praxis has been convincing those with a techno-determinist view that there's more to mojo than technology, namely the *techne*, or the literacies that support praxis. Digital discussion "usually revolves around how new technologies are changing the skills necessary to partake in digital culture" (Park 2012). This usually assumes that a new literacy will completely replace our old set of "basic tools needed to read and understand mediated messages" (ibid). My attitudes are influenced by years of shifting television production styles and skills. Similarly, my approach to mojo retains many legacy skills still relevant in the digital ecosphere, especially story development, shooting and editing.

Tech has always accompanied new ways of working and influenced theories that determine why we do a task a particular way. Fixed lenses meant that for a close-up (CU) early cameras were moved close to the subject. Turret-mounted cameras and rudimentary telephoto lenses meant that cameras could remain stationary and lenses could be swapped from a wide angle (WA), to a mid-shot (MS), or CU. The invention of editing meant that shots could be filmed out of sequence and programs could be scheduled and produced more economically.

In the 1960s, documentary pioneer, the late D. A. Pennebaker, broke the tether to his sound recordist partner Chris Hegedus. This enabled more freedom for both and a new, more exciting, direct cinema form of evolving coverage that enabled films like *Primary* (1960), *Don't Look Back* (1967) and *The War Room* (2001). At about the same time, in the name of cinematic truth, the Maysles brothers were experimenting with direct-camera styles. Works like *Beatles USA* (1964), *Gimme Shelter* (1969) and *Grey Gardens* (1976) let the action and the psychology of the moment evolve in a cinematic adventure. In the 1970s, Ross McElwee began adding his own musings from behind the camera in films like *Charleen* (1978). His direct style provided a slice of life and his commentary connected him to the story as it did Frederick Wiseman (*High School*, 1968). In the 1990s, Nick Broomfield developed the style further by chasing elusive characters. Working as sound recordist/journalist, his questions in *Heidi Fleiss: Hollywood Madam* (1996), designed to help guide the complicated investigation and to catch the interviewee off guard, were as revealing about him as they were of Fleiss and other interviewees. In 2002, Michael Moore's *Bowling for Columbine* added staged sequences to create punchy social commentary. These varied styles of verité were a development of direct-camera film literacies and designed to deliver a form of realism in part enabled by the more portable technologies.

The invention of small DV cameras and portable edit suites made video journalism (VJ) popular. Video journalists developed skill sets and filmmaking literacies to enable them to work alone (develop, shoot, write, edit and publish). In 2007, smartphones and advanced camera apps changed the game again. Accessibility meant that very soon there were 2.5 billion potential mojos on the planet who could shoot and upload user-generated content (UGC) to ready-made publication platforms. When film director Steven Soderbergh produced feature films using a smartphone, the mobile space was abuzz with comments like "look what this technology is capable of." Soderbergh is very experienced and employs story and film literacies to tell his mobile feature films.

As digital media expanded into human communication, the ability to use them well was crucial to a person's participation in the digital society. One difference between traditional and digital media literacy is that the former focuses on understanding media messages (Potter 2010) while the latter is challenge-based, more interactive and immediate (Burum 2018). We carry our communication arsenal—our mobile—in our pocket and we don't need to find a telephone box to change into our super-publishing self, like my old journalism teacher used to do.

There are two misleading assumptions about digital: that access to technology will overcome information gaps; and that owning the technology ensures effective use and a politicised voice. The digital divide can sometimes be bridged using technology, but it can often highlight a more serious epistemic gap if the knowledge base is too low for the user to utilise the technology to its potential. Like the digital divide, an epistemic divide can lead to a form of social exclusion (Park 2012).

It has been found that even in communities with access to technology, how it's used can lead to a second-level digital divide (Gentikow 2007). An example of this occurred in Australia in the late 1980s when the federal government installed radio and video recording and broadcasting equipment in 80 remote Indigenous communities but didn't provide the level of training needed to use it effectively. For many of those communities, video became a Hollywood horror flick they watched on Friday night, an experience that defined video as passive: something they watched, rather than the intended active practice of producing video.

In 2020, when literacy is no longer defined along textual language parameters alone, a broader multi-literacy representational digital pedagogy that accounts for text, video, audio and other multi-media elements on social media is required (Cazden, Cope et al. 1996). Technologies are a type of literacy imbued by cultural and social capital that enables their use for social meaning making. In this sense literacies are also technologies and in a multi-media environment all forms of literacy are, by default, multi-media (Lemke 1998). Participants in these new network societies, "netizans" or "produsers," take on new identities and forms in their communities of practice (Bruns 2005, Wenger 2007). Hence, new communities potentially develop their own specialised literacies. Print, radio and television producers use their skills and cultural and social capital to determine the style and nature of their digital and mojo immersion and the degree to which technology, or story, impacts their output. These new communities require new approaches in educational practice where trainers receive the upskilling we need to better address the needs of digital communities. This must include an interplay between social and the new literacies that emanate from new technologies.

PRACTICAL PERSPECTIVE

I have produced a lot of primetime cross-genre TV and many more video stories. While stylistically different, this content is all driven by a focus on story. The various styles and literacies required to produce each genre form the basis of my mojo style. The following techniques, the key points in my mojo training courses, are based on my experiences as a traveling TV producer and journalist and a decade of global mojo training.

Research

The key to any successful factual story is a research focus, to develop structure and interesting characters. Sometimes I know the story well; other times I develop a structure based on quick research, which generally alters on location. Research, as a key component of story development, is discussed in Chapter 3. However, from a production point of view, effective research results in effective structure, scheduling, filming and, dare I say, editing.

Tip: Make your research uniquely your own so that your story stands out from other stories on the same topic.

At the research stage I outline SCRAP (see Chapter 3) and make my structural mud map to create a strong narrative. Once I am happy the story is focused, I create a schedule before checking that my budget will enable me to shoot the story. *Four Corners*[2] producer Wayne Harley says, "We don't go anywhere until we are assured of being able to obtain 60% of the story. Primary, is identification/clarification of the narrative. Next is talent" (Harley 2019). I look for the most relevant talent, then the most interesting, next the most important and, finally, smart people. Talent has to be available and most importantly willing to talk on camera.

A structural mud map of the Beginning, Hook, Middle, Climax and End helps clarify key editorial milestones (see Chapter 3). I use this as my guide and scribble all over it before, during and after I shoot to help decide which sequences and or talent are working and how my edit will roll. Harley says, "A written structure is paramount, it's not set in stone but if nothing else it will make apparent what WON'T work" (ibid). If you can't state what your story is in two sentences or less, then you don't know what your story is.

Tip: The best research happens when you hit the ground running, that's when you use your five-point structural plan to adjust for talent and scope and stay focused.

Pre-production

Pre-production is a crucial stage that occurs on every story, even news, where it happens much more quickly and often in transit. There are a number of key focus areas during pre-production.

Talent focus—**is a critical aspect for pre-production—who will I interview and are they available? Harley asks, "How many 'players' do I need for my story? Identify the minimum sequences you need to add matching talent to, then add your own on-camera appearance." Do the sums; it sounds calculating but planning like this creates a lifeline that's liberating.**

Structural focus—**during this phase I am all about fine-tuning my structure based on who is available—when, what will they say, why, how and where? If it's a planned story, not breaking news, I usually talk with talent, arrange archival video and photographs, check my facts, ask about locations, permissions and visas. It's as much editorial as it is about logistics.**

Equipment focus—**pre-production is the time to make sure your mojo kit is story specific. Will you need a hybrid approach, a DSLR with a long lens for shooting sport or wildlife? Have you got spare power banks and is charging possible on location? Are you carrying a transfer stick to move your media if your phone is full, or when crossing check points? Do you have a spare phone?**

Safety focus—is the location and shoot dangerous and have you checked the location with the Department of Foreign Affairs in your country? Here are the steps I take to ensure safety:

- Check with Department of Foreign Affairs and Trade Australia.
- Check about immunisation and prepare a medical kit.
- Take out comprehensive travel insurance.
- Check the location of local hospitals.
- Tell someone at home what I'm doing, where I will be and when I expect to be finished.
- Make contact with a local fixer and give them accommodation details, shooting dates, shooting location and interviewees. Get their mobile number and email.
- Advise my consulate that I am in country and will be filming.
- Ensure I have relevant contact numbers in case of an emergency.

Production

Production begins way before you get to location—choosing talent, equipment and sourcing archive are all elements that impact production. In this short section below, I describe how I work in the field.

Hotel—many hotels generally take your passport and make a copy of the front page before returning it, while others keep the passport locked in their hotel safe. I always travel with at least two passports—one for the hotel and one to use at the foreign visa office to obtain travel documents for the next country. In reality, the second passport is your way out if things go pear-shaped, and if they do, go to your consulate or leave, then sort any issues from a safe distance.

Location—every location is different, and language, customs, food, climate and culture need to be accounted for in planning. The first thing I do when I get to a location is to connect my phone and call my fixer. Next, I tell my office that I've arrived before going to a cafe to talk to a local to get the lay of the land. After I've learned the result of the local football final and the state of politics, I have my ice-breaker question and it's time to call talent. A big question is whether I hire a driver. Having an extra hand and someone to ask about local custom is helpful. Will you need a translator (fixer) and can that person also be your driver? Do you have an exit strategy?

Lighting—making your subject pop out of the frame is a skill, especially when working fast and on your own. Harley says, "it's about playing with planes of light and it's the job of the cameraman (mojo) to see and feel it and to use it quickly." When working quickly it's all about using natural light wherever possible. I worked as a field producer and on some stories as a camera person on an international current affairs series, *Foreign Correspondent*, where natural light was used to film eight out of ten times. We'd occasionally pull out a flexi fill, other times we'd shoot with source light only. Being able to sense natural light quickly—where it's coming from and the impact of shadows—is critical. Here are some basic tips:

Exterior lighting is difficult to control because of shadows and weather. The most interesting light occurs in the morning, or before sundown, and is called the "golden" or "magic" hour. This soft light hits subjects at an angle, unlike noon light, which is stark. Given that mojos run-n-gun and will not be able to control all shooting situations, here are a few simple tips for shooting on location:

- Always know where your light (sun) is.
- The middle of the day is high-contrast light so avoid it if possible. Wait, and if you need to shoot, try and use shadows.
- Use a small flexi fill to reflect light.
- Will your lens take a neutral density (ND) filter (which is like giving your camera sunglasses)?
- Film at 45–90 degrees to the sun so the light splits your subject. Have a friend hold a flexi fill on the shadow side and create a two-point lighting set-up.
- At night use moonlight or streetlamps.

In an outdoor location clouds can cause light to vary so try and film in a location, or at a time, when the light source is constant. In this situation it's always simpler to have the sun over your shoulder facing onto the subject.

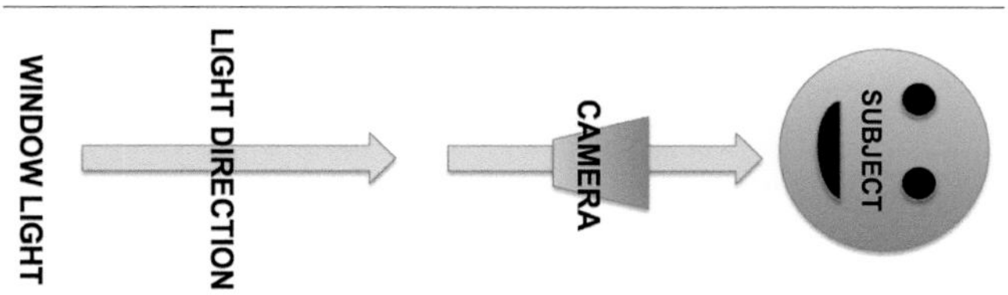

Figure 4.1 **Light source map.**

Ivo Burum

Interior lighting offers much more control. I try and use natural lighting where possible—a window as a key light and a flexi as fill. Mojos will rarely have time to pull out a back light, nor will they have the space to carry one. It's important to expose correctly, to have enough light so you might supplement natural light, especially indoors at night, by using room light, table lamps or on-camera portable lights (see Chapter 2). If I'm working alone, recording a static interview and need light, I gaffer my flexi to a tripod.

Three-point lighting—a key, fill and back light—can be used for sit-down interviews. It takes time to set this up, so I rarely use this on mojo work and I rarely used it in international current affairs. However, being able to set up three-point lighting for high-value interviews is handy, but so is being able to light that interview simply, quickly and effectively using natural light and a flexi fill. Here's a three-point set-up:

- Set an imaginary line between camera and subject.
- Place the key light on one side and the fill light on the other. Placing the key at 45 degrees to the subject provides a modeling light that casts shadows on the opposite side of the subject. The closer the key is to the camera, the flatter the subject.
- The fill is a softer light used to minimise the shadows created by the key, hence it is generally placed closer to the camera so as not to create more shadows.
- The level of intensity between the key and the fill determines the dramatic impact of the lighting.
- The back light generally lights the back of the head/hair and the shoulders to separate the subject from the background.

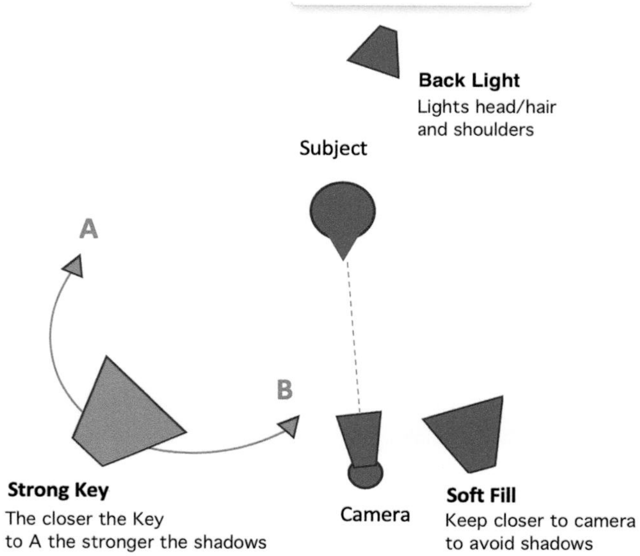

Figure 4.2 **Three-point lighting set-up.**

Ivo Burum

Shooting the Interview

When working with talent there is a fine line between being agreeable and caving in. You are producing the story not your talent, so don't be afraid to tell them that you need a particular angle, location or style. Being sure of yourself, especially admitting what you don't know and asking for guidance, is very important. The other key aspect is not wasting time—theirs or yours. Chapter 6 details various styles and a series of points to remember when conducting an interview. Here's what I do when I meet talent for the first time at an interview location:

- **I always accept a cup of tea or food if offered, but I always ask if the water is okay to drink, yes even boiled water, even in an office. If they can't convince me that the water is okay, I always politely decline, and they understand it's a health concern, not rudeness. I never eat fish unless I am filming near the ocean.**
- **I always tell interviewees very briefly what the story is about and what I want from them.**

- **I let them have the questions if they really want them but prefer to read out one or two and I never give out the "bomb" question.**
- **I ask interviewees to answer as a statement because we might not use my voice.**

In choosing your interview style and location be mindful that your interviewee is relaxed. If you don't see their character on screen you may as well be writing an essay. Wayne Harley adds,

> If it's an interview and it's in a room, always try to make the corner of the room your background. From a pictorial/editorial viewpoint, is the location itself symbolic, do cut-aways (B roll) of the location represent "silent comment" e.g. a park with a statue in it, or a kids playground (carefree happiness)? If it's outside, be careful of the noise—flight path, traffic—both human and vehicle, the light and shadows progressing as you shoot.
>
> Interview with I. Burum (2019)

Covering a walk-and-talk interview with a sound recordist is generally easy. Reporter and talent are radio-miced and the sound recordist might swing a boom for safety. However, how does a mojo operate the camera and include themselves in the interview on camera? Difficult, but not impossible. Of course, you'd radio mic the talent and if you stand close enough the talent mic will pick up the interviewer's questions. If you use a Rode S6 or S6-L splitter you can run two radio mics, one on the talent and one on the interviewer. You'd film the talent walking and talking, then put the smartphone on a tripod in a wide shot (WS) and cover part of the walk-n-talk, again asking a few of the questions. Then you'd intercut the two shots. The next option is to get someone to hold the camera in a mid-two-shot as you walk-n-talk.

Harley says,

> if you're recording two other people in a walk-n-talk, get someone to watch your back, have a gimbal of some sort; sound wise, use Rode Wireless Go Radio mics. When you've finished, walk the talent back to where you started, position yourself behind them with a "back-quarter" angle on the major talent, start walking, start filming. Repeat on the other talent if necessary. When you've finished that, get them to walk again but frame them in a big wide shot (static).
>
> Interview with I. Burum (2019)

Coverage

Coverage is a critical aspect of video production. There are two types of event that need to be covered—that which you set up and actuality, which doesn't need to be set up. You will set up interviews, stand-ups (PTC), some scene setters, explainer shots and specific B roll shots. Many of the set-up shots can be shot using a tripod (sticks) especially when shooting pans, a PTC of yourself, or long lens and close-up (CU) work. RTÉ mobile journalist Philip Bromwell rarely uses zooms, pans or tilts; his excellent coverage looks stylised with a focus on his characters and clean shots (https://vimeo.com/philipbromwell). I try and achieve the same focus with a moving hand-held camera that mirrors the talent's emotion and tempo, especially when shooting actuality. I find this can make stories more fluid/dynamic. I look for events that are self-contained, in effect have their own narrative (beginning, middle and end) and contrasts those against events that are just illustrative and need to be stitched together with other events.

Actuality is the event that happens in front of you—the meeting, the accident scene, the birth of a baby. Your style needs to facilitate coverage of evolving actuality while you cherry-pick story moments. My experience working as a producer and cameraman on current affairs shoots for *Foreign Correspondent*, in difficult global locations, is that we rarely pulled out a tripod when filming actuality. This is because it painted us as targets and slowed our work rate. Of course, tripods are handy for long interviews and long wide pans and that long-lens close-up. But much of a mojo's work will be close-quarter hand-held, so practice those skills.

Basic shots you need to consider are shown in Fig 4.3.

Extra Wide Shot (EWS) establishes the scene and location.

Wide Shot (WS) sets journalist in location. Sometimes called a long shot.

Mid Shot (MS) is an interview or demonstration shot especially effective if the interviewee waves their hands about.

Medium Close-up (CU) is the most common interview shot because it shows emotion without having to zoom.

Close-up (CU) is a dynamic and highly emotive shot.

Figure 4.3 **Shot sizes and usage. (a) Extra Wide Shot (EWS) establishes the scene and location. (b) Wide Shot (WS) sets journalist in location. Sometimes called a long shot. (c) Mid Shot (MS) is an interview or demonstration shot especially effective if the interviewee waves their hands about. (d) Medium Close-up (MCU) is the most common interview shot because it shows emotion without having to zoom. (e) Close-up is a dynamic and highly emotive shot.**

Ivo Burum

When shooting handheld, for smoother filming press your elbows into your sides and hold the smartphone with two hands. This triangle creates added stability in much the same way that a smartphone cradle, like a Beastgrip, does. (Yes, it feels like a Dalek, at first.)

Figure 4.4 **Hand holding with elbows locked and braced.**

Ivo Burum

Irrespective of the type of coverage, it's important to consider these questions:

- **How will the story be set up—a dramatic close-up, telling wide shot, dynamic B roll actuality, narration, an interview grab, a combination? Start with your strongest element.**
- **What B roll is required to introduce interviewees, to cover interview edits and highlight points?**
- **What B roll will you use to cover narration?**
- **What B roll and interviews are needed to give the story currency?**
- **How will you end the story finish and what vision and audio is required for this?**
- **Are you prepared to react to location inputs?**

Following are a couple of templates for thinking about shots and sequences.

Take a look at the three shots in Fig 4.5. It is the same shot cropped. Each frame provides a different feel. Choosing framing is essential to telling the story. Which shot would you begin with and what difference does it make? In a 3, 1, 2 order we get the following: a close-up (CU) that captures a moment of decision; a wide shot (WS) that sets the location drama as the crowd reacts; and the mid shot (MS) is the moment of truth. Starting with 1 suggests a

Figure 4.5 **Three opening frame options. (a) Establishes focus on game. (b) Focus on the star in action. (c) Increase stakes, higher emotion.**

Ivo Burum

different beginning dynamic. Of course, we are talking editing here, but as all editors will tell you, the edit process begins in the field, with coverage.

The five-shot rule is a way of exploring a scene in coverage. Shot in an order that facilitates unfolding actuality, this template could be used to cover simple activity at an event. The order in which shots are edited and juxtaposed with narration and other elements gives the piece its pace and gravitas. Add an interview, narration, relevant B roll and, if you've planned right, completed SCRAP, and captured all important "emotion," you'll have a strong story to edit. The five types of shots described in Fig 4.6, plus the main interview and narration, will tell a basic story. But your story may have anything from 5 to 13 sequences, each identified by the style of shot(s) and a structural role that provides meaning.

Where possible, whenever planning shots/sequences, it's best to consider these in the order they might be edited. Hence, my tip is to learn sequence coverage by filming something that has a definite process and structure—we call that a process shoot. Philip Bromwell (2017) says, "I always encourage people to do the simple things well if they want to achieve a polished piece."

Tip: Simple process shoots like cooking a pasta, where structure is evident, enable a mojo to practice coverage and, in particular, sequencing—emotion, information, B roll, interviews and the elements required to shorten a 30-minute process, into a powerful 2-minute film.

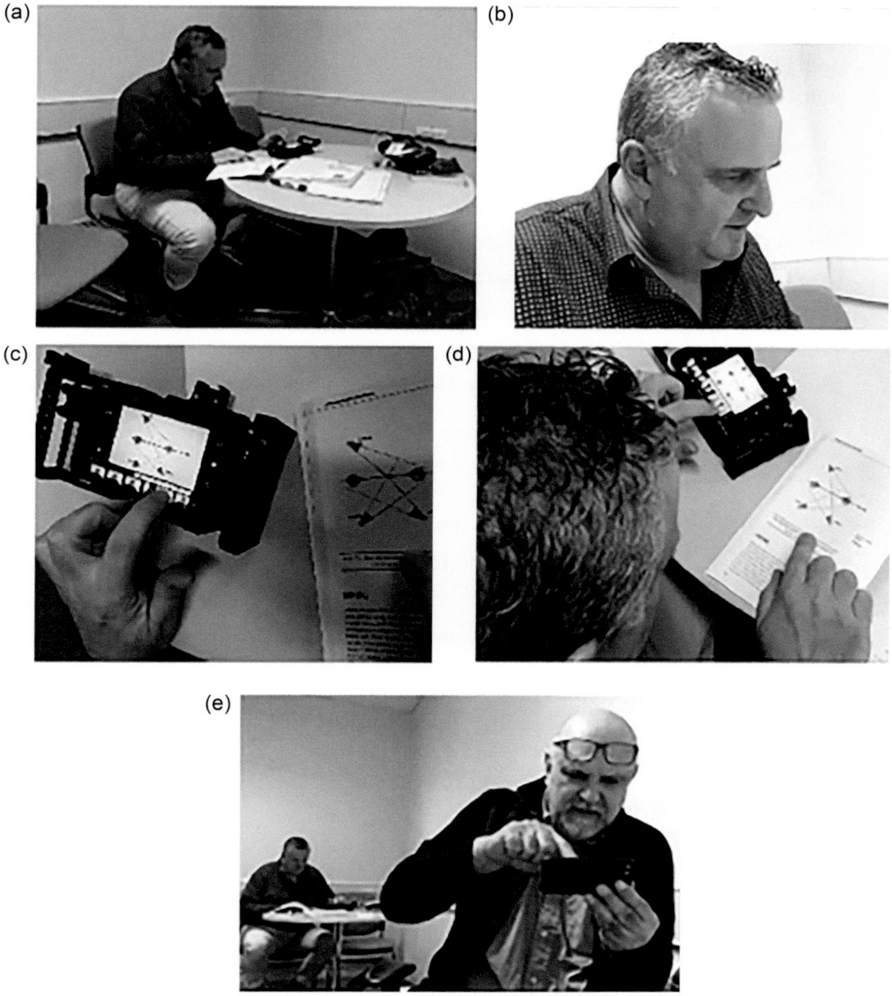

Figure 4.6 **Sequencing (a) Wide shot (WS) that describes where the story is happening used to establish the scene or later in the scene. (b) Close-up (CU) of what's happening offers a dynamic and informative perspective. (c) Close-up (CU) of who's doing it. Try an avoid profiles like the one in this picture. Being more front on to the subject is always more revealing and more dramatic. Watch head room. (d) Over the shoulder (OTS) of how it's being done references "where", "who" and "what", in one shot. This is often quite dynamic and can include a second person watching/ interacting. (e) A special shot that might, or might not, include the main character. In this case someone struggling with similar activity.**

Ivo Burum

I look at it this way—if a shot is like a word, a sequence of shots is like a sentence, and a number of sequences is a scene, like a paragraph. Here are some principles to think about when shooting sequences:

- **The shots must form a sequence.**
- **The sequence must tell the story.**
- **The script must enhance the sequence.**
- **Don't be too literal. Don't over-explain.**
- **The voice-over should add info to the shots to enhance a sequence.**
- **You do not need a shot to show every occurrence or step.**
- **Edit pictures in a logical sequence to answer questions the audience will ask.**

Exercise

For example, practice filming someone (the talent) cooking pasta (the process), or making eggs and bacon, or using a lathe to shape a block of wood into a table leg. How many different sequences are required to cover each of the above activities? To feel the emotion, the frustration and the concentration. How do you include an interview grab and shorten the sequence using B roll and or narration?

B roll is the overlay, or cut-away footage, used to intercut with the main actuality or interview. It is used to highlight aspects mentioned in the interview, cover jump cuts and color narration—essentially to compress and expand sequences. B roll should never be shot mute. It is best used with sound mixed slightly up to provide atmosphere. Harley says, "Do not underestimate the importance of sound, the police siren, the church bell, kids laughing, dogs barking, doors slamming, wind in the trees—they're all very effective punctuation marks." Sound-ups—little rises in sound in between interview grabs or narration—punctuate the story and give it a sense of reality.

I don't always button off when filming unfolding actuality and B roll basically because when the camera is rolling, I'm thinking about story and not shots. I'm still recording shots for my sequence, but when I'm rolling, I have one eye open for evolving story. I'm also rolling and listening for unexpected sound bites. Harley says, "even though the camera might not have the person in frame, someone screaming 'He's got a gun' is going to be remembered

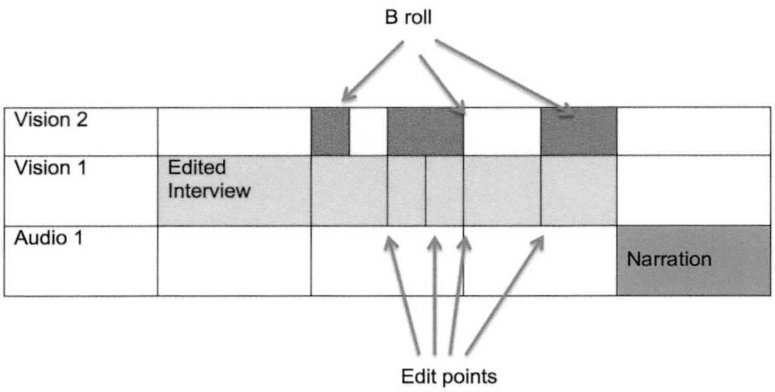

Figure 4.7 **B roll used to cover edits.**

Ivo Burum

forever and a day. Camera whips can also be useful and provide energy for a transition, 'especially if there's clever music underneath it'."

Here are some useful tips for recording B roll:

- **On the way into an interview record the exterior of the interview location.**
- **If you see the main character (a famous stamp collector) interacting with a customer, record that even before the interview.**
- **When recording an interview make notes (mental or on paper) on what's said. If it's an important point, record B roll that describes it immediately following the interview. Ask the interviewee to show you. It's okay to briefly slow them, "show me that again," and then "carry-on."**
- **Never shoot B roll without audio, you never know when that unexpected sound grab might happen.**

Tip: You can never have too much B roll and when you think you have enough, shoot some more.

The Piece to Camera (PTC) or Stand-up is a useful device that establishes a journalist's presence in a story.

Figure 4.8 Ivo Burum reporting from Yangon, Myanmar.

Ivo Burum

The PTC is used for a variety of reasons:

- **When you don't have enough pictures to describe a scene.**
- **Adds credibility and authority to the story (the reporter is there, so she must know what's happening).**
- **Can be used as a bridge between parts of the story.**
- **Illustrates emotions and feelings.**
- **Works to illustrate props (e.g. the new iPhone).**
- **Can be used in a roving walk-n-talk style to describe/show a location.**

Writing the PTC:

- **Make it very brief—8–12 seconds. If it needs to be longer, add the remaining information as narration. In that case read a few words longer (include part of the narration) and make the head of the narration a few words longer to include part of the PTC. This is for inflection and flow and to optimise edit point options.**
- **Keep it current—the point you make can't alter with time.**

- **Keep it in context—you must be able to predict the information that will come before/after the PTC.**
- **Keep it conversational—because the alternative is report-like and horrible.**

Your PTC is almost like you in the middle of an event, a chain of thought without quite reaching a conclusion.

When shooting a PTC follow these tips:

- **You have the luxury of the "re-take"—but remember, the more takes you do, the more you're likely to lose spontaneity.**
- **Dress appropriately for the situation (a PTC in the outback vs one at parliament).**
- **A little movement helps, even if it's a few steps to camera. Always begin talking in motion (after the first step).**
- **Write your PTC—try and keep it short and remember a word or a key phrase in each paragraph. If you can't remember it, use a note pad, but don't try to hide it.**
- **Talk to the camera like it's a friend/colleague; use your hands to inflect.**
- **Notice your location if something is happening around you.**

Tip: When shooting a stand-up (PTC), keep the script short, one thought per sentence and one sentence per paragraph. Choose a key word for each paragraph. Roll into a retake without buttoning off. If there is a problem, it's generally in the script. If you fix the script and still fluff it, put a sharp stone in your shoe and when your concentration is on the stone, record the piece to camera. It works.

Screen Direction—Understanding eyeline is important. If you set up for a single camera location interview, you might consider the front-on eyeline set-up in (B) in Fig 4.9. In many regions it is quite acceptable to hold the camera in front—at chest or waist height—and have the interviewee respond over the camera. Other times it needs to be at eye level (B). In this case it's difficult to shoot completely from the front because you might lose eye contact with the interviewee. In this case, place the camera as close to front-on as possible, and place the journalist (mojo) next to the lens (B). This is traditional location interview eyeline.

You would not, as has been suggested, have the camera sit behind your eyeline (C), especially if you are working solo. This is done when working with a camera person, who checks the frame.

If you need the shot to be profile (A), it can be, but avoid profile shots for the following reasons:

- **You get a greater variety of shots, without moving, if you shoot from the front.**
- **You can move the camera in on the wide lens to an MCU or CU.**
- **You can even zoom for a close-up (not advisable unless imperative).**

The almost front-on shot (B) is powerful because you see the person's face, their eyes and their emotion, all without moving the camera away from their eyeline.

Shooting around a table is an art. Figure 4.10 shows person A on Cam 2 talking left to right (from left of frame into the right of frame looking at person A). Person B on Cam 1 is talking right to left to person A. As long as our cameras stay where they are on one side of "the line," persons A and B will always talk to each other. If we cut to Cam 3 on the other side of

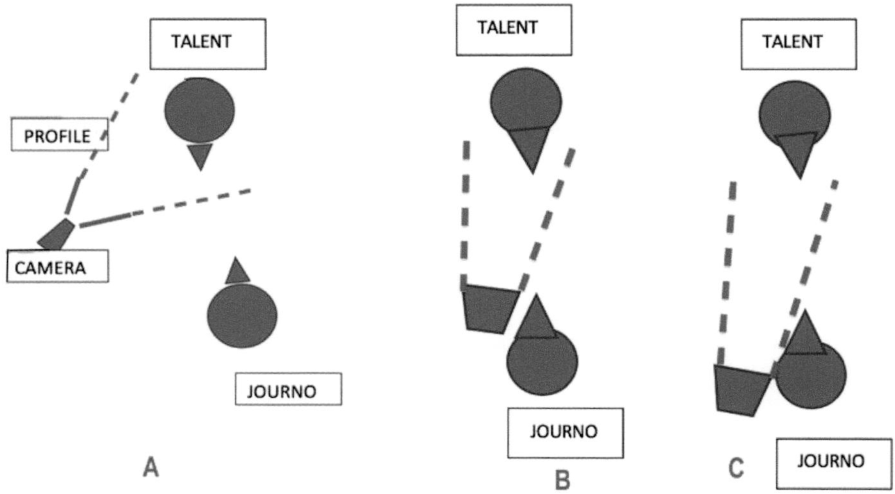

Figure 4.9 **Interview eyeline options.**

Ivo Burum

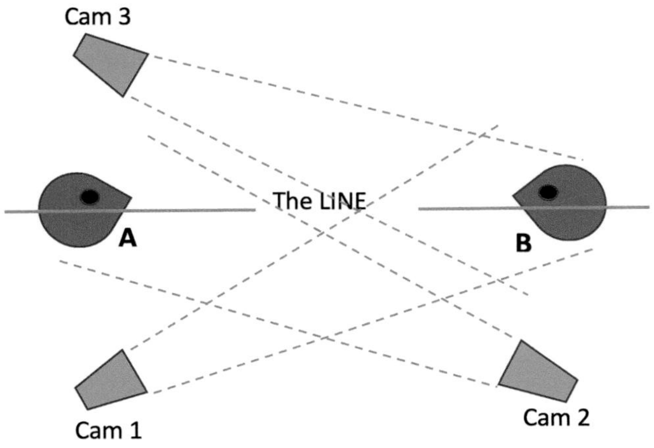

Figure 4.10 **Screen direction and line crosses.**

Ivo Burum

"The Line," person B is now talking left to right, the same as person A. In this situation they are talking to no one.

Tip: If you want to cross the line—break the 180 degree rule—cut to a neutral shot, like a crowd shot or a scoreboard, or a CU on the table, then cross the line.

Here are a few tips for recording shots and sequences:

- **Make sure your battery is charged.**
- **Make sure you have space on your phone.**
- **Let someone know where and when you will film.**
- **Switch to airplane mode to avoid unwanted calls and WiFi interference.**
- **Use a plan to indicate clearly what you have filmed and what's left to film; this will help during the shoot and the edit.**
- **Prepare specific research and questions for your interviewee and set these out against your structure, so you know how they might be used in the edit.**
- **Shoot with the light over your shoulder and on the subject.**

- Don't use the tripod unless you have to because it will slow you down.
- Learn to hand-hold the shot, something that is helped by using a wide lens and creating a 'V' (see Fig 4.10).
- Always press record and wait for the counter to roll before you ask questions, so you don't miss the beginning of the answer.
- Ask open-ended questions that don't give you a yes or no answer, unless you want yes or no.
- Frame your interviewee in MCU unless they move their hands about, in which case choose a MS.
- Try and hold B-roll shots for 10 seconds to ensure they are steady and to enable multiple sections to be used.
- Always shoot a few seconds of static shot before and after a panning shot so your pan is steady at both ends and so you end up with three potential shots.
- Shoot B roll before the interview, for example, as you enter a building, during actuality with interviewees and immediately after the interview.
- When it gets busy, think about information and story and not shots.
- Movement within a frame, or that which is created by moving the camera, can create more dynamic shots. Be careful ... be steady.
- Be aware of screen direction and the 180-degree rule, but learn how to break rules by using, for example, neutral close-up shots to cross the line.
- Use the correct gear (see Chapter 2).

Aspects that should be considered are:

- How will interviews and narration be structured to create story bounce?
- What type and how much B roll do you need to set the scene, cover interview edits, and highlight and shorten specific moments? Don't forget the detail, or location-setting shots. When you feel you have enough B roll ... shoot more.
- Do you need additional audio, like a buzz track of the atmosphere in a room? This is usually recorded for at least 30 seconds and used in the edit to smooth contrasting audio edits.

- **Will graphics be required and how and where will these come from?**
- **If it's a historical piece, or an update to an existing story, will archive be used and where will this come from, will it be copyright cleared and how much will it cost?**
- **Will PTCs be needed and if so, why? PTCs can be effective when there is no B roll, interviews or actuality, and to establish the journalist on location.**

AUDIO PERSPECTIVE

Recording audio in the field is about being ready with the right microphones and a sound strategy to enable quick reaction to location inputs (see Chapter 5). The audio recording task is made more complex because mojos predominantly work on their own. While placement is important in all types of recording it is especially difficult when recording video, where the microphone often needs to be hidden (see chapter 5).

I'd suggest:

- **Always have a shotgun mic attached to your phone and a lapel mic in the bag.**
- **If you need an interviewee to walk and talk, use a radio mic (see Chapter 2).**
- **If you need your questions cleaner, use a splitter and mic yourself with a lapel mic. Remember that both the interviewee's and interviewer's microphones will generally be recorded onto the same track on a smartphone.**
- **If you need a true split track, use a device like a Zoom H1 to record a second audio track. Use a hand clap on camera to create an edit point and sync the track to the video in the edit.**

Tip: If you need translation, do it in the field, just in case pick-ups are needed, something you won't know until media is translated.

Here are some final tips from Wayne Harley and the prolific RTÉ mojo, Philip Bromwell.

Wayne Harley provides this Break-out Box of tips:

- **A written story structure is paramount; it's not set in stone but if nothing else it will make apparent what WON'T work.**
- **Characters are critical. If you don't have characters you have an essay on your hands.**
- **Follow the action, identify a player in the action, follow the player—what they do and say makes them the "real-time" commentator.**
- **Make light soft, make it natural, side light, limited back light.**
- **Make sure your questions are very precise/concise as you may well end up using them.**
- **Emotion is a result of a factual event. If you just have emotion without facts, you don't have a story, and you're not a storyteller—you're a voyeur.**

Philip Bromwell provides this Break-out Box of tips:

- **Learn to shoot sequences... the classic five-shot sequence can form the basis of most stories.**
- **Shoot more close-ups than you think you will need... close-ups provide detail and draw your audience in.**
- **Learn how different platforms will require different shooting techniques. For example, shooting for social may require a different style to TV.**
- **Natural sound is underused and underrated. Learn how to capture it well and know when to use it.**
- **Look to capture "moments"—and learn to link them together in your writing. This will make your story memorable.**

In summary, video stories are more than radio with pictures. Understanding the rubric nature of combining video elements to create a seamless story is a key step in the mojo workflow. As Bromwell says, "You need a certain discipline in your approach to successfully bring everything together."

Working as a mojo is a holistic and organised process. You need to be smart and ready to react to location inputs. You need to think and plan like a journalist. You need to focus, record and edit the story like a filmmaker. Staying ethically and legally healthy is crucial.

Understanding the technology, but not being limited by it, is part of the job. Knowing how to do all this is difficult, but the control this holistic skill set provides is uplifting. Give it a go and you'll grin broadly at the outcome.

Go mojo ...

NOTES

1 Westlund, O. (2013). "Mobile News: A Review and Model of Journalism in an Age of Mobile Media." *Digital Journalism* **1** (1): 6–26.

2 *Four Corners* is Australia's longest-running and most prestigious investigative journalism program.

REFERENCES

Bromwell, P. (2017). Interview with I. Burum.

Bruns, A. (2005). *Gatewatching: Collaborative Online News Production.* New York, Peter Lang Publishing.

Burum, I. (2018). *Democratising Journalism Through Mobile Media.* Abingdon, Routledge.

Cazden, C. et al. (1996). "A Pedagogy of Multiliteracies: Designing Social Futures." *Harvard Educational Review* **66**(1).

Elia, I. (2012). Interview with I. Burum, London.

Gentikow, B. (2007). "The Role of Media in Developing Literacies and Cultural Techniques." *Nordic Journal of Digital Literacies* **2**: 78–96.

Harley, W. (2019). Interview with I. Burum.

Lemke, J. (1998). "Multiplying Meaning: Visual and Verbal Semiotics in Scientific Text." In J. R. Martin and Robert Veel (eds.) *Reading Science: Critical and Functional Perspectives on Discourses of Science.* London, Routledge.

Park, S. (2012). "Dimensions of Digital Media Literacy and the Relationship with Social Exclusion." *Media International Australia* (8/1/07–current) **142**.

Potter, W. (2010). "The State of Media Literacy." *Journal of Broadcasting and Electronic Media* **54**(4): 675–696.

Sabbagh, Rana. (2017) Interview with I. Burum.

Wenger, E. (2007). "Communities of Practice: A Brief Introduction." In *Communities of Practice.* Cambridge UK, Cambridge University Press.

CHAPTER 5

RECORDING AUDIO ON A SMARTPHONE

SUMMARY

Recording audio on a smartphone is not unlike recording audio for video, except mojos will generally not work with a sound recordist. This chapter explores recording audio situations including actuality and interviews, recording narration, hardware and software, and includes recording tips and developing an audio strategy. In particular, we look at how to record a location interview and we explore the various microphones used to record mojo audio. Award-winning sound recordist Roger Van Wensveen provides expert opinion and a Break-out Box.

OVERVIEW

Recording clean, usable sound on location requires technique, practice and the right equipment. Basic sound recording principles apply—the right microphone and proximity to the sound source—but mojos need to shoot video and record audio without a camera person or sound recordist. When I first needed to record sound on a documentary, I saw my old sound recording teacher who said, "put the microphone close to your subject." I did as I was told, and the sound was almost too clean. In reality, it's almost that easy, but not quite.

We're bombarded with noise and our senses are detuned to filter out sounds that we hear but don't want to listen to. In essence, what we do when we record clean audio is to filter out noise. If music clips have taught us anything, it's that while we are happy to watch flashy whip pans, or blurry close-ups, audiences want clean audio. Sound recordist Roger Van Wensveen (2019) says, "It is pretty simple, we'll watch wobbly shots, but we want our sound clean, so up-skill, know your tools, be prepared and get close to the source." Have an effective sound strategy that includes the right equipment, microphone placement and monitoring. The following sound notes will help mojos record clean audio in a variety of locations.

BASIC SOUND THEORY

The relevance and value of sound recording to the filmmaking and storytelling process is not in question, so it's kind of strange that sound recording is often an after-thought. Walter Murch, the famous Hollywood feature film sound editor and mixer, reminds us that "the most important thing students must learn is 90 percent of film is sound ... The picture is far less important" (McDonald 2014). While it's important never to come home without the video (pictures), Murch is absolutely right, especially when it comes to factual, location-based filmmaking. Having said that, today we produce videos with text explainers, not because sound is not important, but because consumers want to watch videos anywhere without using headphones. These videos work at the expense of sound which, as Murch says, is a critical storytelling element that can bring the viewer to the heart of a film.

Sound on film has a historical connection with studio sound recording that often made it heavy with personnel and equipment, and cumbersome and slow in the field. In the TV business we have a saying, "waiting on sound," and no truer words have ever been spoken. Whether they're dragging cables, waiting for a noisy plane to disappear, or just getting rid of loud fluorescent light noise, the sound recordist is often working in the background, but when they speak, we always stop and listen. Notwithstanding the obvious benefits of using a sound recordist, we needed a faster, more modern approach to, in particular, location sound recording. Van Wensveen says, "As a mobile journalist you need to cover ground fast, you need to record your sound fast and to get work out fast. You need to know how to use your tools, on the run, and quickly."

As early as the 1960s, film sound "offered an untheorized and relatively unchanged set of practices that were inherited artifacts from the studio system of production" (Beck 2002). At about that time filmmakers, like ex news cameraman D. A. Pennebaker, changed all that when they literally broke the tether between camera and sound (Stubbs 2002). Severing the cable—the umbilical cord—in some ways released sound recording from its legacy connection with studio practices, into a yet unexplored realm called location sound recording. The film cameraperson was now free to roam among the action, while the sound person, recording on their crystal-sync Nagra, had the freedom to roam and collect important atmospheric audio and dialogue. In a sense it was now the job of the sound person to anticipate where the camera would head and to make sure they were there and ready with that perspective. "As the sound recordist you learnt to watch the zoom stick on the barrel of the lens to tell whether the cameraman was on a wide shot or a close-up" says Van Wensveen. "Then you could drop your microphone into frame knowing what the shot was and get perspective sound to match the shot." Perspective sound is, according to Van Wensveen, a key to filmic immersion. Because the camera was no longer tethered it was not waiting on sound as much as expecting sound to be ready. But the camera was not yet recording its own sound, so recording audio was still the role of a sound person.

The fact that documentary filmmakers like D. A. Pennebaker chose to reconfigure practices of sound recording during this period was as much a desire to break free from the restrictions of the studio system as it was to provide audiences with a more immersive experience. Filmmakers working in this new era resisted models that may have "dictated certain accepted structural aspects of how to correctly make a film" (Beck 2002). This new technical freedom eventually enabled the production of immersive documentaries like *Primary* (1960), *Don't Look Back* (1965) and *The War Room* (1993), which challenged audience perceptions of what film could be. These filmic experiences, with very real soundscapes, required audiences to engage in new, more realistic levels of access to the "action," predominantly because the relationship between the camera and sound had shifted to enable a more enveloping experience.

In the process, practitioners like D. A. Pennebaker paved the way for a new approach to seeing and hearing documentary, news and factual media. New microphone strategies and location sound, in lieu of post-produced dialogue and FX, gave films a sense of the real and changed the aesthetic forever (Beck 2002). During this period cinema practices were deconstructed into emergent styles like *cinéma vérité*, direct camera and new forms that exposed the way professionals made stuff. These looser styles were precursors to the current reality genres and obs-doc formats and led to the various self-shot series I produced in the 1990s.[1] Later, when many practitioners moved from film to video, it was, as D. A. Pennebaker said, like the difference between using "the pistol and the rifle" (Stubbs 2002).

Mobile provides even greater close-quarter recording opportunities, especially when it comes to sound. Unlike feature films and some large documentaries, which use post-synced sound and dialogue, a mojo needs to know how to record clean audio in the field, especially in noisy locations. A decade ago it was much simpler because, ironically, everything was more complex. You either knew what you were doing, or you hired a professional sound recordist. In the late 1980s and early 1990s, new DV cameras further impacted the way we recorded content on location.

The word location has a number of connotations when used to describe sound recording. In the first instance, it has a topographical meaning that suggests you are not in a studio. It also describes the proximity of the subject to the reporter/filmmaker, suggesting they are both in the same location. This presupposes an ability to communicate directly and to feel the full emotional weight of the auditory experience in a way that watching silent pictures never did. Hence, an important rule of recording location sound is to get in close to capture the "reality" of the situation. Exactly what I was told to do all those years ago on my first sound recording job.

There are basically two distinct concepts of sound recording, realism and reality. Both are essential to creating the level of filmic immersion required to suspend belief for the audience. Realism can often be post-produced sound, or soundscape, that creates an illusion of reality. This form is not limited to the representation of truthfulness and authenticity (Murray 2010). Reality, on the other hand, is a real-life portrayal, or what I call "actuality." Unlike drama, where every sound can be post-produced, in documentary and other factual productions location sound is generally real—live and actual. Of course, in some documentary moments we use post-produced sound and music, but essentially, documentarians, news crews and video and mobile journalists, aim to record authentic location sound to provide a sense of the real. An ethical dilemma can occur in the dialectic between *realism* and *reality,* where artistic discretion is used to slightly misrepresent the real sound to create a pseudo-reality that audiences are more accustomed to. Audio in factual programs has mostly been an amalgam of reality and realism, and often relies on what an audience perceives as real.

In fictional narrative viewers construct meaning from what they see or hear on the screen, something they also do in factual programming. The degree to which we interfere with reality sound is driven by a desire to impact an audience's aural senses. Seen by Altman (1992) as events—the amalgam of location sounds impacting a primary sound—these include "multiple sounds, each with its particular fundamental array of partial sounds" (1992). While we will all probably hear and feel a scene differently, we can be manipulated one way or the other through the combination of sound and vision events. "The production of any sound is a material occurrence that takes place in space and time, and involves the disruption of surrounding matter" (Remael 2012). And that is one of the roles of sound in video, to heighten and/or clarify any scene we are watching by selecting the level of audio disruption, which plays on an audience's perception of reality.

Mojos, like video journalists, work alone and need to know the basic principles of sound recording—which microphone is best and where to place it. He or she will also need to understand to what extent working as a one-man band will compromise their ability to record clean sound. For a mojo, as with any journalist working in radio or television, recording location dialogue correctly is vital because, in most cases, it's the only dialogue the project will have. The key to recording clean dialogue on a smartphone is

- **Technique**
- **Strategy**
- **Equipment**
- **Access**

The following information is based on what I have learned over many years producing a variety of television programs (nighty turnaround public affairs, current affairs, news, documentaries, reality, magazine content and docudrama) and also working as a sound recordist, video journalist and mojo.

Tip: Never misrepresent the truth in your embellishment of sound but feel free as a program maker (within network and ethical parameters) to use sound to focus the emotional context.

PRACTICAL PERSPECTIVE: RECORDING AUDIO SITUATIONS

Mojos can find themselves in a variety of audio situations everywhere from recording unfolding actuality in a riot, to a controlled sit-down interview in a studio. Recording clean sound is not that difficult if you prepare and understand the job parameters. This means you have the right microphone, develop a sound strategy (know who you are interviewing and how you will mic them), react positively to location inputs (how will you deal with unwanted noise, extra interviewees, people, authorities and weather). "Compromises will be made when working as a mobile journalist," says Van Wensveen, "but knowing how to use your tools of trade will help you make compromises to your advantage."

Tip: To record clean sound, prepare the right microphone, react positively to location inputs and develop a sound strategy.

If you're recording speech on the cheap, one of the dynamic microphones or cheaper lapel mics described in Chapter 2 might be right for your job. If you want a softer, more acoustic sound and have some extra cash, choose a phantom-powered condenser microphone. At a press conference where cables can be an issue, a wireless microphone might be best. But whether your mic is lapel, shotgun or wireless, it helps to understand the basic recording characteristics of different microphone types, and to understand how they work.

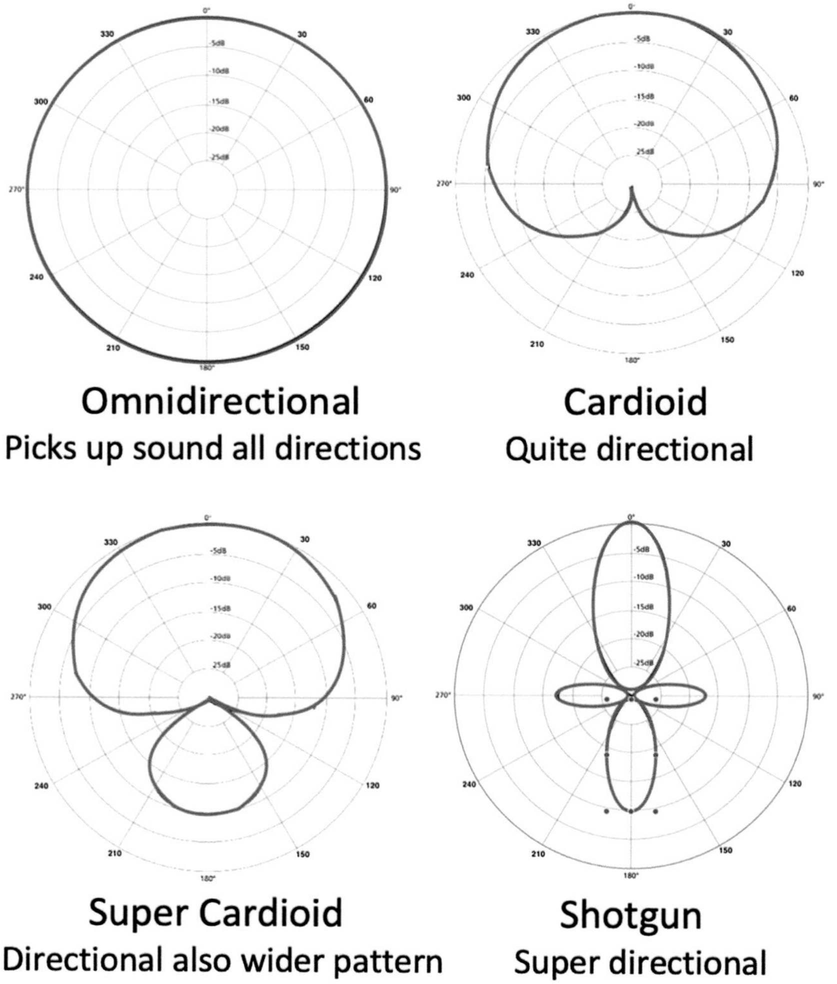

Figure 5.1 **Polar patterns.**

Ivo Burum

A microphone's polar or pick-up pattern determines how it picks up sound—at the front, the side or behind the microphone capsule:

- ***Omnidirectional microphones*** **have a 360-degree pattern and are excellent for placing on a table, to record a number of sources, or for use as neck mics.**
- ***Cardioid microphones*****, sometimes called shotguns, have a narrower pick-up pattern and are often found in handheld microphones or on video cameras used by news and documentary makers, especially those working solo, as video or mobile journalists.**

Tip: Microphones work on proximity. The closer to the sound source and the more focused (directional) the pattern, the richer the sound.

Recording Actuality Audio

Actuality is the time-sensitive content that you don't need to set up, and not full of the journalist's questions, like police, ambulance or screaming people at an accident. Mojos generally record their actuality sound as part of their video, and much of their work mostly occurs among the evolving action. This enables mojos to record more dynamic location sound because they can feel the scene developing and can see the type of story tension and activity forming that causes sound to happen. Being close to the action has some drawbacks: it's difficult to control sound that's bombing in and out of your audio perspective, which can cause the bigger picture perspective to be lost. When working close, mojos can be bumped and pushed in ways that impact sound recording quality and working close can make it difficult to relax talent. "It's important to build a rapport with your talent because you're going to be in their personal space, but if you build that rapport, working within a meter of them shouldn't be a problem," says Van Wensveen. In these situations, it's important not to panic and to work the specific problem.

Tip: You need to plan for this possibility, have a strategy and use a shotgun microphone, so that you can roam without dangerous cables, to capture a tight audio perspective that matches your pictures.

Figure 5.2 **Student at La Trobe University using Rode Video Micro shotgun microphone.**

Ivo Burum

Shotgun microphones may be a smart option for a mojo who's covering an evolving event, primarily because mojos normally work close to the source and not on a long lens. These on-camera directional microphones, often found on top of big ENG cameras, have a cardioid (narrower) pattern that potentially alters the source audio vs background noise ratio, in favour of source.

Tip: Remember, you are mobile, you can turn the talent 180 degrees to background noise so that the background noise is shielded by your body and penetrating the back of a shotgun microphone and away from its recording pattern.

It's not immediately true that all location sound recording needs a boom operator, who traditionally dropped their boom into an interview frame to record close-up perspective sound. Even when we use sound recordists, we often choose to use radio microphones or a shotgun microphone on top of the camera. This is how mojos work and it enables a level of unrestricted movement required when recording sound at a riot, an accident, a sporting event, or during a practical demonstration. In a fast current-affairs shoot, when it gets busy, a tethered cameraperson will pull out the sound recordist's cable and record audio using shotgun mic only, like mojos do. The sound recordist will keep recording on a digital recorder while the cameraperson roams freely to pick up time-sensitive video content while it's actually happening.

See Chapter 2 to determine the type of microphone you need. However, if you are recording a loud event, like a music concert, use a microphone with attenuation. You'll need to carry a dead cat (furry windshield) for recording audio in windy outdoor locations. Shotgun microphones placed on the camera will work fine as long as they're positioned within a meter (1000–750mm) of the interviewee and there is not too much background noise.

Figure 5.3 **Shotgun mic showing 3-step attenuation.**

Ivo Burum

Individual actuality interviews are generally recorded in a medium close-up (MCU) shot that's cut off around chest area, close enough to feel emotion and to enable a sound recordist to swing their boom close to the edge of frame. If the subject is stationary, microphone choice and placement is relatively simple. Lapel, or lavalier, microphones are preferable for recording interviews. Pinned on the chest 6 to 8 inches (the spread of a hand) from the interviewee's mouth, they are close to the sound source and shielded from the wind by the subject's body.

Figure 5.4 **Indigenous mojo trainee doing a piece to camera.**

Ivo Burum

Tip: A wide lens will enable mojos to get their microphone closer to the subject while retaining, for example, an MCU interview frame.

Zooming in on the video won't zoom audio or match the audio perspective from where a shotgun microphone is located. A better option is tracking/moving in closer to the source and staying on the wide lens, which makes a handheld shot much steadier and less grainy.

Tip: In a crowded situation aim to minimise your kit and your footprint. One way I do that is to exclude tripods and booms and go top or shotgun mic for most of the filming, changing to a lapel or radio mic when an interview calls for it.

Recording Interview Audio

The interview is a mojo's stock in trade and provides the information and the emotion in a story. The reporter provides the background via narration and lets the person being interviewed give their opinions, beliefs, reactions, feelings—their side of the story. Recording audio for interviews can be impromptu, as happens in a door-stop or walk-and-talk interview, or it can be more controlled, as in a sit-down interview (see Chapter 6).

Audio Considerations in a Sit-down Interview

- ***Location*** **The correct setting requires a balance between aesthetic, audio and light. What's required is constant audio and light and this can prove difficult in a long outdoor interview. Outdoor locations need to be chosen for audio controllability—no trains, no changing traffic noise, away from busy malls or schools. Noisy locations might mean stopping at crucial moments and risk breaking flow, or it might mean repeating important information, or simply using the location distraction as part of the interview by shooting B roll to show where the noise is coming from (the train, the crowd).**

- ***Microphone choice* is important in any interview situation. Will you need an external microphone, or can you use the device's onboard microphone? The simple answer is that it's always better to have an external microphone close to the sound source. However, that's not always possible when working fast on an unexpected breaking story, or when working alone. The answer is to get as close as possible to the sound source with whatever microphone or recording device you have that will record the audio as cleanly as possible.**

Renowned journalist and radio mojo pioneer Neal Augenstein, from Washington DC all-news radio station WTOP, concluded that speaking into a built-in microphone on the iPhone was "approximately 92% as good as using an industry Shure mic" (Augenstein 2016). Augenstein also found that by the time audio travels through "the broadcast processing chain," its inferior quality "was not noticeable to the listener." This is true in a relatively quiet location when working and placing a microphone close to the sound source, which is increasingly difficult when shooting video actuality and walk-and-talk, or door-stop interviews. Having said that, if your smartphone microphone or the microphone in your headphones is all you have, get as close as possible and go for it. "If you are within a meter of your source a shotgun mic with a dead cat is excellent, but if you're stuck, the smartphone mic with a fluffy velcroed on it will also work outside and close to your source," says Van Wensveen.

Audio Considerations in a Walk-and-Talk Interview

One key concern in any walk-and-talk interview, especially a door stop, is how to keep the interviewee in frame and close to the lens and your shotgun microphone. Hence, it's best to use a wide-angle lens where you can get closer to your sound source (subject) and still maintain an interview frame. Because mojos operate their own smartphones, it's difficult to be on camera with the interviewee (see chapters 4 and 6). Questions worth considering in this situation are:

- **How will that impact your interview, will you need an extra-wide shot (EWS) that is not lip sync, or B roll of you or the interviewee's walking POV?**
- **Will you need your questions on camera?**
- **Are you using a gimbal (see Chapter 2) for stabilisation?**
- **Are you walking on flat ground so that you don't fall?**

In this situation, knowing what archive and other B roll you have is essential. If there isn't much B roll, I would record the interview focusing on the interviewee. I would get an extra wide shot (EWS) of the walking and talking that wasn't lip sync and ask a few key questions, getting the interviewee to answer each for 10 about seconds. Once the interview is over, I would record one or two walking and talking questions and some listening shots. Or, get a friend to help (see Chapter 6).

Be careful when you're trying to hide the lapel or radio microphone that you don't get clothes rustle. "Become a bit of an expert at listening to a person's wardrobe" says Van Wensveen.

Following are a few common sound recording scenarios, suggestions for equipment, and tips for recording audio as a one-person band, or mojo.

Figure 5.5 **Rode SC6-L splitter showing two-mic input.**

Ivo Burum

- ***Interviewing two people:*** **try two lapel microphones plugged into a splitter (the SC6-L from Rode has two mic inputs and one headphone jack). If there is no background noise and interviewees are sitting next to each other, try an omnidirectional microphone on a stand placed between them. Or place the transmitter from your Wireless Go (with its inbuilt mic) on the table between the two interviewees.**

    Recording two microphones with video directly onto a smartphone results in one composite video/audio track. If you need each interviewee's audio separate in the edit, you'll need a second recorder, like a Zoom H1 or another smartphone.
- ***Handheld microphones*** **come in two categories—wired and wireless (see Chapter 2). They are often used in very noisy location reporting where they are pivoted between the reporter and the interviewee, a little like a boom operator swinging a boom. With practice, solo operators can use this technique.**

Tip: Avoid giving handheld microphones to interviewees who will inevitably move them away from their mouths and wave them.

Radio microphones, also called wireless, are mostly lapel or handheld microphones. They use a transmitter rather than a cable to send a signal to a receiver that sits on a camera or smartphone up to 150 meters away. They are excellent when the reporter, or the interviewee, is mobile.

I use the five wireless systems pictured in Fig 5.6. The Wireless Go is the cheapest (US$200), next is the Filmmaker(US$399), probably because it's plastic and larger than the XSW (US$550) or the D11 (US$600), or AVX (US$850) which also ships as a combo kit that includes a transmitter, receiver, lapel, and a handheld microphone.

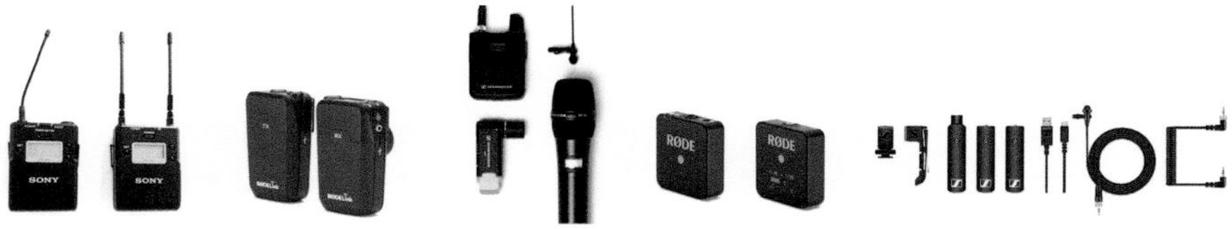

Figure 5.6 **Wireless microphones I own and use at price points.**

Ivo Burum

Tip: Buy the best radio microphone you can afford. If you can't afford a decent set, try the alternative, described here: www.youtube.com/watch?v=lQrbHpkTK9c. It uses your old smartphone and a lapel microphone to create a wireless system that works perfectly even if you are hundreds of meters from the camera.

Digital recorders can be handy when two audio tracks are needed, such as in a boat-to-boat situation or on a small plane where there's only room for one. The Zoom H1 (US$100) is small, cheap, and excellent. I also use the Tascam DR-10C PCM recorder (US$350), which fits into the palm of a hand.

Tip: If you are panning between two interviewees, ask them not to talk over each other when they speak.

Recording Narration Audio

Narration is usually recorded during an edit, either as live sound or more of a voice-over feel. One of the first questions you ask is what is the narration going over? If it's location vision, maybe it's best to record it live on location. "Narration is meant to enhance the vision, so the last thing you want is for it to distract" says Van Wensveen.

Before pocket edit suites were available, we would write and record narration in the car—which is acoustically quite dead—parked off the main road, or in a hotel room between two pillows or mattresses. If you can't get into a car or room, pull a towel or jacket over your head and record narration under there. In the mobile ecosphere it can happen at the scene where your five-point plan, which contains your location scribbles and your edit and narration notes, will be invaluable. Don't record it in a stairwell or anywhere there is echo, like a toilet.

Tip: Hold the mic without moving it and if you clip it onto a shirt do a test to make sure there is no clothes noise.

Irrespective of whether it's live or a voice-over feel, read the narration script into an external microphone, either a shotgun or lavalier, positioned 6–8 inches from your mouth. If you are using a makeshift studio, you might try a studio mic. Narration is best recorded in a dead quiet location.

Tip: Except in very special circumstances, where you need audio at super-high bit rates, above 48Khz (see Chapter 9), or in specific forms, you won't need to use a separate audio app to record narration for a video story, where it's recorded as part of the video track.

Figure 5.7 **Studio mic price points.**

Ivo Burum

On smartphones, video (with audio) is recorded and stored into the camera roll (iOS) and in the gallery (Android). When working quickly it's best to record narration into the same location as video. The easiest way to do this on a smartphone is to record narration as video. Place your hand over the lens so that the shot is black and easily recognisable as narration in the camera roll or gallery. Doing this means that all assets (video and audio) are found in the same folder (app) so that you don't have to search for your narration when editing. If needed you can detach the audio from the video during the edit and cover it with relevant B roll (see Chapter 7 for tips on writing narration).

Tip: Make sure your microphone is platform-ready. Smartphone-compatible microphones use a TRRS (tip, ring, ring, sleeve) plug with three rubber rings. A catch with TRRS is that poles can vary between CTIA (newer) and OMTP (older) standards, so check—do a test before you buy. Rode makes a set of TRS-to-TRRS and TRRS-to-TRS adaptors (see Chapter 2). Rode also has new mics like the VideoMic NTG that self-switch from TRS to TRRS.

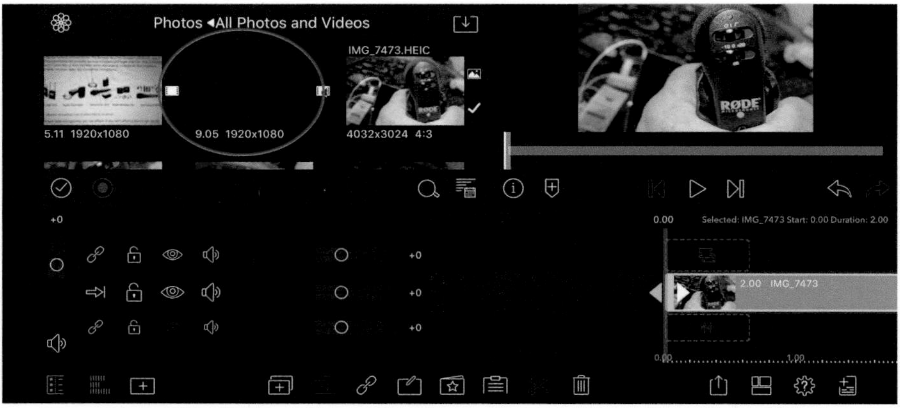

Figure 5.8 **Voice-over recorded black showing easily recognisable in *LumaFusion* gallery.**

Ivo Burum

In summary here is my list of sound recording do's:

- **Always switch on airplane mode so you don't receive calls and so WiFi doesn't distort your audio.**
- **Always have a directional microphone on the smartphone just in case.**
- **Always carry a lapel microphone especially for recording narration.**
- **Always carry a windsock or dead cat for filming outdoors.**
- **Always get the camera close—within a meter—of the interviewee to avoid background noise.**
- **Always point your microphones at the sound source.**
- **Always record audio clean in the field.**
- **If you need a true-split audio track, use a device like a Zoom H1 to record a second audio track. Using a clap, sync the two tracks in the edit (see www.youtube.com/watch?v=lQrbHpkTK9c).**
- **Time permitting, get a buzz track—30 seconds of natural on-location audio. This can be laid under a series of B roll shots, or used in a montage to smooth audio transitions between shots.**
- **Always check your audio before you leave each location.**

Tip: If you need translation, get it in the field, just in case pick-ups are needed, which you won't know until the translation is completed.

Roger Van Wensveen Break-out Box

1. **When recording narration indoors, look for a room with carpet on the floor, curtains and soft furnishings that deaden the room.**
2. **Outdoors, look for a location without background noise or wind; both will ruin your audio and your shot.**
3. **Don't use a boom or a shotgun microphone when recording audio in a live room because it will pick up reverberations; use a lapel or radio microphone instead. In a dead room, within a meter of your source, the shotgun mic will be sufficient.**
4. **In a walk-n-talk, if you stay within a meter, for convenience, the shotgun is the choice of microphone.**
5. **Start with a basic kit of microphones (lapel and shotgun) and then, as you get more experience, extend your tool kit and explore the boundaries of each microphone.**
6. **The most important tip is record perspective sound relative to your framing.**

In the post-production chapter, you'll find specific information on listening to each piece of audio and adjusting and mixing levels before rendering.

In conclusion, treat every shoot like an international job, where you can't go back; and record audio clean on location. When you have shot your interviews, or actuality, and before you leave the location, check your audio—in fact check it before you record your interview. The best tip I ever got about recording audio is to get the microphone close to the sound source and to listen to the location—this is still key to recording dynamic on-location audio.

Go mojo …

NOTE

1 Burum experimented with self-shot formats in the 1990s and 2000s, where citizens were given an opportunity to produce their own stories for primetime TV.

REFERENCES

Altman, R. E. (1992). *Sound Theory, Sound Practice*. London, Routledge.

Augenstein, N. (2016). Interview with I. Burum. GIJN. gijn.org.

Beck, J. (2002). "Citing the Sound." *Journal of Popular Film and Television* **29**(4): 156–163.

McDonald, S. (2014). "Introduction to Location Sound Recording." AFTRS. www.aftrs.edu.au/short-courses/introduction-to-location-sound-recording/U537. AFTRS.

Murray, L. (2010). "Authenticity and Realism in Documentary Sound." *The Soundtrack* **3**(2): 131–137.

Remael, A. (2012). "For the Use of Sound. Film Sound Analysis for Audio-description: Some Key Issues." *OPEN—Expertise Centre for Accessible Media and Culture*.

Stubbs, L. (2002). "D. A. Pennebaker and Chris Hegedus—Engineering Nonfiction Cinema." In *Documentary Filmmakers Speak*. New York, Allworth Press.

Wensveen, R. (2019). Interview with Ivo Burum.

CHAPTER 6

RECORDING AN INTERVIEW

SUMMARY

We live in an interview age where everyone with a mobile is a potential interviewer. In this chapter we define interview styles, explore interview questions, learn how to prepare and record a video interview and consider ethical aspects. Former foreign correspondent and Australia's leading interviewer, Walkley Award-winning journalist and broadcaster Tony Jones provides specialist comment and a Break-out Box of tips.

OVERVIEW

During my time as a television producer, journalist and mojo trainer, the nature of interviews has both changed and stayed the same. A journalistic interview still takes the form of a conversation between two or more people, where an interviewer asks questions to elicit facts, statements or emotional responses from interviewees. However, one of the major shifts that's occurred in the mobile era is that those who once were solely the audience are now part of a converging production process and talking to each other online. But are these exchanges interviews?

Tony Jones has an interesting perspective: "Interviews must be story driven. An interview about your personal interests is a conversation. Such conversations can be interesting, but they are generally outside the scope of conventional journalism. You should always assume the audience is uninterested in your personal opinions" (Jones 2019). Yet reality TV is a ratings winner and very personal video user-generated content (UGC) continues to be uploaded online at the rate of more than 500 hours every minute. These citizen witness moments, generally captured as a result of being in the right place at the right time, have their own use value. If they are event driven they are often subsumed by legacy media, who use them as free color for their stories. However, with very little training citizens can learn to produce grassroots witness moments into powerful citizen journalism and transform their conversations into powerful interviews and user-generated stories (UGS).

One key aspect of this transition from curious conversation to structured interview begins to occur when our questions are used to

- **Elicit or check information (general and news)**
- **Provide an explanation or a decision (informative)**
- **Gather expert or general opinion (political)**
- **Draw out insight into a personality (profile)**
- **Source reaction (vox pop)**

Historically the news interview has been used to put someone on record and to hold them to account. Jones says interviews are about setting the context. "We often interview people to find out what they know about a story we're investigating or exploring. You find witnesses to events or people affected by those events and you ask them to describe it using straightforward, brief, logical questions. Be guided by your natural curiosity. Curious people often make good interviewers."

The stock in trade of journalists and documentary producers, interviews are used in almost every type of media production for the following reasons:

- ***Accountability*: Why did you claim for the helicopter flight when it wasn't official business?**
- ***Discovery*: What was going through your mind when you first told your parents you were gay?**
- ***Information*: What did the murderer look like?**
- ***Currency*: The election results are in. What does that mean for your family?**
- ***First-hand account*: Tell us what you saw when the helicopter crashed.**

One characteristic of media interviews is that they work to represent the questions of an audience, even if that audience has not yet thought the questions through. Knowing the audience is listening and watching creates pressure to perform and to acquit oneself well (Montgomery 2008). Even though there is a distinction in roles—between the questioner and the questioned—both feel they need to perform well. The interviewers, who historically came from an institutionally supported position, held an advantage and a responsibility for setting the agenda and the discourse, the length and even style of the interview (Montgomery 2008).

Over the past 100 years interviews have become their own genre across a range of print, broadcast entertainment and confessional formats, and online media (Montgomery 2008). In the 1990s I pioneered a style of television in Australia called "self-shot." We gave citizens cameras, and their self-interview and confessional pieces became a hallmark of this style of production. In the current converging media space, where the distinction between the audience and the interviewer can be even more blurred, the interview does often manifest more as a subjective chat and not the neutral objective tool that it was once thought to be.

However, asking a series of articulated questions that focus filming around a story theme is the art of interview. This process of structured purposeful investigation can transform kludge like UGC into structured and politicised UGS. As explained in Chapter 10, in the section on the Arab Spring, much of the UGC uploaded by the Springers, which media called citizen journalism, was not so much journalism as powerful witness moments: being in the right spot at the right time. The media that used this free UGC to color their Arab Spring stories justified their use by suggesting they were promoting citizen journalism. In the process the UGC often lost its unique diversity by being flattened into the prevailing image/doctrine. This chapter provides an easy-to-follow set of concepts and skills to enable mojos to create their own powerful interviews that helps transform their UGC into more diverse and purposeful UGS.

THEORETICAL PERSPECTIVE

Considerable attention has been devoted to the role of the interview as a way of holding people in power to account. However, the formal interview plays numerous roles in society, from challenging the status quo, as described above, to providing color and currency-pop to social media. This chapter will suggest there is a set of defining principles that sit at the core of all strong mojo interviews, which can enhance their commercial and public sphere use value.

At the heart of any interview there are clearly defined roles:

- **one person asks questions and the other responds**
- **the interviewer has generally invited the interviewee, which by default provides an advantage**

- **the price for this is that the interviewer carries the weight of public and institutional responsibility for setting the agenda**
- **for this the interviewer generally gets to choose the style, duration and rules of interview engagement**

Fundamentally, the interview is a series of assumptions made when recording the real to compose context. The interviewer, even in vox pops, where interviewees provide an unselfconscious outpouring, is validated by the quality of the interviewee. For example, on a nightly television series I produced, *George Negus Tonight*, we interviewed 200 studio guests each season and probably three times as many in our packages. George used his star power to attract many guests, and online responses indicated that our audience felt that each studio interviewee had somehow earned the right to be there with one of Australia's leading interviewers, something Myers (2000) calls "communicative entitlement." As executive producer I hoped the reverse was also true, that our host was legitimised by what I call public worthyness of our interviewees. The interviewer is legitimised by having a high-caliber guest, who acknowledges the interviewer's position by responding carefully to a line of questioning designed to show that producers were right in their choice of interviewee. The theory is that prominent interviewees mean more relevance and hence more viewers.

The reality is that relevant interviewees are as vital as prominent ones. Moreover, interviews are not mythical neutral tools, but "negotiated accomplishments of both interviewers and respondents that are shaped by the contexts and situations in which they take place" (Fontana and Frey 2000). The struggle with any interview, especially for mojos, who mostly work as one-man bands, is to maintain a level of objectivity in relation to the participants and within contextual parameters. The aim of any interview is to describe how "mediated talk about emotion can play a role in defining [an] event" (Myers 2000).

PRACTICAL PERSPECTIVE

Interview Types

There are many types of interview that a mobile journalist might be asked to record. Essentially, all interviews require a question and an answer (even a silent one), but their context and level of complexity varies depending on intended use and an interviewer's preparation and their ability to stay on script. But the line between preparation and choking the interview is fine says Jones (2019):

> Prepared questions are useful but never, never allow yourself to be restricted to a list of questions. The fundamental skill of a good interviewer is to be a good listener. If you're listening carefully to the answers, you'll find you have to go off script when your interviewee says something you weren't expecting … When that happens, go with the flow. You can always come back to your prepared questions later in the interview … My friend Mark Colvin the late, great ABC radio broadcaster, went into many live interviews with no written questions, relying solely on his general knowledge, research and his capacity to simply listen.

Figure 6.1 **Trainee mojos learning to record vox pop interviews.**
Ivo Burum

Jones believes tone is critical in all interviews and the wrong tone, especially in political interviews, can result in angry responses. "It's best always to adopt a neutral tone during a political interview (and most other interviews too for that matter). If you do that you can still be firm and persistent but, whatever you do, avoid getting your own emotions involved." Don't show your angry "tell." Don't twitch, or pull at your collar when you get angry, like one of Australia's foremost interviewers used to do. It was a sure sign, says Jones, that "he was literally hot under the collar." This "tell" had viewers on the same side of politics as the interviewee, thinking "the interviewer's own political views were in the mix and they made claims of bias." Jones says it's important to train yourself to stay cool under pressure when doing interviews for television. "Stay neutral because every nuance of your body language and facial expressions are up on screen in high definition for the viewers to judge."

Careful preparation, being curious and being a good listener are things all great interviewers like Mark Colvin and Tony Jones are renowned for. Preparation provides the context to focus tangential or unexpected information and to go with the flow and come out the other side with useable content. When I produced Jones at *Foreign Correspondent*, the first thing he would do with each of my story briefs was to question every detail, and this was the beginning of the preparation that enabled us to go with the flow. This preparation was a lifeline that enabled us to chase the unknown that our research missed. It helped us stay on track, get back to the core of our interview, and the context of our story. Mojos will often need to do the questioning on their own.

Following are examples of a variety of interview types that require preparation and context:

- ***General***: **Primarily recorded to reveal facts or opinions about a news story, event or person. These interviews are often based around breaking stories (emotion and legal issues) and need to be recorded quickly and succinctly.**
- ***Informational***: **This could be a business interview talking about stocks, or an aspect of health, or science that provides the latest evidence.**
- ***Investigative***: **The subject of the interview is asked a series of questions that relate to a broader context and outcome of which the interview is only one component. Part of a series of interviews recorded over time, in stages, to probe an evolving story, often designed to answer the "why" question.**
- ***Political interview***: **Requires a great deal of homework and a sense of the overall landscape. Politicians will have a pitch they are trying to sell. You'll need to be prepared to go beyond that. Jones (2019) believes that one effective method of preparation is to**

> Look at recent interviews done by the subject or read transcripts of those interviews. If you are astute, you will see the questions the subject wants to avoid, and you will see the questions that rattle their cage. You will also get a sense of the key arguments around the subject of your interview. You should always, if you have the time for research, understand those arguments and the logical weaknesses in them.
>
> Tony Jones (2019)

Ask the politician the question and give them one opportunity to answer. If they don't answer, use your research to find another way of asking the question. If your audience wants to know something in particular, allowing the politician to drag you off point risks losing the audience. If you need to interrupt, to get the interview back on track, do it. But bear in mind that too much interruption can be distracting and not enough might let the politician off the hook.

- *Emotional*: The emotional interview is probably the most complicated. Often the person being interviewed is directly caught up and emotionally affected by complex and often dramatic events that can range from happiness (Olympic gold) to sadness (death of a child). Interviews can be filled with silences, fits of anger or even laughter—emotions that can be more telling than words. Jones believes that "except for moments of terrible tragedy where to be emotionless would not be human, it's never ok for interviewers to show emotion." There is a difference between empathy and emotion, so my aim in interviews is to have empathy and let the interviewee provide the emotion. Allowing time is critical in an emotional interview—time for the interviewee to feel like they can tell the story. In Germany Tony and I interviewed a rape victim from the Bosnian camps. We did this in a small apartment with family supporting her. We allowed time and we used a small camera to make it less confronting for the interviewee and her family.
- *Vox pops*: The short ad hoc grab works when the person being interviewed shows an entitlement to the feelings they express about a subject, or they show an expression of feeling that ordinary people will relate to. Even impromptu vox pops require a degree of preparation to set the context—purpose, style and use.

When chasing a jaw-dropping response, mojos must tread carefully across the thin line that divides journalistic excellence and gratuitous voyeurism. "The best interviewers," says Jones, "have the confidence to remain in control of the process. By being clear, polite and firm you can ensure that interview subjects answer the questions. Nothing is more frustrating for viewers/listeners than listening to an interview go off track when the subject is ignoring the questions and going off on a tangent." On the other hand, if the interview subject, who's made a tacit agreement to answer questions, steadfastly refuses to do so, Jones feels "it is absolutely fine to keep asking the same question (without rancor) over and over again. The question repeatedly unanswered is often as telling as the question answered. The audience will make their own judgments of evasive interview subjects."

Journalists can be accused of exploiting emotions, but in the end, no one is forcing people to talk (especially not politicians who are practiced avoiders). The grey area between coercion and confession is the domain of the journalist. Navigating this challenging area takes great skill and commitment to ethical practice, especially for mojos who often work alone without a sounding board (see Chapter 12).

Interview Styles

There is a big difference between interviewing for print and video. Print journalists are invisible to their readers and on-video journalists are often front and center. One of the biggest differences with video interviews is that we need moving pictures. This generally means that for a planned interview you need to make an appointment, coordinate your crew, drive somewhere, find the interviewee, choose a location, set up camera and sound and warm up the interviewee before you can record a frame. It's a lot to think about.

Figure 6.2 **Dr Anne Spoerry flying her plane to a remote clinic in Kenya.**

Ivo Burum

Conversely, if you have camera and sound skills and have some journalistic experience, the lack of a crew can be a blessing. In some cases, working alone is the only way to go. While on assignment for *Foreign Correspondent* in Africa, I chose to send our crew home when filming a story about the oldest flying doctor at AMREF, in Kenya, Anne Sporrey. Mama Daktari, as she was known, flew her small single-engine plane to her clinics, which required a small crew. This was a lot more work, but it also meant we could work much quicker in confined and rugged locations. The result was a more intimate portrait.

Notwithstanding the type of job and the location imperatives, there are basically three types of interview styles that a mojo might encounter.

Sit-down interview: This is your standard set-up used across the various genres. The advantages of this style are that you chose your location for ambience, sound and light.

A controlled environment means interviewees are captive, miced up and at your disposal for a defined period of time. This level of control can benefit interviewer and interviewee.

Figure 6.3 **George Negus sit-down interview with Gerry Adams.**

Ivo Burum for **Foreign Correspondent**

Things to be mindful of when choosing a location for a sit-down interview:

- ***The sun*: If it's outdoors, you need to know when and where the sun will shift over the course of the interview. You could screen the interview using lightweight scrims, or film in a shady location, which can have its own exposure issues unless you shoot tight on the subject.**
- ***Changing audio*: The outdoor audio situation needs to remain constant for the duration of the shoot.**
- ***Talent*: Maintaining interest in a sit-down interview is important. If the interviewee is not very strong you might need a more dynamic style (see p xx).**
- ***Length of interview*: Monitoring how much you record as there is a tendency to over-record in sit-down interviews.**
- ***Relevant B roll*: Note the B roll that you need to shoot to highlight specifics and shorten the interview and note required archival material.**

Door stop: This is an "ambush" type interview generally with a politician or other public figure that looks informal (because we see the interaction/stop on camera), often as they enter or leave a building. Like vox pops, door-stop interviews can be full of emotion and very personal comment about a just completed event, like a court case and verdict.

This type of interview is sometimes "planned to look unplanned" to add a dynamic to the program. At other times it's spontaneous and used because the journalist has no time to prepare. Potentially this results in a real on-camera moment where the interviewee wants to

Figure 6.4 **Mobile journalist door stops policeman at suspected drowning in Norway.**

Ivo Burum

fight or flee. Even in these unplanned situations research can help determine that the person will actually be there, what to ask them and how they might react. Ask them the right question and they will probably fight, which is what you want. Door stops can be used to force a connection with the interviewee, for example, sidling up to a politician who is on the hustings and has been hard to lock down. In this case a key concern is not to slow the politician down and not to make them look stupid, unless you want the reaction of them walking away. Once the interview begins it can become a walk-n-talk, if they agree to continue.

Figure 6.5 **George Negus in a walk-n-talk interview with John Hume in Ireland.**

Ivo Burum

Walk-n-talk: This is where the interviewer and interviewee walk and talk and is generally used in a situation where the surroundings are important for the interview. For example, walking through a warehouse with 400 dead bodies to show the devastation of genocide; or walking through a series of flowers in bloom for a gardening story; or through a mine field; or over a blue-screen map to show the progression of a pandemic, or an army. In Fig 6.5, George Negus, an Australian broadcaster, is seen interviewing John Hume in Ireland for *Foreign Correspondent*. John Hume's hallway was packed with historical memorabilia, so I asked him and George to begin at one end and move through the hallway talking about specific pieces related to the new peace in Ireland. In this situation you film the interview in a wide covering shot, pushing in for specific close ups. Later you pick up choice B roll. It's okay to ask your talent to repeat something occasionally as long as you don't slow them or deviate off point (see Chapter 4).

Unless you're indoors, a shifting light source might be an issue (see Chapter 4), maintaining clear audio is another (see Chapter 5). Walk-n-talk coverage needs a degree of planning to create edit points—will it be covered in a master two-shot and what will you use for B roll (see Chapter 4)? Walk-n-talk interviews are generally more dynamic and should have a more relaxed feel about them.

Tip: As a mojo, one of your main considerations is who will operate the camera if you choose a walk-n-talk frame that includes you. Another consideration is how you will cover both audio feeds (see Chapter 5).

Preparing the Interview

In preparing the interview consider the following factors:

- **How much do you know about the interviewee and their position on the issue?**
- **What are the opposing views and who has these?**
- **What facts and figures do you need for the interview and for the edit?**
- **How will you record it?**
- **What B roll will you need?**

Figure 6.6 **One of two survivors of the Laniste massacre in Bosnia tells Ivo Burum about the genocide while looking for his family.**

Ivo Burum

Here are my thoughts on some questions I am asked about interviews:

Are comments in email exchanges, Skype chats or Google Hangouts "interviews"?
They are, or can be, but the person supplying the answers needs to know and agree.

What should ground rules for interviews be?
I always tell the interviewee how, where, when and by whom the interview will be used. I am always in charge of the interview. The interviewee knows that they are not obliged to answer but that their response will be filmed. Before the interview I ask the interviewee to sign a release or acknowledge their agreement to the interview on camera.

What about requests for questions in advance?
I treat this on a case-by-case basis. It's difficult to send the "bomb" question in advance and I'm not sure I ever want to. It depends how much you want before you drop the "bomb" because you don't want them to walk out before you have the answers.

Should reporters pay for interviews?
My view is we shouldn't pay for interviews. But I have worked for shows where it happens. Would you pay for interviews and if not, why not?

Covering traumatised people?
I have filmed with traumatised people looking for relatives in rivers, bodies in the forest and digging through mass graves in war zones. I find it difficult but have no problem doing this. I ask for permission first and have rarely been refused. In Fig 6.6 is a survivor of the massacre at Laniste in Bosnia. I approached him through a policeman. I only asked him to tell me what he was doing at the grave, what happened in the minutes before the massacre and who did it? I asked for the facts and he provided the exposition and emotion. Keep it simple and don't pretend to know their pain.

Does a promise of anonymity become irrelevant after the interviewee dies?
Not in my book.

More specifically there are at least nine stages to developing and recording a structured mojo interview and each stage is a milestone that sets up the next:

1. ***Definition of purpose*: It's important to know what you want to achieve from the interview. Do you want to reveal something new, support an existing view, set**

the record straight, get a comment on a current event or explore someone's inner side?

2. *Choice of respondent*: Knowing who is best to interview requires research. Will you need one or more interviewees to get a perspective? In all my years of producing interviews for video, TV, Web TV and mojo, I have learned that dynamics rules. If you have a choice between a smart but boring interviewee, and an interesting emotive person, I'd choose the latter; the "smarts" can always be added using narration.
3. *Pre-interview research*: Once you've shortlisted potential interviewees and before you sign off, even on a door stop, you'll need research. I always try and pre-interview to ask leading or difficult questions, to gauge how far I will be able to push the interviewee.
4. *Planning your interview*: Structuring the questions in a logical order, knowing what to ask first and when to ask your difficult questions is important. In structured interviews I always use set-up questions to relax the interviewee while I'm setting up.
5. *Making an interview appointment*: This sounds very basic, but can be a deal-breaker. Video requires pictures and this requires scheduling. Your deadline and an interviewee's life might not sync up. Time is one of the biggest issues when shooting video and you need to bear this in mind when planning interviews and when choosing interview styles.
6. *Maintaining a friendly conversational rapport, like old friends talking*: You'll need to decide on the tone of your interview very early on and not shift from your focus. Maybe use ice-breaker questions—about their child's soccer team's win—before you ask a series of questions to find out why they are accused of harassment. Your role is to keep the interview on track and the best way to do this is to avoid confrontation. I generally treat interviews like structured conversations—friendly but focused.
7. *Getting down to business—your first planned questions*: Once I'm done with set-up questions, I pick up on what the interviewee is thinking and saying and lead with that before shifting focus back on to my structured series of questions. Research will define a series of questions that you will ask in an open-ended form unless you want a closed "yes" or "no" answer. For example:
    a. Closed question: Did you like the car? Answer: Yes or No.
    b. Open-ended question: Tell me what you liked or disliked about the car.

8. *Tangential/supplementary questions*: It's important to keep the interview on track especially once you get flow. But maintaining structured flow may require the interviewer to go with the odd unexpected answer as long as the interviewee has not shifted off point to avoid the answer. LISTENING is the key, so that you can refocus.
9. *The "bomb" and potentially embarrassing questions*: These must be handled carefully and in a timely manner—asking too early may end the interview. Generally, the interviewee will expect the "bomb" question.

Producing the interview is dealt with in Chapter 4.

Here are Tony Jones's five best tips for interviewing:

1. In unfamiliar countries find a translator/fixer you can trust and pay them appropriately. Unless you are multilingual this person will be your window into the lives of others and your instant guide to their own culture. Your questions will go through them. Your answers will come back through them.
2. Always ask simple questions. That may sound silly, but so many people conduct interviews by making statements and expecting a response.
3. In conflict zones make sure the person you're interviewing will not be put in further danger by talking to you.
4. If you are filming current affairs or documentary style, make sure to speak on camera to people in every location, otherwise you could end up with a lot of lovely, lifeless footage which you'll have to explain with your own boring voice-over. This is important even if you are filming some dramatic event that you assume will be intrinsically interesting to anyone who sees it. Anyone watching those scenes will want to know what the people in the middle of it are thinking/responding. I remember filming a great drama in Kabul as heavily armed Mujahideen took over the presidential palace. My ABC cameraman Neil Maude did a brilliant job filming the confrontation. It was a dangerous situation, but we missed opportunities to interview their commander and the commander of the presidential guard who surrendered to them. I've always regretted that.
5. Preparation for "on the road" interviews is all about research. I have found many times that it's good to rely on the advice of an intelligent fixer.

In closing, I have interviewed people in war zones who have lost families, killers who were repenting, and small children in kindergartens laughing at clowns. Some I couldn't understand, and some couldn't understand me, but what got me through every interview is an empathy I have for the people in my stories. It's a gift to be able to talk to people about their lives. The way we use the interviews we collect can sometimes change lives. It's our job as journalists to push the plus side of that ledger as far as possible. Make every interview you do count.

Go mojo …

REFERENCES

Fontana, Andrea, and James Frey. (2000). "The Interview: From Structured Questions to Negotiated Text." In N. Denzin and Y. Lincoln (eds.) *Handbook of Qualitative Research*. Thousand Oaks CA, Sage: 645–672.

Jones, T. (2019). Interview with I. Burum, Melbourne.

Montgomery, Martin (2008). "The Discourse of the Broadcast News Interview." *Journalism Studies* **9**(2): 260–277. https://doi.org/10.1080/14616700701848303.

Myers, G. (2000). "Entitlement and Sincerity in Broadcast Interviews about Princess Diana." *Media, Culture & Society*, **22**(2): 167–185. https://doi.org/10.1177/016344300022002003.

CHAPTER 7

WRITING MOJO STORIES

SUMMARY

Aristotle said, when story dies we are left with decadence. The responsibility of the press, recognised by its Fourth Estate[1] role as advocate and political watchdog, is to investigate the facts and write and report the story. In a convergent ecosphere where video is critical to driving traffic across screens and platforms, writing is still a key binding agent. Mojos write video and audio scripts, pieces to camera, and narration to segue between grabs and bridge story moments. They write headlines and introductory paragraphs for online stories. These skills enable mojos to write in and out of pictures and sound bites. This chapter introduces these skills and provides Break-out Boxes of tips by eminent radio and video journalists, including award-winning RTÉ mojo Philip Bromwell.

OVERVIEW

Telling stories is one of the earliest forms of expression and writing them down is a way of imbuing the oral telling with a sense of permanence to enable stories to travel in time with a degree of commonality and certainty. The advent of the printing press enabled stories in books and newspapers to be mass-produced and transformed publication and the news business. Authors and journalists produced forms of words to suit a variety of tastes and people began to check for news daily. Now that computers have morphed into smartphones and print has converged online, the multi-media content produced across platforms and screens requires its own styles of writing.

In the converged world stories can be presented in a variety of multi-media formats (Chung 2006). Often referred to as digital storytelling, the new multi-planar forms of online content creation require their own dynamic language. The flexibility and universality of digital storytelling suggests anyone with technology can become a producer (Yan, Hyungsung et al. 2011). The reality is that producing and writing for the Web, and in particular for the mobile ecosphere, has its own peculiarities. The Web is permanent and accessible to anyone with a connection. It's elastic, with almost infinite capacity to grow interactivity. While retaining legacy styles and forms, writing for the Web is an evolving form that needs to account for surfing, quick retention, text, video and audio, and boredom.

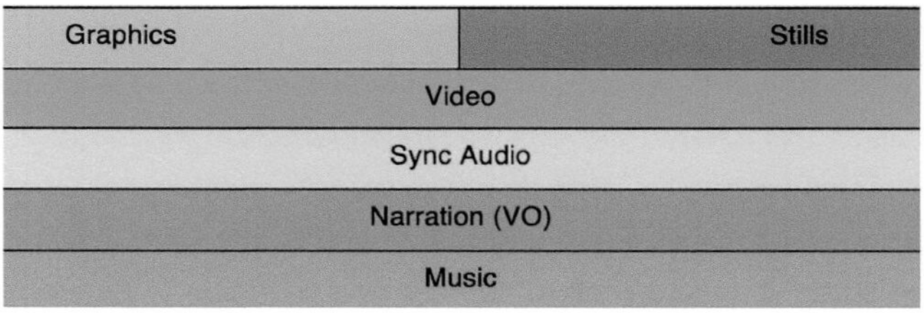

Figure 7.1 **Multi-planar track matrix.**

Ivo Burum

The current generation of writers who have grown up with the Web understand this. Many of their concepts of media—immediacy, presentation, interactivity, capacity, flexibility and permanence—are developed in and for a multi-media environment. This chapter provides an overview of writing skills used to glue multi-media elements into cohesive story.

THEORETICAL PERSPECTIVE

One of the benefits of working in a convergent space is accessibility to screen technologies that enable cross-platform production and diverse publication from source. Source diversity is measured in terms of diversity in ownership of media outlets, workforce and content (Napoli 1999). User-generated stories (UGS), which are produced and published by mojos at source, can overcome what media scholars have described as media's gatekeeping practices (Bruns 2005, McKee 2005, Shoemaker 2009). Hence, a key to the editorial ownership of story is completing a story at source. Writing is a key component of this process.

At universities writing teachers rely on decades of experience and listening to student needs to help shape their lessons (Hicks 2009). However, teaching writing in a multimedia space requires a challenge-based real-world approach (Johnson and Brown 2011), where students choose topics, get constant feedback, where publication occurs beyond the classroom and assessment includes process and artifact (Hicks 2009). This can often mean working in groups where individuals have specialist skills.

In a multi-media environment, where numerous people can construct a story, it can be difficult to know exactly who the writer among them is. There might be a specific writer whose job it is to make sure the script works, but who is doing the digital writing? Who is writing the script and deciding on the balance between pictures and words—the edit points that can often be the difference between a ratings hit and a miss? In the digital world, unlike the analog world, the writer's role might be morphing continuously as different hands play with the various media used to produce a digital story. But, where does the role of the digital writer begin and where does it end?

Writing for the Web is about getting used to a multi-media system of content creation and delivery where the phone, a central production tool and carrier, is accessible 24/7. In this neo-journalistic space, writing is the most difficult skill to learn, especially writing to pictures. Students and journalists can easily be taught technical skills—to shoot video, record audio and to edit basic sequences, but it's their ability to write "in and out of pictures" that enables journalists to work in a digital space. Hence, the focus of my mojo training workshops is storytelling, and writing is a key component.

My writing process begins when I first conceive a story, when I begin to think about the pictures (what and who we'll see) and interview grabs (what will be said). SCRAP, which is discussed in Chapter 3, is a useful tool for developing and writing a structural treatment of your story. Knowing the story enables the writer to compose an intro, and knowing what the structural points are enables writers to outline a set of narrative links that bounce the story between structural points and story milestones.

According to BBC mobile editor Nathalie Malinarich (2017), journalists have always believed that every word counts. This is especially relevant when writing for the mobile ecosphere. "News online needs to be clickable, readable and engaging on any size screen the user chooses." The impact on how a journalist writes should not be that different for news, where it's important to strip writing back to the 5Ws. This is more critical when writing on mobile. "Tolerance of padding on mobiles is a lot lower—so people are even quicker to drop out. You have to get their attention instantly; grab them from the first sentence. It's too easy to click away" (Malinarich 2017). Malinarich adds, "If there's an important story about Iraq or Syria where 50 people have died, don't say 10 were killed on Tuesday, 20 on Wednesday—just say 'this week.' It is not a new discipline—it just got tougher."

A recent Reuters survey of 70,000 respondents (Newman, Fletcher et al. 2018) indicates that mobile's ability to deliver news anytime anywhere is bringing revenue back into the news business. That requires writing the story for mobile first, then including extra information and features to enhance the user experience on tablet and desktop. It's generally thought that the mobile experience impacts the length of story, its structure and the length and type of intro. You need to write into the story quicker, and while the story needs to be tight, the length of story is dependent on quality. Yes, users surf, but they are all looking for a wave to ride all the way to shore—they'll stay if the quality is there. Quality on the Web is a holistic bag that begins with strong story, engaging characters, dynamic structure and sharp writing.

Convergence is the age of interaction where relationships between journalists, sources and audiences are undergoing transformation (Pavlik 2008). Whether it's a story using repurposed or original content, based on traditional or new digital design concepts, produced for small or large screens and across platforms, writing plays a key role in developing story signature and the level of diversity in the story.

PRACTICAL APPLICATION

I ran a mojo workshop in a seaside town in Norway for a mixture of citizen and print journalists and public relations people. The theoretical and practical components went well. Students went out to film their 1½- to 2-minute mojo stories about aspects of the town. The sun was shining so there was some focus on the water and the sailing boats. It is, after all, Norway.

Participants returned beaming, excited to begin writing and editing. They jumped right into it with crows of "wow, it works," "it's (mojo) so quick." One very experienced investigative journalist was, however, wandering around the patio enjoying the sun and smoking a lot. After an hour he still hadn't begun his edit. What was it? "I shot too much," the journalist said. He'd shot about 15 minutes of footage. Too much is 900 hours, not 15 minutes. The journalist stared at the water unsure of how to begin the edit. So I asked how his story would start? He knew that. So I asked, "If you were to write a few words to encapsulate that beginning, what would they be?" He knew exactly; he was, after all, an award-winning journalist. I said, "record that as VO." "But it might be wrong," he replied.

"Then we'll change it," I said. He recorded that VO, inserted it into the timeline and 15 minutes later his draft edit was complete. Writing an opening line, whether you ultimately use it or not, narrows your parameters and gives the story edit focus, making it easier to see what is relevant and what is not.

Tip: Writing is the key to story structure and when in doubt, write a draft script and record narration, insert it to pictures, then, if needed, rewrite it.

Irrespective of the type of story, whether you are writing for news, current affairs, live programs, comedy or documentary, the following principles apply:

- **Find your ANGLE—what's your story focus?**
- **Be CLEAR—the viewer gets one pass at the story**
- **Be CONCISE—a snappy phrase hits home**
- **Be DEFINITE—wishy-washy annoys**
- **Write the way you SPEAK, and it will sound true**
- **ONE idea per sentence**
- **ONE sentence per paragraph**
- **Read your work ALOUD before committing**
- **REWRITE if it doesn't bounce the story along**

Here are a set of tips that will help when writing in various situations.

Active and Passive Voice

Irrespective of the format or the style of segment, write your narration, headline and story intro in active voice.

Active voice is putting the subject doing the action first. An example is, "Betty hates Fred." Betty is the subject doing the action of hating Fred, who is the object of the story.

An interesting example is the Marvin Gaye song "I Heard It through the Grapevine." "I" is the subject, the one who is doing the action. "I" is hearing "it," the object of the sentence (Taylor 2013).

Passive voice puts the target up first. For example, "Fred is hated by Betty" or "A speech was given by Prime Minister Scott Morrison."

Using passive voice is not wrong but some people find active voice easier to understand because it's less wordy and therefore less awkward. Notwithstanding this, sometimes it can be preferable to use passive voice:

- **When the subject is unknown as in a crime story**
- **In fiction to emphasise detail**
- **In scientific writing to create objectivity—to take writers' opinions (the subject) out of results**

Writing Narration In and Out of Pictures

Mojos work with video and need to know how to write in and out of pictures. In some respects, journalists have been doing this for years, writing a few words of context that leads to a quote, and then writing out of the quote. In video the quote is generally a sync interview grab in vision. It may also be what we call an UPSOT[2]—a scream, the sound of a car skid, a word from someone that acts as story punctuation.

Writing narration to compress or expand interviews, segue between story elements, and bounce the story forward by relating to the outgoing video and introducing the incoming video is a key to creating seamless story transitions and maintaining a dynamic story structure. Called "writing in and out of pictures," it is one of the most important editorial skills a journalist can have.

Narration may be as simple as an RVO (reporter voice over pictures) where the mojo reads narration covered by B roll. It could be complex structural narration that drives a video package that the mojo shoots and edits. Writing narration is a learned craft that, like a metronome, provides the story bounce. Here are a couple of examples of the same piece written differently.

Version 1 Basic—more literal relying on words

Narration: When he stopped coughing, all he could see were dead bodies.

Interview Stan: I was sick in the stomach and the bloody stench was unbelievably strong and before long I was dry retching until I threw up ... weak as piss!

Narration: Lying in his own vomit he began crying.

In script form Version 1 looks like this:

Stan is coughing. He stops looks up and ... Stan's POV dead soldiers	Nar: When he stopped coughing all he could see were dead bodies.
Stan grab re being sick San dry retching Stan on all fours throwing up before he falls ...	Stan 100%: I was sick in the stomach and the bloody stench was unbelievably strong and before long I was dry retching until I threw up ... weak as piss!
Stan flat on his face ...he starts to cry	Nar: Lying in his own vomit it became too much.

Version 2 Dynamic—shorter, not so literal and relies more on the video to tell the story. In written form:

Narration: He looked up still coughing and was immediately sick.

Interview Grab. "... Weak as piss!"

Narration: Stan eventually threw up when it all became too much.

In script form Version 2 looks like this:

Stan looks up coughing and ... Stan's POV bodies Stan dry retching	Nar: Stan had never seen so many dead ...

Stan grab re being sick	Stan 100%: "… Weak as piss!"
Stan on all fours dry retching and then throwing up. He falls flat on his face. Stan crying.	Natural Sound (Natsot)

Writing effective narration requires planning at the structural stage and altering it once interviews are recorded and again at the edit stage. Written early, even in draft form, narration helps structural introduction of a scene: "The small island, which is nine kilometers long, was used by the German army as a supply base during the war." It can be used to make a more specific segue from one scene to the next: "After the war it became a thriving oil producer. Today Sipan's economy is driven by tourism."

Producers often use narration on longer programs to link a complete set of stories in an episode. On *Missing Persons Unit*, a TV police series, where five stories in each episode were interlaced like a soap (not run back to back), narration was critical to help with geography and timestamping. I would let story producers write the first narration pass and when I segmented and interlaced the stories into a program, I rewrote all narration so that it became one voice. Using one person to write the narration helped lessen confusion when stories were interlaced. Mojos mainly write and record their own narration and will write for their own voice, delivery style and audience.

Tip: When writing narration for a reporter, make the words simple and get them to read the narration out loud before it's recorded. Alterations are often made at the reading aloud stage. As long as these changes are not editorial, reporters should alter words to suit.

Here are some basic tips for writing and recording narration during a location edit:

- **Get draft narration down as soon as possible to help create story bounce and to narrow story parameters.**
- **Speech is more informal, so write spoken English.**
- **Write in the present tense and active voice so the audience feels the currency.**

- **Use mostly simple phrases and sentences—one idea per phrase or sentence.**
- **Sentences should be about 5–25 words.**
- **Usual reading pace is three words per second.**
- **For "how-to" videos, use words known to the viewer.**
- **If needed, use your hands to help inflect and punctuate the rhythm.**
- **Don't inflect every second or third word like a newsreader.**
- **Don't read and report, tell us a story.**
- **The first couple of words at the head of a story are often not heard, as the audience tunes into the story.**

Tip: Narration shouldn't repeat what is said in the first words of the incoming sync audio. It should lead into the video and form one cohesive thought, which drives story from one structural, editorial or emotional point to the next.

For more detailed information on writing and recording narration, see chapters 5 and 8.

Writing the Piece-to-Camera (PTC)

How to film a PTC (sometimes called a stand-up) is addressed in Chapter 4. PTCs are generally used at the head or the end of a story, but can work at any point during the story. PTCs are almost always shot on location to:

- **Place the presenter and/or the network in location with their unique spin on events.**
- **Cover a sequence where there is not specific footage.**
- **Add emotion or a personal view from a reporter experiencing a hurricane.**
- **Illustrate something in a "how to" segment.**
- **Summarise a complex theory.**
- **Add clarity by bouncing from one phase of the story to the next.**

For example, filming for *Foreign Correspondent* in Sicily, we didn't have footage of a kidnapped child and were not allowed to film in the house where he was hidden, so an emotive PTC, walking around the house, gave us a way to explain the child's last hours. It was more interesting than narration and looking at video of walls and windows.

A good PTC usually adds credibility to a story and segues between structural moments. When you write a PTC, keep it:

- **Current—the point you make can't alter with time.**
- **Short, at about 8–15 seconds unless it's at the end of a story with lots of background action. If you need more information, add it using narration. If you do, overlap the last words of the PTC and the first words of the incoming narration (Chapter 4).**
- **In context—relate it to information that comes before and after the PTC.**
- **Conversational—the alternative can be formal and turgid and alien.**
- **In your style to make it your PTC with not too many newsy inflections.**
- **Dynamic and walk-and-talk if that is required to demonstrate.**

Key is to be invested in the moment, the story and the need to do a PTC.

Writing Across Genres and Screens

Writing is the same but different across genres. In radio we talk about "writing for the ear" and in TV we "write for the eye," or more to the point "with the eye." We have to learn how to see the story in our pictures and not clutter these with too many words. Mojo work is a bit of both. Mojo stories, like any video news story, may be watched with or without audio. Stories need to make sense structurally and may use written text as well as, or instead of, narration.

Tip: Structure is a form of writing and writing is an integral part of structure.

As mojos get more involved in creating longer pieces and even TV-like programs, they will need to write across a variety of genres. Some will require the following styles of writing (check your own country's terminology):

***Live Read*: This is where the mojo or presenter reads a script on an autocue (see Chapter 2). There actually are no pictures. The writing must be strong enough to hold an audience. If the mojo is in vision, it's effectively a PTC.**

***Reader Voice-over*: This is where the mojo, or presenter, reads a script on an autocue but pictures are put over the top of the voice.**

***Recorded Package*: This is what has been described as a UGS and includes the various elements, from various sources that we discuss in this book, edited into a story.**

***Off the Cuff*: This is where the chat can appear to be unscripted but in reality the in and out cues are scripted, and between these are a series dot points, around which mojos ad lib. These may relate to structural aspects of the story, link to graphics or even through to packages.**

Whether it's a live read, a reader voice-over, a recorded package, or an off-the-cuff type of script, it will have been written with an objective in mind. The difficulty for mojos is that because they often work alone, they might not have a sounding board to bounce ideas off. Below is a list of tips from a number of experts across a variety of genres: news, radio, current affairs.

Writing for Audio Formats

I like to describe the scene when writing for radio or for an audio podcast—a mixture of voice, sound FX, music—sounds and silences to create a mood in the listener's mind. The idea is to help the audience feel the emotion rather than tell them in an expository style. However, don't be afraid of exposition. Used sparingly, in a manner that doesn't slow flow, it can be very useful to contextualise action and provide explanation and backstory.

Award-winning radio producer and journalist Dr Nasya Bahfen from La Trobe University provides the following Break-out Box of tips for writing radio stories:

> 1. **Use language you'd use in everyday conversation. No one uses "due to" in day-to-day speech—so it shouldn't be in your broadcast copy (use "because" instead). Imagine you're meeting a friend—how would you tell this story to your friend?**
> 2. **Read the story out loud to yourself. If a paragraph sounds strange the first time, change it.**
> 3. **Stick to one idea per paragraph. If there's a dependent clause, get rid of it—split the paragraph so it's two shorter paragraphs.**
> 4. **Get your head around the past perfect or present perfect tense. These tenses are the ones with a "has" or a "have" in front of a verb in simple past tense.**
> 5. **Break the rules where necessary. Active voice is awesome—it's how we learn to speak if we are native English speakers and it is how people who learn English as a second language learn to speak. But use passive voice if it suits the story—for example, when the object of the paragraph is better known than the subject.**

Writing for Video Formats

When writing for TV and any form of video, like mojo stories, you use sound and image to tell the story. The trick is to find a balance between the two so that the pictures do the heavy lifting and narration supports and bounces story from one structural point to the next. Writing is used to help plug structural or information holes and to provide context or a quick jump in focus.

In mojo or video work the writer is a filmmaker. Your job is to have the images stay in people's mind long after the story has been telecast. "If it's a good movie, the sound could go off and the audience would still have a perfectly clear idea of what was going on" (Alfred Hitchcock).

Tip: Never let the voice get in the way of the pictures telling the story.

Award-winning RTÉ video journalist Philip Bromwell, part of the ground-breaking RTÉ mobile team and arguably one our most prolific mobile journalists, provides this Break-out Box of tips for writing mojo videos:

1. **Aim for a solid narrative arc about one central character. There should be a clear beginning, middle and end.**
2. **Write and "unwrite." Look at what you have written and strip back the superfluous stuff. Good writers know when to shut up!**
3. **Write to your pictures—there should be a rhythm between words and images. Short, simple and clear sentences will allow your pictures (and any natural sound) to breathe.**
4. **You are not giving a lecture. You are telling a story. Lead the viewer through the narrative. Be their companion, not their professor.**
5. **While facts are essential, try to write so that the audience *feels* something too. They will remember what they feel longer than what they know.**

Excellent advice! However, don't be afraid to build secondary characters in the arc around the main character. Support characters that validate your primary character and develop story focus are essential, especially as stories develop from news to feature lengths.

Scripting Formats

Irrespective of the genre, when writing for visuals, keep the language informal and conversational. Table 7.1 describes an example of formal and informal writing.

Table 7.1 Formal and informal text Version 1

Formal text	Informal text
The relationship between cable and television grew increasingly competitive in the 2000s as cable companies invested heavily in movies and series.	As cable increased investment in movies and series in the 2000s it began to compete with television.

Or you can go further and completely rewrite:

Table 7.2 Formal and informal text Version 2

Formal text	Informal text
The relative disadvantage of Indigenous Australians with regard to health standards and levels of home ownership indicates that they are still marginalised by many basic economic standards.	Indigenous people don't live as long nor do they live as well as other Australians. Why?

A Variety of Script Approaches

How you set out your script will often depend on the format, and in video that can occur in a number of the following styles:

1. ***Standard host approach*: used for stories that are being introduced by a host or anchor.**
2. ***A presenter's introduction*: This is often written by the journalist or mojo after they edit the story and before they send it to the network. The intro will be impacted by the first words or any sync at the head of a story. This will be added to the autocue script back at the studio and be altered to suit the back announce from the preceding story and the anchor's particular feel. Your intro should:**
    a. **Outline the main point of the story (i.e. its newest element)**
    b. **Provide some context (but not all)**
    c. **Throw to the package (you're trying to keep viewer's interest here)**
3. ***The story package*: This can begin any number of ways: B roll with narration followed by a sync grab; or an emphatic sync grab followed by narration and B roll; or actuality and short sound-up followed by narration and B roll. Here is an example of a simple story bounce for a short package.**

    PACKAGE:
    Nar Script and B roll
    Sync Interview Grabs
    Nar Script and B roll
    Sync Interview Grabs
    PTC from the reporter 100% and sign-off

Table 7.3 Starting with narration and B roll

Vision	Audio
WS—Police cars screaming through frame In: 11:25:08 CU—police car In: 11:30:10	Nar: Seventeen residents have been confirmed dead in what's been described as Melbourne's worst fire
Police Sirens over CU p/car In 11:35:18	Sound-up—police sirens In 11:35:18 Out 11:38:18
Grab: Fire brigade spokesperson Super: Captain Fred Bloggs	In: 11:18:10 We have 15 trucks here... Out: 11:26:15 ... on the top floor.
Rep to Cam:	In: 12:10:14—Fire-brigades dealing with our biggest death toll in decades, Ivo Burum, ABC News, Richmond—Out: 12 15: 20

Another option could be to start with sound-up—natural sound you recorded that we used to call NATSOT (natural sound off tape). This is not a grab, but it can be vocal or another sound. If you are working with a network, you might be given a style guide. The rule of thumb at ABC and SBS in Australia is to always finish the story with the reporter's voice and B roll, or a final PTC (stand-up).

For example, in a swimming story about a record-breaking swim the sign-off PTC might be, "The boy from Queensland now firmly in the international spotlight. Ivo Burum, ABC News, Brisbane."

Here are a series of writing tips:

- **The first rule of writing is, have something to say—your story angle and focus—can you summarise your story and angle in one short sentence?**
- **Use short, one-syllable words—can you write your script in one syllable words?**
- **Writing in and out of pictures—narration must not say what the sync is saying, they must complement pictures. Does your narration and sync grab feel like a sentence or phrase?**
- **Is the style a straight news information piece, or more a feature with more feeling?**

- **Write short narration sentences. Count the number of words, if the average is more than 20 your sentences are too long.**
- **Be clear and precise. If the cost is high, say it is.**
- **Never use a metaphor that doesn't fit with context.**
- **Make your script conversational—write the way it's spoken not the way you think it should be written.**
- **Never let words get in the way of pictures—let pictures and audio do the heavy lifting.**
- **Read scripts aloud before finalising and you may need to rewrite to simplify the thought and the language.**

EXERCISES

These simple exercises will strengthen some of the points in this chapter:

In these exercises:

1. **We'll get to practice writing to some vision.**
2. **We'll get you to shoot some vision on your mobile device, and write to it.**
3. **We'll get you to start writing your TV news piece.**

Exercise 1

Part 1: Vision shooting (on mobiles)/writing exercise

- **On your own, or with a partner, shoot some footage of someone rushing upstairs, possibly late for class. Get a few shots to be able to edit a dynamic sequence (see sequencing in Chapter 4).**
- **At the top of the stairs, before they rush off, get a grab from them about why they are running and how they feel.**

You have 5 minutes to shoot.

Part 2: Write to the pics—before and after the grab (e.g. the person is rushing up a corridor because the tutorial ran over and they are late for a lunch date, or something—why?).

You have 10 minutes to write.

Part 3: Record narration and edit—you have 10 minutes to record narration and another 15 minutes to edit the sequence with narration.

Tip: Narration can't repeat what they have said to camera. More specifically, the last words of the narration can't be the same as the first words of the sync grab.

Show the class and discuss if the narration works with the shots and the grab, and whether the shots work. Re-do and fix up.

Part 4: Record a sequence of shots of where you are running to (the class, the date—where?).

Get a comment from the person there (waiting "S/he is always late" etc; or a teacher "You will all need to be here on time next week …" etc).

Part 5: Edit—now intercut these sequences with the previously shot media, writing narration in and out of pics as needed. How many ways can you cut this? How does the positioning of the narration alter the piece? Continue the piece to develop a story.

Exercise 2

Cook a pasta.

- **Shoot a variety of shots to enable you to shorten the process.**
- **Get three short grabs—beginning, middle and end from the cook.**

- **Write three pieces of narration to help bounce the story and the process.**
- **Edit the material, which could be 30 minutes long, into a short two-minute story.**

How many shots will you need and are three grabs and pieces of narration enough?

In both exercises ask:

- **Did the narration script help you understand the vision?**
- **Did the narration script get in the way of the vision?**
- **Was the script overwritten (did it leave enough room for the pics to tell the story)?**

In conclusion, writing for the convergent mojo space, even in factual-type storytelling, needs to address the fundamentals—every story needs a protagonist who struggles to overcome external forces and who experiences a form of change as a result of their struggle. Whether it's a fence dispute, local fire or the farewell of a football star, each story will have a character who overcomes obstacles to achieve their goal. Their struggle is the emotional heart that fascinates the audience and it's the writer's job to capture that journey and the associated emotional shifts. In short-form storytelling, mojos must develop these story elements quickly and find a balance between sync, narration and actuality. One of the most useful tools and skills for this is writing in and out of pictures and one key to this is understanding the power of narration.

Go mojo ...

NOTES

1 Fourth Estate refers to the press and news media and the earlier historical division of the Three Estates of the Realm: the clergy, the nobility and the commoners.

2 UPSOT is an early TV term that stands for raising a piece of sound on tape.

REFERENCES

Bruns, A. (2005). *Gatewatching: Collaborative Online News Production*. New York, Peter Lang Publishing.

Chung, S. K. (2006). "Digital Storytelling in Integrated Arts Education." *The International Journal of Arts Education* **4**(1): 33–50.

Hicks, T. (2009). *The Digital Writing Workshop*. Portsmouth NH, Heinmann.

Johnson, L. and S. Brown (2011). "Challenge Based Learning: The Report from the Implementation Project." *The New Media Consortium*. www.learntechlib.org/p/49837/.

Malinarich, N. (2017). "Writing for Mobile: Bite-size Basics." www.bbc.co.uk/academy/en/articles/art20141202144618106.

McKee, A. (2005). *The Public Sphere: An Introduction*. New York, Cambridge University Press.

Napoli, P. (1999). "Deconstructing the Diversity Principle." *Journal of Communication* **49**(4): 7–34.

Newman, N. et al. (2018). "Reuters Digital News Report." Reuters.

Pavlik, J. (2008). *Media in the Digital Age*. New York, Columbia University Press.

Shoemaker, P. (2009). *Gatekeeping Theory*. New York, Routledge.

Taylor, C. (2013). "TechCrunch Disrupt Berlin Backstage with Tim Armstrong." Berlin, AOL. https://techcrunch.com/video/techcrunch-disrupt-berlin-backstage-with-tim-armstrong/

Yan, X. et al. (2011). " New Approach Toward Digital Storytelling: An Activity Focused on Writing Self Efficacy in a Virtual Learning Environment." *Journal of Educational Technology & Society* **14**(4): 181–191.

CHAPTER 8

EDITING VIDEO STORIES

SUMMARY

This chapter looks at the various forms and stages of an edit. More specifically we explore edit theory, edit preparation, beginning an edit, the story cut, editing narration, editing B roll, various types of cuts, the fine cut and edit apps, before discussing rules of editing and associated workflows. Award-winning feature, documentary and TV editor Steven Robinson ASE, who has also worked as a video journalist/producer, provides tips and a Break-out Box.

OVERVIEW

From the earliest days, movies were hamstrung by technical limitations and because the language of visual storytelling was still being developed. As film language and tech developed, so did our realisation that we needed a mechanism to manage story perspectives. Editing was that construct. Steven Robinson is an award-winning cross-genre editor who's cut everything from news to documentary and comedy features. He sees editing as a set of possibilities where, irrespective of the genre, its essentially about "Working out what you need to tell the core story, your narrative—cutting out the bad bits and putting the good bits in the right spot of the structure to tell the story best" (Robinson 2019). Like all great art forms, this simple-sounding statement is supported by years of experience. The editor's job is to take that experience to merge the absurd, the creative and the editorial into an emotive and informative structure the audience will watch and feel.

Editing is a way of thinking about converging states of immediate possibility, something John Berger might call "ways of seeing" (1972). Robinson says, "the main narrative is your freeway and you can only divert so many roads away from that highway before the audience wonders what's going on—keeping audience focused is an editor's job" (2019). More specifically, it is a visual language, a form of digital writing that constructs and shapes realities from raw content and settles perceptions, or ways of seeing, for an audience.

Today, if we have the skills, we can create complex edits on smart devices that we carry in our pockets, which the Lumière brothers, Eisenstein and Pudovkin, would have killed for. We use these smart devices to upload more than 500 hours of mostly raw user-generated

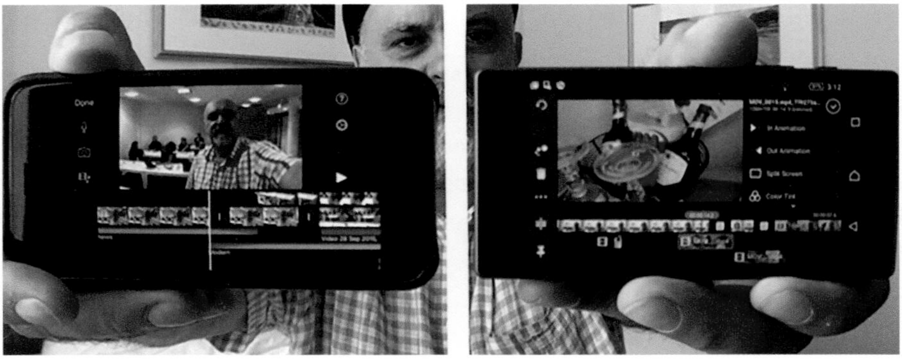

Figure 8.1 ***iMovie* and *Kinemaster* timelines.**

Ivo Burum

content (UGC) to YouTube every minute. I wonder what could be done with this footage if the people who shot it knew more about video storytelling and editing?

Some experts believe that because of our techno-determinist predisposition to gadget worship, the craft of editing, traditionally passed on from one generation to the next, is being lost (Reisz and Millar 2009). Being able to shoot, edit and publish stories on a smartphone is a skill that can potentially increase immersive cross-border reporting and local representation from the marginalised world. Rana Sabbagh, former executive director from Arab Reporters for Investigative Journalism (ARIJ), believes all journalists should learn to edit stories on a mobile: "Editing generates diversity in storytelling and a local point of view and in the Middle East working on a mobile is often safer than carrying a large camera and laptop edit suite" (2017).

Former *Newsday* reporter T. C. McCarthy said that his approach to finding the right mobile tool was "trial and error" (Belmaker 2013). With respect to editing, that's not the case today. We have the ability to create and slide B roll, alter transitions, grade video, duck audio, mix music, create versatile titles, dynamic graphics and animation, and render and send projects to various targets. Journalists and citizens who are trained in video storytelling can edit professional stories on their smartphones and publish them from almost anywhere. But to leverage the power of smartphones we need to wrap the technology in a literacy that I call a common digital language (CDL). Being able to edit and publish quickly from location is a key aspect of that CDL, and that's what we discuss in this chapter.

THEORETICAL PERSPECTIVE

From the first days of cinema, when the camera was in a fixed position providing one point of view, the need for more and varied story perspectives was apparent. In essence, editing is a language that harnesses film technique into a dynamic, entertaining and generally marketable form that enables films to be shot discontinuously. Russian director Vsevolod Pudovkin called this "the creative force of filmic reality" (cited in Dmytryk 2019). Editing is not only a post-production language, but as Murch (2001) observes, it's a major talking point during the whole filmmaking process.

If one filmic reality is that we are filming either real time or real constructed time, as we do in drama,[1] then editing is the glue that positions characters and compresses or expands real time to create a desired mood and drama, even in a factual program.

Early edit theories were built around mechanical developments—stop-start frame changes, multiple exposure and time lapse (Reisz and Millar 2009). George Méliès's *A Trip to the Moon* (1902) used these tricks to create a sense of being there. A year later *The Great Train Robbery* (Porter 1903) used simultaneous action edited in parallel to link two separate realities in the same story.

By 1912, Russian film theorist and founder of the Moscow Film School, Lev Kuleshov, was telling students that it wasn't acting that mattered as much as the way acting was cut together—the juxtaposition of shots. Kuleshov also determined that eyelines (looks) can provide reference even if the B shot (cutaway) is nowhere near the A shot (person looking). This became known as the Kuleshov effect and was the beginning of screen direction theory. One shot gives relevance and poignancy to the next. In shot A the person's eyes look up and we cut to shot B, a streetscape, suggesting that's what he is seeing. This enables a new set of meanings to be constructed (edited) between shots A and B, but also shot B and a slew of other shots.

The role of editors is to place these shots—either hold onto a shot or cut to a contrasting one—in such a way as to produce an emotional response from our audience. Murch says that it's all of the above, but it's also about cutting out the bad bits. The more experience an editor has, the better they become at deciding if "a bit" is "bad" or not. In essence, when an editor looks at a pile of rushes, she is looking at raw DNA. The level of the editor's experience provides a degree of sequencing tools used to construct the chimpanzee DNA into monkey, a human, or an Oscar-winning film.

As we build sequences in the edit, we create and settle constructed realities for our audience in a way that gives meaning to a particular line of questioning, a script, a structure, a series of shots. Sergei Eisenstein, a Russian editor and filmmaker, argues that "shots and scenes each contain their own ideas, concepts and feelings. But when strategically placed (montage) against one another, the viewer is able to deduce a third and entirely new meaning" (Zunitch 2015). This concept, which he termed the "intellectual montage," is well represented by *Battleship Potemkin* (Eisenstein 1925). Intellectual montage uses images that exude cultural, symbolic and political impact. A central concern of his was how a series of images carefully composed by the filmmaker can produce an abstract response from an audience. His American contemporary, documentary film maker D. W. Griffiths, used montage in another way: to create a greater narrative continuity to enhance clarity in the unfolding story.

At about the same time a contrasting movement called *mise en scene* was developed, mainly in France and Italy. *Mise en scene* suggests the best way to capture reality of the moment is not to cut. An early proponent, André Bazin,[2] believed "the camera should essentially act as the eyes of a neutral viewer, and yet still portray the filmmaker's meaning." More recently, the opening nine-minute shot of Peter Altman's *The Player* (1992) is an example of this. However, in reality, unless it's a news cameraman capturing an unfolding event like an accident, in *mise en scene* or observational styles, *mise en scene* shots will be choreographed around frame and movement. In a sense they are edited in-camera and constructed using scripted or choreographed action. Mojos will often find themselves in situations where actuality is unfolding as they shoot, and they will use an observational form of one-eye-open, unplanned *mise en scene* that is driven by the unfolding actuality of the story. We often shot this way on *Foreign Correspondent* (1998), an international current affairs program, when we rolled onto evolving actuality. When this happens, your edit will require cut points and these will need B roll (see Chapter 4).

As edit theory developed, so did a set of editing methods designed to help editors tell the story. Some of the earliest of these ways of creating/seeing varied perspectives (edits) on the timeline were proposed by Sergei Eisenstein, and these sit at the core of editing theory (Hess 2017):

1. ***The metrics method* of editing is all about pace and is determined by, and determines, the length of a shot and the tempo of the film.**
2. ***The rhythmic montage* method is based on length and how the action or dynamics of a scene is portrayed by editing to the rhythm of the scene using music or action to motivate the cut. Mojo editors will use this method with or without music.**
3. ***The tonal method* focuses on the representation of temporal shades of a scene using lighting and colors in the sequences to change the feeling of the scene and impact the viewer's emotion. Mojos may not have time to light, but can use natural lighting, a sunrise, sunset, cloudy day, a streetlight, bedside lamp, angry and happy characters and juxtapose these in the edit.**
4. ***The combination method* seeks to find balance between 1, 2 and 3—metric, rhythm and tonal—to impact the feel of a scene.**
5. ***The intellectual method* creates new meaning through editing by combining shots on the basis of a conceptual connection between them, which is often full of metaphor and symbolism helped by narration.**

At Film Australia there used to be a sign that read, "When the shooting stops the film-making begins." To a certain degree this is true. My cross-genre production background required many different approaches to editing: in observational and documentary films, structure was often fleshed out in the edit room; the comedy editor is often cutting for a balance between pathos and laughter; in drama, editing can add a nuanced perspective to an otherwise dry script; and current affairs relies on the edit to juxtapose intellectual and legal arguments with character and dynamic action in a way that drives story, makes meaning and minimises litigation. On some of the above genres the edit begins in the producer's or journalist's head or their notepad in the field even before shooting. I call this an "edit map" and it helps me use the raw DNA to make, as Murch says, either the chimpanzee, or the monster, but not a construct of both … unless of course that's what I want.

PRACTICAL PERSPECTIVE

Mojo workflow is often story currency and/or corporate-specific, which impacts the level of editing done in the field. Chapter 9 outlines a variety of mojo workflows. In this chapter we deal with the offline edit that's completed on a smartphone in the field.

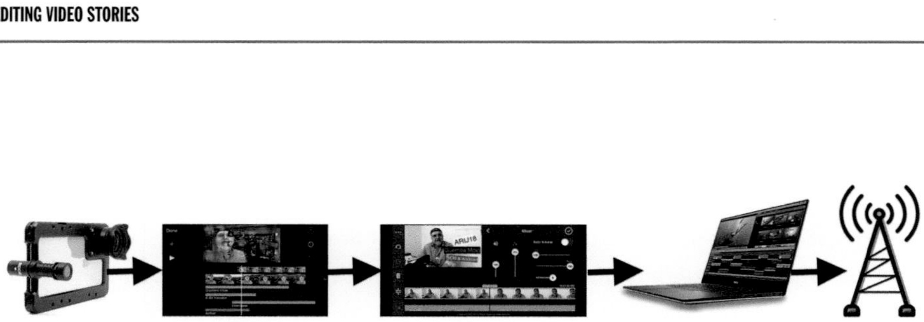

Figure 8.2 **Various mobile editing workflows.**

Ivo Burum

Planning for the Edit

Irrespective of whether you are editing on your smartphone in the field or in your hotel room on a laptop, or sending a basic edit and raw footage back to base, planning your edit is key. I use the SCRAP story development tool from my research stage to help develop my edit plan (see Chapter 3). SCRAP unlocks my reflective process where I evaluate story, character, structure, possible shots, sequences, order of interviews, who says what to whom, why, where and how. I think about what content I'll need—actuality, interviews, B roll or archive. This process always begins well before the edit so that I plan a shoot that captures the media I need for my edit. Robinson (2019) says a strong editing process always begins with careful field preparation:

- ***Presentation*: why and how will the final story be presented?**
- ***Beginning*: where, when and how will the story be introduced dynamically?**
- ***Coverage:* how will the scene be structured and covered—WS, MS, CUs, reverse questions, noddies and a variation of shot sizes to tell the story and to facilitate edit options and why?**
- ***Structure*: what is it and where will a sequence fall in the story—beginning, middle or end?**
- ***Location*: where is the story or scene set and how can we show a sense of place and location that gives us an emotional context?**
- ***Ending*: how might story be finished?**

Location, or shoot, imperatives (availability of talent, conflict, weather, emotional turmoil, time on the ground) and perspectives (who's making the story, the political view, freedom of speech) always impact the edit (the story and the structure). Mojos work alone so the

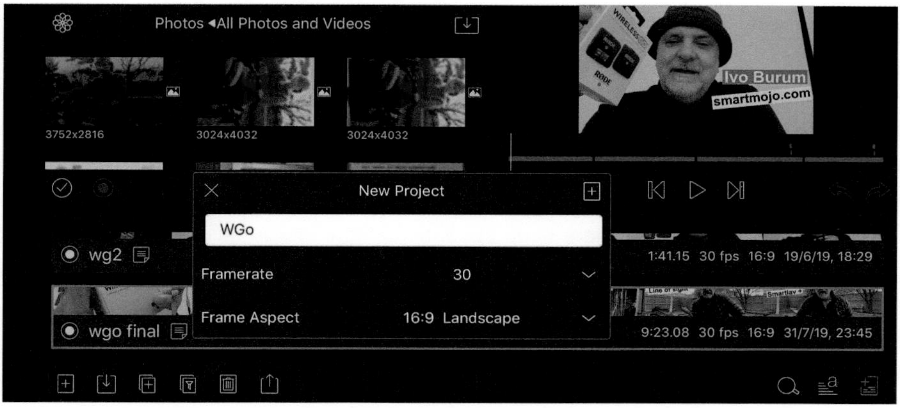

Figure 8.3 **Starting an edit on *LumaFusion.***

Ivo Burum

impact of these influencers will be manifold. Hence the need to develop a workflow, where every facet of the production cycle is considered at each stage of that cycle.

I do this using my initial story outline, or structural mud map (graphically shown in Fig 8.3). I scribble on it, indicating what media I have, what's missing and what still needs to be recorded, how and where it might best be used in the edit, and whether I need archive and graphics. My mud map includes aspects of my SCRAP research.

I number the structural arc 1–5 and note the elements I record—my interview questions, actuality and B roll—against certain story points (see Chapter 3 for a detailed description of SCRAP).

One of the key edit elements is B roll (see Chapter 4). Having enough story-specific B roll[3] increases the number of structural options in the edit and increases your ability to use narration to breathe, shorten, explain and segue between story moments. Robinson (2019) sees B roll as an essential element in any type of edit. "A montage (B roll) allows you to use a series of disconnected images to create transitions in films and show a passing of time … it breaks up the rhythm of storytelling and allows an audience to relax before taking in the next scene."

Beginning the Edit

Starting an edit is important, especially when you can't decide how to start. "Put something down because you can't change anything until you have something down; the second shot will follow naturally," says Robinson (2019). Ironically, even though digital editing is nonlinear and a completely malleable process, it's even more important to be well prepared. In a nonlinear edit suite where there is no spool time, there is also little or no think time, so mojos need to be prepared to choose the first shot and to start editing. One of the biggest mistakes I've noticed in the nonlinear environment is that producers play with possibilities, usually because they are unprepared, and lose valuable time.

Ulla Ryghe, Ingmar Bergman's editor, and my edit teacher, taught me the hardest lesson in filmmaking more than 30 years ago when she said, "Ivo you need to learn to kill your babies." It's another way of saying dump shots if they don't move the story forward. As the story begins to unfold on the timeline, many shots and sequences that you loved and thought important become redundant once you start focusing on the various realities that exist at the beginning of each edit.

Tip: The best way to eliminate these shots is before you get to the edit suite, because once you see them on the timeline you invariably fall in love with them all over again. After all, you shot them.

Start your edit with your strongest shots—actuality, interview grabs, overlay, music and/or narration. Something "real" from the story that captures emotion is better than a piece to camera (PTC). But a PTC can be dynamic and very effective if the journalist is in the middle of a riot or walking and talking at a mass grave. In this case you might pan off the unfolding actuality (see Chapter 4). Don't get bogged down by finessing the edit before you find the structure and the emerging story. At this early stage you are trying to lay down a structure on the timeline. Robinson's advice is, "don't worry about the B roll, overlay, or GVs at first, do it as a radio play … If I am doing an edit for 10 weeks, I won't put the nice stuff in until week 8 … get the structure down and don't finesse too early" (2019). Try to understand or see the story on the timeline and know that you have the footage to cover it. If you don't have it, and

Figure 8.4 ***LumaFusion* showing a full palette of tracks and FX.**

Courtesy of LumaFusion

are editing on location, you might have time to get it. Having an edit map during shooting is helpful so you don't forget B roll.

Tip: Structuring a story to answer what you expect listeners' questions might be, in the order they might arise, creates an engaging initial draft story structure.

The Story Cut

Using an edit app with at least two video tracks (V1 and V2) means the story can be edited on V1, leaving V2 to add B roll once the story cut is tight. This places the initial focus on story—writing in and out of the interview bites and actuality—rather than on B roll. However, two video tracks also enable B roll to be added early and slipped (positioned) in the fine cut.

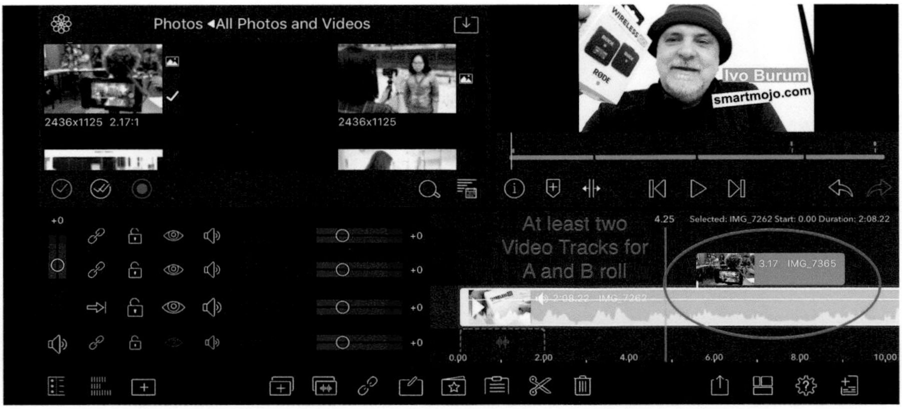

Figure 8.5 ***LumaFusion* has six video/audio tracks and another six audio tracks.**

Ivo Burum

This is called the "tight is right" method and is used when you are working to a deadline. It's key to get a draft narration down as quickly as possible to help with timing, structure and story bounce.

Figure 8.6 describes checkerboard editing, where video checkerboards with narration. This is done so that you can easily replace, shorten or extend B roll shots (wide shot, CU1 and CU2) when they are eventually inserted, something that is difficult if you have only one vision track and all shots are slotted into gaps on V1.

The example above shows how you might extend the wide shot to overlap some of the interview (J and L cuts; see p xx) and do the same with CU1 (close-up) or CU2. This provides a more dynamic feel to the edit. But if the wide shot was on V1, squished between the PTC

V2		Wide Shot		CU1 CU2	
V1	PTC 1		Interview		PTC2
A1		Nar1		Nar2	
A2		Add	music here		

Figure 8.6 **Checkerboard edit map.**

Ivo Burum

and the interview, it would be difficult to extend without first detaching the PTC and interview audio. A2 is left blank, but you could add some music here. The story cut is the time to check the rhythm, or story bounce, to determine if there are any clunky bits, where the story stops.

The rhythm and story bounce are created (in part) by the juxtaposition of narration and sync interview grabs, punctuating UPSOTS and, importantly, B roll, so I always write, record and lay a draft narration down as quickly as possible and before inserting interview grabs. This is key to focusing the story on the timeline. At this stage, and before I add B roll, I play with the structure of the grabs and the narration (see p xx for more on narration).

Tip: Your B roll will enhance story bounce, so if it's working without B roll, rest assured it will be right with B roll.

Editing B Roll

Supplemental footage intercut with an interview grab is called B roll, overlay, or cutaways. B roll covers an unwanted zoom, a jump cut in a shortened interview, a whip pan and mistakes in shooting. B roll is also used to compress and expand sequences and to cover narration (see Fig 8.7).

Figure 8.7 **B roll map.**

Ivo Burum

Look for story B roll that works to supplement your story message. One great advantage of editing on your smartphone on location is that if you don't have enough, or have shot the wrong B roll, you can quickly shoot some more (see Chapter 4 for tips on shooting B roll).

Tip: When you think you have enough B roll, get some more and make the shots special—varied and unusual angles and story-specific.

Types of Edits

Russian director Vasevolod Pudovkin concluded that in addition to edit methods there are a number of styles of montage. While mojos working quickly might mostly use a straight cut, or butt edit, they may find the time or a need to experiment with a variety of edits:

- ***Montage*: joining and contrasting straight cuts, or butt edits, is where the outgoing shot butts up to the incoming shot. This hard-cutting montage style is the most-used form of editing. It can be made more dynamic in the following ways.**
- ***Jump cut*: usually we look for continuity in a cut so that one shot follows the next; a person is standing in one shot and we see him sit in the same shot before we cut to him sitting. Jump cutting can jump from a person from standing to sitting, without the transitional movement. Jump cuts often occur when we shorten an interview, where we use B roll to cover them. But an editor might choose not to cover a jump cut and use it as a creative motif.**
- ***L cut*: is when you hold onto the audio of the outgoing shot and cover it with video from the incoming shot. The effect is to speed up the scene and to help with flow by maintaining a voice we know over new vision before we hear the voice from that vision. An example is the door squeaking and the boy counting in *The Tree of Life* (Malick 2011).**
- ***J cut*: is the opposite to the L cut and introduces incoming audio while holding onto outgoing vision. The effect is to create a sense of urgency about the sequence and pre-empt the incoming shot. It's used in interview situations. An example is the chest-banging Ohm scene in *The Wolf of Wall Street* (Scorsese 2013). Matthew McConaughey can be heard banging his chest before we see it.**

- *Cutting in action:* is when the editor matches action from one cut to another. This could be action in wide shot of a person beginning to sit; cut to a mid-shot of him sitting. This is mostly done in drama or multi-cam coverage.
- *Parallel action*: often called cross-cutting, is when two elements in the same story are intercut. For example, two cars racing to get to the same destination. Having parallel action means that you don't need as much B roll. In essence, the parallel action becomes the B roll.
- *Match cutting*: is when two edits are matched, for example, to transition a story. A well-known example occurs in Stanley Kubrick's *2001 A Space Odyssey* (1968), where an ape throws a bone into the sky and the editor cuts to a space station. Another great example occurred in *Lawrence of Arabia* (Lean 1962). Can you guess what it is?

The split edit in Fig 8.8 is an example of an L cut. And Fig 8.9 is the same sequence shown as a J cut. J cuts are used in dialogue edits when two people are intercut while talking. We might stay on the vision of the person listening (Shot 1) while hearing the incoming audio (Audio 2), before cutting to the vision of the person we can hear talking (Shot 2). It effectively speeds up the exchange.

Tip: If your edit is feeling a bit flat, J and L cuts will create a more dynamic pace and dramatically shorten the cut.

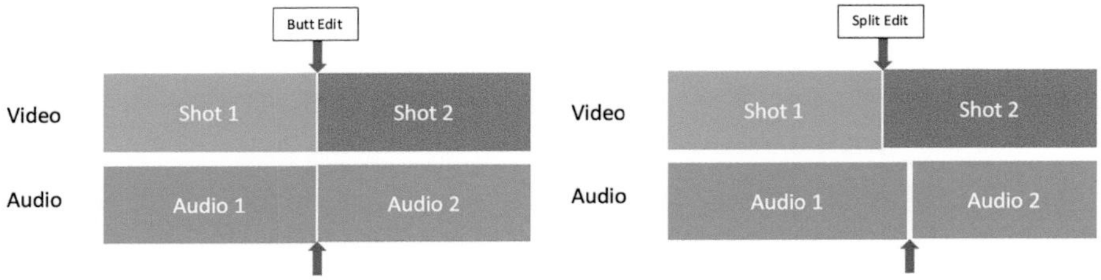

Figure 8.8 **Butt and split edit.**

Ivo Burum

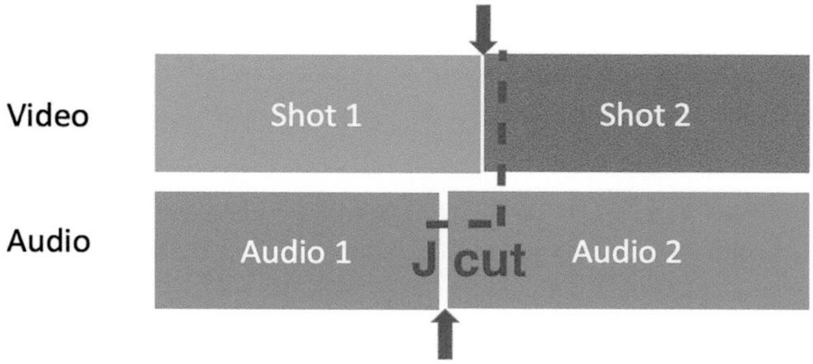

Figure 8.9 **J cut.**

Ivo Burum

Examples of J and L cuts can be found at www.youtube.com/watch?v=eyH-a964kAs.

Editing Narration

Narration is the glue that binds the various elements in story. Usually written and recorded during the edit, narration enables the editor to compress and to expand sequences, to segue between story milestones and to provide a third-party perspective. See chapters 5 and 7 for how to write and record narration.

Narration is used to compress rambling sync dialogue by enabling the mojo and editor to cherry-pick and write into choice interview grabs. Narration bounces the story forward by relating to the outgoing video (a back announce) and introducing the incoming video (throwing to). This is called "writing in and out of pictures," and is one of the most important skills a mojo, editor and/or producer can have.

When writing and timing narration, work to three words a second, the speed at which we generally read for television. If your video is seven seconds long, you'll need between 19 and 21 words of narration.

Narration shouldn't repeat what is said in the interview grab, especially the first words of the incoming audio. It should lead into the sync video grab and form one cohesive thought that drives story from one structural, editorial, or emotional point to the next. For example, if the first words of the interview grab are "Football is the root of all evil," the narration that leads into this grab can't end with the word "football." If it does, you'll have this: Nar: "His mother feels that it all happened because of Football." Interview grab: "Football is the root of all evil." You'll have Football mentioned consecutively. This might be better. Narration: "His mum blamed the game." Interview grab: "Football is the root of all evil."

Here is a summary of basic tips for writing and recording narration during a location edit:

- **Write the narration down so you can alter it if it doesn't work.**
- **Speech is more informal, so write spoken English.**
- **Write in the present tense and active voice so the audience feels the currency (see Chapter 7).**
- **Use mostly simple phrases and sentences—one idea per phrase or sentence—so that your mum and dad will understand.**
- **Sentences should be about 5–25 words long.**
- **If possible, use your hands to help inflect and punctuate the rhythm.**
- **Don't inflect every second or third word, like a bad newsreader.**
- **Don't read and report, tell your audience a story.**
- **Remember that the first few words are often not heard, as the audience tunes into the story.**

Tip: Get a draft narration down quickly and as early as possible in the assembly, to establish timing and structure in the edit.

The Fine Cut

There could be many reasons why the story might not be working, but when it's not working it's generally because the sequence includes redundant shots and/or information. Robinson is very particular about his process at this time: "Often when I look at a story and see a problem, I see that there are too many shots. In this case your emotional push should be guiding the narrative." He adds,

> Usually I reduce my edits … question, why have I cut … I'll try and simplify things mainly because what you are trying to do is tell the narrative and too many cuts can confuse. If

> I have cut MS, to CU, to MS I might decide I don't need all those cuts. Cutting can add to the emotion, but it can also be jarring. I look at the fine cut and ask do I need to add or pull back on the emotion.
>
> (Robinson 2019)

The truth about editing, as Walter Murch pointed out, is that you are not being paid to cut, you are actually being paid to decide whether to cut, or not. When you cut, you cut for story, that's what you are being paid to create. Once the rough story cut is completed with narration, interview grabs and B roll in place, and what I call cutting music, you're ready for the fine cut. More often than not, if the story bounce stops, the fix is to remove footage, close the edit and check by watching the sequence. Obviously if you are editing a quick news story in the field, the above process becomes a little more truncated. But mojos who work alone will need a checking mechanism and a version like this might work. The steps I use at this stage are:

- **Go back and watch the edit but don't change anything yet.**
- **Make notes about what you feel at each section, especially the story bounce.**
- **Go back to the beginning and start fine cutting. This may require:**
  - **shortening shots to lose any dead air after someone finishes talking**
  - **lengthening shots to provide think time**
  - **ensuring that words aren't clipped**
  - **sliding B roll shots left or right in the timeline for correct placing and impact**
  - **adding or replacing interviews and/or B roll**
  - **in some cases, you will need to re-record the narration**

Story bounce, or flow, is complicated and is different for everyone and every project. But the following is what some editors and producer/directors look for in a cut:

- ***Emotion*—the cut evokes moments of emotion from the viewer**
- ***Story*—the cut focuses and bounces the story from one structural moment to the next**
- ***Rhythm*—cuts occur at the right time, either driven by screen action, music or narration, to assist story bounce**
- ***Eye trace*—impact of location and the level of the audience's distracted movement within the fame**

- *Screen and story relativity*—that we understand the story continuity within scenes and between scenes and across the story structure

I always ask:

- Why am I cutting to a new shot?
- Is the new information, structurally right?
- Where does it take the story?

Tip: Structure your story to answer what you expect listeners' questions might be in the order they might arise.

Steven Robinson's Break-out Box of Tips:

1. Get your coverage cutaways wide shot for location, close-up of hands, eyes, bits of detail to provide cut points and a sense of the person and setting.
2. Get clean audio—don't talk over the questions and answers, especially if you are not going to be part of the program. Clean audio will override bad vision.
3. Think about the order of shots and how the sequence will be edited together; think about how to start to develop and use a sequence.
4. Give a sense of location and place.
5. Think about transitions and montages to give yourself a couple of shots.
6. Shoot for what you want. Don't overshoot—get what you need for your edit and get the @#$% out.

Edit Apps

Edit apps are introduced in Chapter 2 and discussed in detail in Chapter 9. In summary, here are the three apps that I use for my story edit:

- *iMovie* is a free app that is quite powerful, despite what people think. You will be able to do most of your work on *iMovie*. However, its titling tool lacks power

Figure 8.10 **Variety of mobile edit apps.**

Ivo Burum

and there's no audio ducking or grading tool. In 2019, Apple added a green screen feature.

- *LumaFusion* is a paid iOS app that's loaded with features; it has a difficult interface which takes some time to learn, but is well worth the effort. Once learned it is relatively intuitive. It is great on an iPad. I use it for advanced training and work.
- *Kinemaster* is a fully featured iOS and Android app that has an excellent UX (even though B roll is below the timeline), powerful onboard graphics, audio ducking and even does green screen.
- *VN* is a free cross platform edit app with many pro features.

What should you look for in an edit app?

Check out chapters 2 and 9 for a complete list of important features. However, you might look for apps that offer the following functionalities:

- **Multiple video tracks to enable B roll to be added separately and moved around easily and to enable graphics layering**
- **Ability to import a variety of formats**
- **Multiple audio tracks to enable track laying and mixing**
- **Audio ducking tool**
- **Simple titles tool that enables choice of font, sizing and background creation**
- **Export in a variety of formats and resolutions**

Editing is the creative and fun part of filmmaking and should be enjoyable. Whichever genre of story you're editing, the following summary of basic edit principles will help create flow in your cut:

1. **Never make a cut without a positive reason.**
2. **When undecided about the exact frame to cut on, cut long rather than short.**
3. **Whenever possible, cut in movement.**
4. **Current is preferable to the "stale."**
5. **Substance first—then art. Don't use a shot unless it moves the story forward editorially, with new information or heightened emotion. Cut for story rather than shots, even in fast montage sequences.**
6. **Interview grabs help to tell the story—they can make the story.**
7. **You can have five inserts in a short news story, more in a current affairs story and many more in a documentary.**
8. **Keep sound bites short: 5–15 seconds in a news story and longer only if they are amazing.**

Exercises

Option 1: Sequencing—shoot some shots of a person exiting a door; walking up some stairs; finding $5—deciding whether to pick it up, picking it up, walking off.

- **How many and what shots and perspectives do you need?**
- **Can you create drama around the decision and what shots do you need for this?**

- **Can you create a sense of pace in the edited sequence?**
- **How do you use sound?**

Option 2: The Interview

1. **Record an interview with a sports person and ask about**
   a. **Their early love for sport**
   b. **Their sport**
   c. **What they do besides sport**

2. **Edit this into a one-minute interview**
3. **Cover the edits with relevant B roll**
   a. **Early life**
   b. **Sport**
   c. **Life outside of sport**

Option 3: The Meal

1. **Record a person preparing and cooking a meal—say a pasta:**
   a. **Preparation—actuality and sound bite**
   b. **Cooking—actuality and sound bite**
   c. **Serving and eating—actuality and sound bite**

2. **Edit this into a one- to two-minute sequence**
3. **What B roll will you cover your edits with?**

In closing, even after decades of video production, editing still feels like magic. Only 20 years ago editing was still relatively cumbersome and costly; now we carry our very own smart creative suites in our pockets. We need to learn to use these smart tools to write digitally, in essence, to edit.

Steven Robinson and I worked together for many years. We spent hours struggling through sequences shuffling cards and doing trial cuts. We have worked on programs shot at a 2:1 ratio, and others where we've had 900 hours of raw documentary material to sift through for a half-hour program. In fact, in my capacity as producer, and at times working as an editor,

I've watched more than 80,000 hours of rushes. So, when you are struggling through 10 minutes of raw smartphone footage, know that we have all been there, at the precipice, staring at an empty timeline. Don't panic—start the cut.

Walter Murch worked out that on *Apocalypse Now* (Coppola 1979) he and his edit team looked through 1,250,000 feet of film, which was a ratio of 95:1, and only averaged 1.47 cuts a day (Murch 2001). But for each of those cuts, many more, which Murch calls "shadow" cuts, were contemplated before he arrived at a desired cut. So even the greats like Murch need time.

You'll be just fine; take a breath, check your structural map and edit list, and *make the cut*. You can't fix anything if you don't have anything on the timeline to fix!

Go mojo ...

NOTES

1 A time reference measured by the interaction of characters and scripted dialogue.
2 French film critic and theorist.
3 B roll that relates specifically to aspects mentioned in an interview and or narration.

REFERENCES

Altman, P. (1992). *The Player*.

Belmaker, G. (2013). "5 Ways Journalists Can Use Smartphones for Reporting." www.poynter.org/reporting-editing/2013/5-ways-journalists-can-use-smartphone-apps-for-reporting/.

Berger, J. (1972). *Ways of Seeing*. London, BBC.

Burum, I. (1998). Foreign Correspondent. *Foreign Correspondent*. Australia, ABC TV.

Coppola, F. F. (1979). *Apocalypse Now*.

Dmytryk, E. (2019). *On Film Editing*. New York, Routledge.

Eisenstein, S. (1925). *Battleship Potemkin*. Critical Commons. https://criticalcommons.org/search?q=Battleship+Potemkin%3A++Tonal+Montage.

Hess, J. (2017). "The History of the Soviet Montage Theory: Sergei Eisenstein and the Theory of Montage." https://filmmakeriq.com/lessons/sergei-eisenstein-theory-montage/.
Kubrick, S. (1968). *2001: A Space Odyssey.*
Lean, D. (1962). *Lawrence of Arabia.*
Malick, T. (2011). *The Tree of Life.*
Méliès, G. (1902). *A Trip to the Moon.*
Murch, W. (2001). *In the Blink of an Eye.* Los Angeles, Silman-James Press.
Porter, E. S. (1903). *The Great Train Robbery.*
Reisz, K. and G. Millar (2009). *Technique of Film Editing.* Abingdon, Focal Press.
Robinson, S. (2019). Book Interview. I. Burum.
Sabbagh, Rana (2017). Interview with I. Burum.
Scorsese, M. (2013). *The Wolf of Wall Street.*
Zunitch, P. (2015). "An Editing Theory Primer." www.videomaker.com/article/c10/18020-an-editing-theory-primer.

CHAPTER 9

POST-PRODUCTION

SUMMARY

This chapter explains various mojo workflows and introduces specialist post-production apps. The term post-production in film, TV and online video production refers to work done to embellish the story after the shooting is complete. While story editing is also part of the post-production chain, this chapter describes the work of manipulating the image and sound that might follow the story edit and before the delivery of the finished story or program. This can include picture grading, FX, specialist text and graphics, audio mix and delivery. Drew McPherson, one of Australia's most experienced post-production (online) editors, provides specialist comment and a Break-out Box of tips.

OVERVIEW

Nicolas Bourriaud (2005), in his work *Postproduction*, describing various aesthetics of post-production writes, "Postproduction is a technical term from the audio-visual vocabulary used in television, film and video. It refers to the set of processes applied to recorded material: montage, the inclusion of other visual or audio sources, subtitling, voice-overs, and special effects."

Moreover, discussing production without understanding post-production and the various options, even for mojos, seems incomplete. Producing film and television programs usually occurs in four stages: development, pre-production, production and post-production. Generally, post-production happens after the production phase. For our purposes it refers to the process after the picture edit is completed, which in a mojo context and in a digital workflow, can occur while the picture edit is in progress. Production can be costly and if post-production is not scheduled properly all the good production work can be wasted.

However, production and post-production can often overlap depending on the format. On continuing series, post-production is often scheduled while episodes are still being shot. On *Outback House* (2005), an observational documentary series I produced for ABC Australia, episodic story editing occurred while we were still filming each episode. This was important because each of the documentaries related to the previous episode. Because we didn't have a script, editing a day after each shoot day enabled us to follow developing story lines and to do story pick-ups as they were identified in the assembly edit. It also meant that the assembly cut was well underway after the 10-day shoot of each episode concluded. The fine cut, specialist graphics, final narration, grading and the mix all occurred after all episodes were complete.

Doing post-production is like contracting out to various experts each charging for their speciality—picture grading, electronic FX or audio mixing. One finishes and the next begins the new task in the production chain. Post-production is an expensive part of television and filmmaking. But in mojo work, it's mostly all done by the mojo and often on location as a story is breaking. A post-production suite, which usually comes with specialist operators, could cost US$750 an hour. The post or compile (inserting the various shots and other elements into a program), grading (getting the pictures looking right), mixing (adding music, FX and setting audio levels) and finishing (DVE moves, graphics, titles, end credits), on a one-hour documentary could take 10 or more days.

A traditional post-production workflow might look like this:

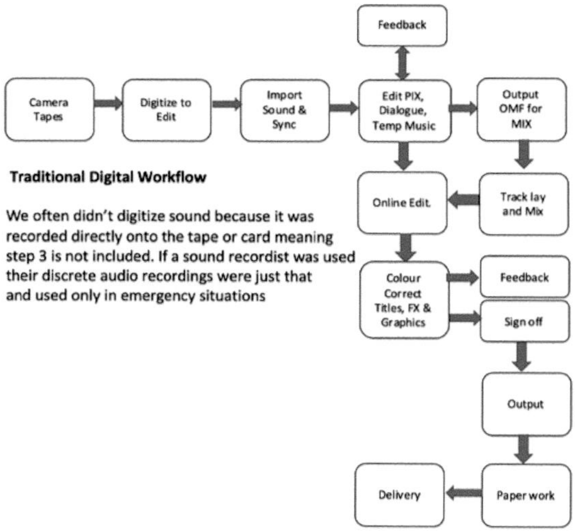

Figure 9.1 **Broadcast digital workflow.**

Ivo Burum

***Assembly edit*: this includes getting the story right, adding interviews, B roll, narration, some FX, some music for rhythm and to highlight story moments. This can take anywhere from a day for a 5–8-minute story to 12 weeks for a one-hour observational documentary.**

***Images, graphics and supers*: building specific name and location supers, images and graphics to enhance the emotion or information flow of the show and to show instead of tell. Insert**

some of these in the assembly to clarify story, provide timing and enable rebuilding, complete in post-production.

***Feedback*: a key element where feedback is provided and fix-ups made, before producers move to what's called a fine cut.**

***Fine cut*: is where we finesse a story to the point of picking UPSOTs (sound ups), sliding B roll, adjusting narration and inserting relevant music and temp FX at appropriate spots.**

***Approval*: a safety check to determine whether all feedback has been considered and to gauge what specific inclusions were required during the next post-production stage.**

***Picture lock*: Generally, after picture lock visual aspects are not changed. I would always schedule final approvals of story and length, any temp music, preliminary graphics or legal overview at this stage. On some programs temp music had to be used in order to get a viable picture lock.**

In the film age picture lock was important as it triggered a number of timely processes around the film negative. For post-production editor Drew McPherson, picture lock triggered his involvement in a project:

> It is where all parties sign off on the "content" and "editorial" of a film before moving on to the finishing stage. Many larger productions would be edited from a low-resolution copy of all of the footage captured to save on hard-drive space. Then only the "picture-locked" film would be matched back to the high-resolution original files and sent off to a sound mixer and a finishing editor (called an online editor). The colorist and sound mixer would most likely be working to a fixed number of hours, and making a change that should have been completed previously would reduce the time they would spend on finessing the film.
>
> (McPherson 2019)

In the digital age picture lock could be slightly elastic because, as McPherson points out, "the film could be finished using the same software package." But it was important to recognise and stick to this and other milestones, because they triggered certain funding drawdowns.

Once the picture is locked we moved into the post-production phase:

- *Conform or compile*: **In the early days of film, video and digital, the assembly was often called the offline because the film used for editing was what we called a low-grade work print. When we went digital in the late 1980s, video footage for the assembly edit was also ingested at a low resolution due to the cost of storage and a lack of computer power. As storage became cheaper and computers became faster at crunching video, the assembly was done using hi-resolution footage and aspects of the compile stage became almost redundant.**
- *FX run*: **We would use the power of the post-production suite to insert high-end FX like green screen, DVE moves and other complex video transitions and graphics or animation. Trimming is frowned upon at this stage, but we were still able to trim if needed and we often did, because the FX and graphics timing could require it. Today green screen can be done using a smartphone edit app.**
- *Track lay and audio mix*: **Final music pieces, audio FX and any changed narration is added before adjusting levels between the various audio tracks: interviews, narration, sound FX, actuality and music. In the early days, audio was replaced, but as we began recording digital, we found camera audio more and more useable. The key is story clarity and enhancement and today many smartphone edit apps contain high-end mix features.**
- *Sign off*: **This occurred for creative, technical, editorial and legal reasons and often triggered budget drawdowns. Mojos working alone make this call themselves.**
- *Export*: **The finished film would be mastered and exported either as film, 1-inch, digital Betacam tape and finally as a digital file (MP4, Apple Pro Res). Today export variables are chosen and completed on the smartphone edit app on location.**

One of the dangers of the homogenisation in production and post-production that results from producing formatted shows is that we stop thinking outside the box. For example, many critics of reality TV believe that it has somehow flattened a generation of production innovation. The democratisation of cameras and computers within smartphones has enabled a variety of experimentation in post-production approaches. New apps enable people to experiment with workflow and this is one of the exciting aspects of mojo. There are a variety of production workflows ranging from basic mojo (raw shots are uploaded) to edited stories (UGS are cut on location and uploaded) and even user-generated programs (UGP).

Mojo Post-production

In the digital era a video journalist became a one-man band and the post-production process became more streamlined to enable editing and publishing from location using just a smartphone. The truth about video journalism is that VJs didn't always edit on location, and sometimes used a story editor to do their cut. Depending on the nature of the project, they might use a post-production editor as well. This is one of the differences with mojo. Many mojos do their own post-production—whether it's a simple edit, or something more complex using advanced edit (*VN, LumaFusion* and *Kinemaster*) and post-production apps.

In the early days of mojo, many of the stages described in Fig 9.1 were flattened into an even simpler workflow: shoot and publish. We were shooting and sending back to base, where an experienced editor would edit. This stopped when journalists began sending too much mobile footage back to the office for video editors to handle. When edit apps became more prevalent and feature rich, mojos could edit the whole story in the field and also send a completed package back to base or publish it from location.

In particular, in mojo work the edit (step 4) might include any simple FX, a simple mix and generally have very little feedback before output. As specialist post-production apps became available and mojos began editing longer projects, some of the above workflow stages began to reappear in mobile workflows.

As mojos begin to produce series, they will be able to licence their formats and their own workflows. The current proliferation of broadcast channels, or publishing platforms, means that tested formats (*Big Brother*, *Idol*, *Project Runway*), with their proven audience pull, are often preferred by networks. But mobile story platforms like QUIBI are challenging this domination with their own short-form series formats shot on and for mobile.

PRACTICAL PERSPECTIVE

On location mojos often work alone, so they rarely have a camera or audio person to act as a sounding board. They often make quick decisions on covering breaking news or covert stories from conflict zones. Mojos often shoot, edit and even publish their stories from location where they wait to update a developing story. Mojos can cross checkpoints and work downrange where they shoot, edit and publish stories. In conflict zones, after the story is uploaded, mojos can wipe the footage from their phone prior to crossing the checkpoint back to safety. There are various levels of mojo, each with its own post-production workflow implications:

- **_Shoot and upload/publish_—recording video and publishing the raw footage immediately from location is the most basic mojo operation. Mojos either send the video in its raw form or put it into an edit timeline to play it out at a lower resolution if the bandwidth is low. Generally, in this situation the edit and advanced post-production will either not occur, or be done back at base, where the footage is integrated in a story and/or a post.**

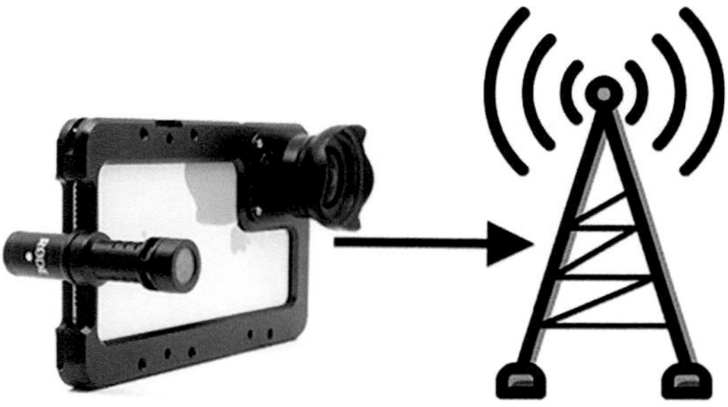

Figure 9.2 **UGC workflow.**

Ivo Burum

- **_Shoot, edit and publish_—video is edited on location using the onboard edit app with little picture or audio post-production. Mojos use onboard titles tools and simple FX if required and they have time. An audio level balance is done if required. A render resolution is chosen, depending on their streaming capability, and the package is sent.**

Figure 9.3 **UGS workflow.**

Ivo Burum

- *Shoot, edit, post-produce and publish*—the edited story is post-produced (video and audio, music, graphics and FX) on location using advanced apps (see p xx). Many of the advanced edit apps include post-production tools—audio mixing and ducking, picture grading, layered titles and network badging. This can all now be done using the smartphone if time permits and a mojo has the requisite skills.

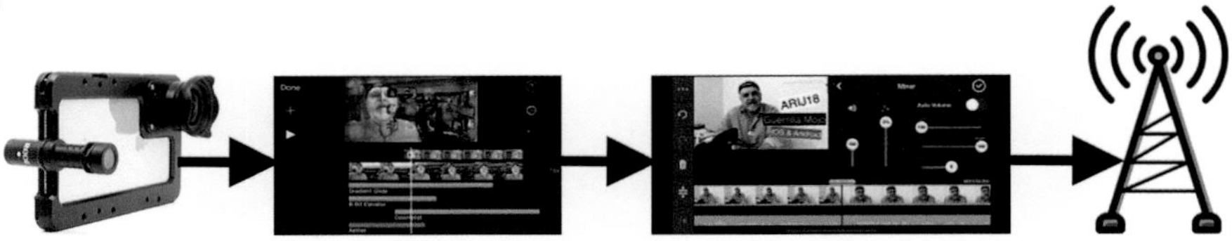

Figure 9.4 **Enhanced UGS workflow.**

Ivo Burum

- *Shoot, edit, post-produce on hybrid systems and publish*—when the story necessitates, mojos will use DSLRs and long lenses (e.g. when filming lions on safari, or sport). In this situation they will transfer the footage across to their smart device using Airstash, or one of the Sandisk transfer drives (see Chapter 2).

Figure 9.5 **Hybrid smartphone-to-laptop workflow.**

Ivo Burum

FILE SIZE AND TRANSMISSION

Irrespective of the level of mojo that's right for you, image resolution of the completed work—the higher the resolution, the cleaner the picture—is a technical aspect that mojos will need to be aware of (see also Chapter 2).

- *Resolution*—if the WiFi, 3/4G pipe is choked and slow, and if you needed to send your breaking news video back to base quickly, resolution, or the size of the information you are sending, may be a consideration. Mojos might need to create a lower-resolution, or smaller version of their shot, sequence of shots, or story.

After editing, a clip can be rendered at numerous resolutions from 640 × 360 up to 3840 × 2160 (4k). The higher number refers to the number of pixels

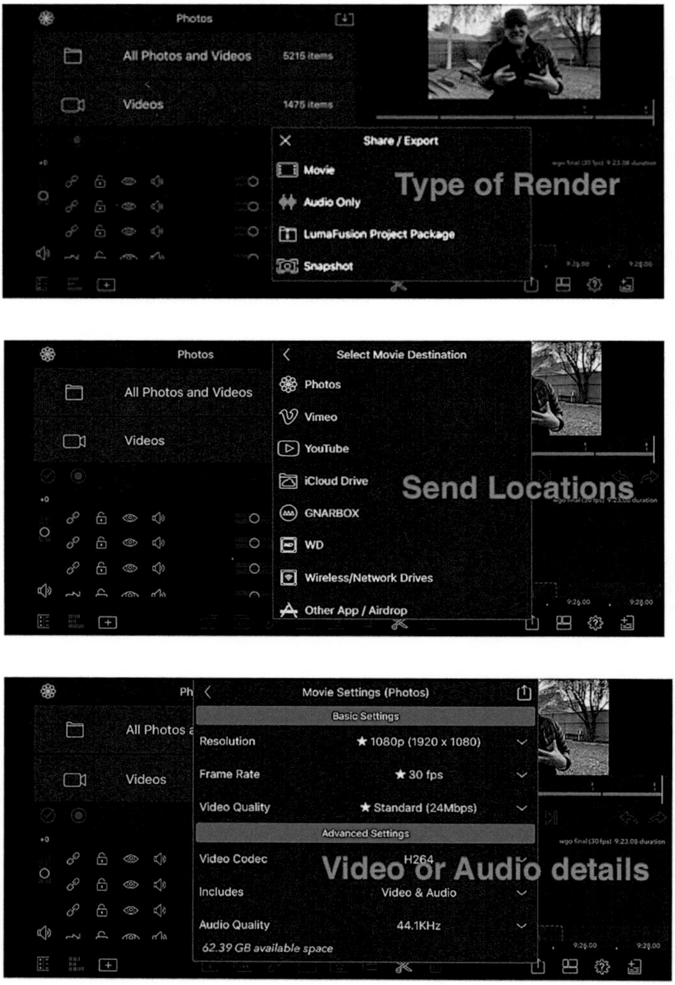

Figure 9.6 *LumaFusion* render screens.

Ivo Burum

across a screen, the smaller number refers to the number of lines on a screen. A resolution of 1920 × 1080 (HD1) = 2,073,600 pixels, whereas 1280 × 720 (HD2) = 921,600 pixels. Lower resolutions create smaller files that are quicker to send, higher resolutions create bigger files that are sharper. McPherson says look at the reality of who's going to be watching: "Most phones would be playing back in HD (1920 × 1089). So in most cases shooting and editing in 4k is overkill. For instance, most movies in the cinema are projected in 2k (a small percentage are in 4k)."

- *Interlaced or progressive*: refers to the way an electronic image is scanned. In the analog days this was interlaced, where odd lines, then even lines of an image were scanned. This left a flicker on the screen. In progressive scanning, universally used in computer screens, all lines are scanned simultaneously resulting in a much cleaner image. The disadvantage of progressive scan is that it requires higher bandwidth than interlaced video that has the same frame size.
- *Aspect ratio*: describes the proportion of the width to the height of an image. There are many aspect ratio sizes, for example, 1:1, 4:3 (which was the old TV size) and 16:9 the most commonly used size today. The first digit refers to the width (16 units) and second refers to the height (9 units). For example, 1280 × 720 is a 16:9 ratio, 120 × 960 is a 4:3 ratio. At https://calculateaspectratio.com you'll find a useful aspect ratio calculator.

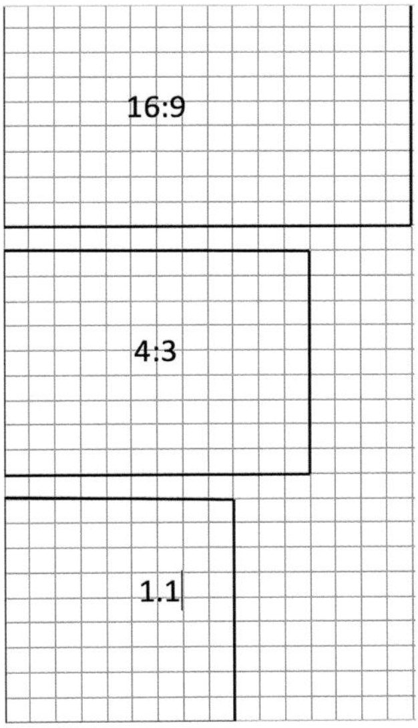

Figure 9.7 Aspect ratios.

Ivo Burum

- *Frame rate*: is the rate of frames per second (fps) at which images appear on a screen. NTSC is screened at 30 fps and PAL at 25 fps. If you record a video shot at 60 fps and play it back at 25 or 30 fps it looks like it's shot in slow motion. Human vision can articulate 10–12 individual images per second; beyond that images tend to be perceived as motion.
- *Codec*: is a computer program or compression technology for encoding and decoding (see Chapter 11) digital data. Codecs are contained in formats like

Quicktime. There are two kinds of codecs, lossless and lossy. Lossless codecs such as PNG reproduce an exact copy of a file and are generally large, so not great for sending video across the Internet. Lossy codecs such as JPEG compress more to make smaller files and trade quality for size. You get a facsimile of the original file that is smaller and faster to send over the Internet. Most of what applies to Web content delivery also applies to video stored on mobile handheld devices. Below are a few options:

- Video
    - *H264/MPEG-4 AVC* is the most common codec used in modern camcorders, digital cameras and mobile devices. Even at lower bit rates it delivers fairly high-quality video. It is possibly the most common codec used on our smartphones because it's a favorite with YouTube and supported by Apple.
    - *H265 or HEVC* (High Efficiency Video Coding) is a new compression standard updated from AVC or H264 specifically built to accommodate streaming and in particular high-bandwidth 4k video.
    - *DV and HDV* is a codec that was developed by a consortium of consumer electronics companies that manufacture and sell camcorders.
    - *WMV* (Windows Media Video) is a Windows codec we are moving away from.
    - *JPEG (JPEG2000)* is a very popular stills codec.
    - *Apple Pro Res* is a very high bit rate professional codec that is almost always used for exporting professional video destined for network broadcast.

- Audio
    - *MP3* is a good lossy audio compression format. But there are royalties on distribution of MP3 content in some cases.
    - *WMA* (Windows Media Audio) is a Windows codec.
    - *AAC* (Advanced Audio Coding) is a lossy codec that is free to use. AAC has excellent compression characteristics and is a preference with mojos who are streaming. The Fraunhofer Institute for Integrated Circuits, a German consortium, have declared AAC the "de facto standard for music download and videos on mobile phones" (Fingas 2017).
    - *Vorbis* is an open-source and patent-free audio codec that's great for streaming over the Internet because it highly compresses data—very lossy, but fast.

- ***WAV*** **(Waveform Audio File Format), FLAC, AIFF or Apple Lossless are uncompressed, or lossless codecs that use more data but produce better audio quality.**

There's a lot of noise about 16-bit vs 24-bit and 32Khz vs 48Khz audio. Both are digital, and once audio has been through the audio chain and played through small smartphone speakers, very few people will notice the difference. Having said that, it's worth knowing what "bits" and "Khz" mean.

The term "bits" refers to the depth of sound, the fatness of the sound. Audio recorded at 16 bits theoretically includes twice the amount of information of audio recorded at 8 bits. The higher the bit depth, the more data will be captured to more accurately recreate the sound. If the bit depth is too low, the reproduced sample will be degraded. Practically, bit depth determines the dynamic range of the signal (Presonus 2019).

Most of my broadcast work was recorded at 16 bit and sampled at 44–48Khz. We didn't see a need to sample higher than that. That said, some engineers prefer a higher sample rate. Specialist camera apps sample at up to 48Khz; if you need higher, you'll need to go to audio apps, but that complicates the mojo video workflow. The question I always ask is when is enough enough? Many people just won't hear the difference in hi-resolution sound above 48Khz.

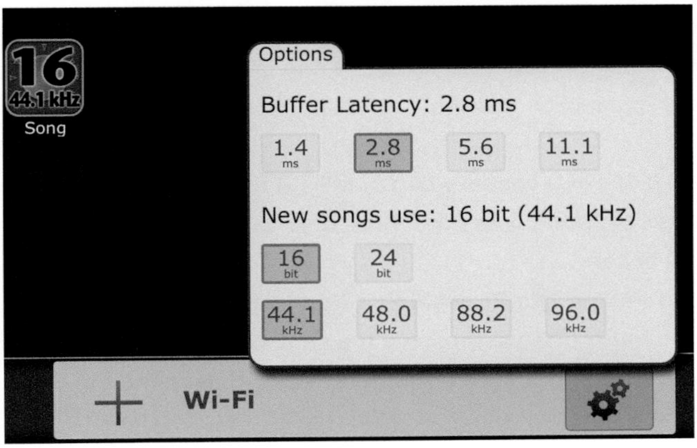

Figure 9.8 **Multitrack DAW showing 96Khz.**

Ivo Burum

EDIT APPS

Edit apps enable media to be rendered as video, or even sound when audio only is required, like in a podcast. Choose the type of render, choose where the rendered video will be sent, either on the phone in camera roll (iOS) or gallery (Android), to social media, or to proprietary websites, choose the resolution or size of the rendered file and press send.

Post-production for a mojo might simply involve an edit of the raw footage and publishing from a phone without too much finessing. If time permits, it might include a simple mix, adding titles and name supers. Often the edit is sent back pretty raw with resolution and send speed being a primary factor.

If time permits and the story necessitates it, the mojo might do a good sound mix, adding music and FX, and a picture grade. Depending on your edit app, there are a number of features and apps to facilitate this, with many having excellent onboard post-production features. I will summarise three of these from different price points and platforms, and focus on their key post-production features.

iMovie Post-production Tools

This free intermediate-level edit app for iOS is one of my favorites. Beyond basic editing it offers these post-production features:

- **Two tracks of video enable video or stills B roll to be included very quickly. Simply choose the shot, press the three dots to select the menu and then choose the B roll style.**
- **Picture in Picture (PinP) enables a box to be placed and sized anywhere on your main track. Choose PinP, tap the shot in the timeline, then tap the "size" or "position" icon in top right of frame to size or place the box in the appropriate area of the frame.**
- **Split Screen (SS) enables the screen to be split and a box to be placed and sized anywhere on your main track.**

- **Green or Blue Screen (GBS) enables certain highlights to be chosen and keyed into a shot. Choose GBS, tap the shot in the timeline, then tap the "Strength sliders" or "Position points" to isolate the area of the key. Shooting your B roll against a chroma blue or green background helps.**
- **Multiple audio tracks—four audio and music tracks can be split, mixed and faded, and an audio track embedded in the video makes five audio tracks. The embedded track can be detached by pressing the "Detach" icon (bottom right of Timeline). *iMovie* doesn't have a ducking tool.**

iMovie also has a set of pre-set filters that can be adjusted so that shots can be treated.

LumaFusion Post-production Tools

LumaFusion (US$29) is an advanced iOS edit app with a vast array of on-board post-production tools including the following key features:

- ***Integration with Storyblocks* provides access to 14 million HD clips, background music and FX. Requires a monthly or yearly subscription through *LumaFusion* in-app purchase.**

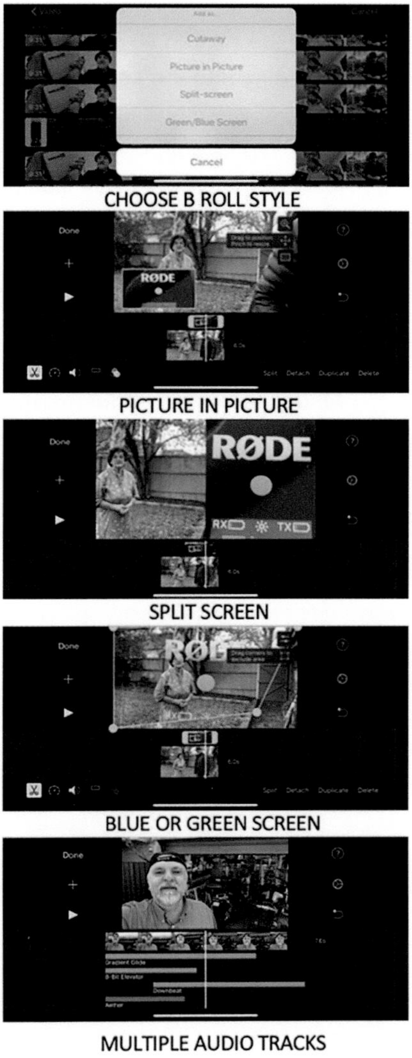

Figure 9.9 ***iMovie* post-production tools.**

Ivo Burum

- *Integration with Western Digital wireless drives* means that high-volume and large assets can be previewed in post-production wirelessly before selectively importing into the *LumaFusion* timeline.
- *Multiple video and audio tracks*: up to 12 video and audio tracks—6 video and audio tracks supporting 4k video in real time, and 6 additional audio tracks.
- *Insert and overwrite style editing*: these professional features enable editors to insert media into a timeline at any point and to overwrite and replace shots or parts of shots.
- *Multiple layers of real-time effects with keyframing:* enables green or blue screen or luminance keying with unlimited keyframes to animate your effect or color at any frame.
- *Motion*: create slow/fast motion forward and reverse at 120 and 240 fps and time-lapse video files.
- *Transition library*: if mojos are taking their stories into post-production after the story edit then *LumaFusion* offers a set of professional transitions.

Figure 9.10 ***LumaFusion* layers.**

Ivo Burum

- *Color correction capabilities*: an excellent color corrector enables video to be fixed without leaving the edit app. This means that, if needed, a quick fix can be done at the story assembly stage.
- *Multi-layer titling*: creating multi-layered titles is an expensive operation often requiring specialist operators and even preparation before post. *LumaFusion* has an excellent suite of multi-layered titling tools to enable onboard creation of professional titles with onboard and imported text, shapes, images, and effects and motion transitions to animate titles.
- *Live audio mixing* feature allows a mojo to hear the mix as it is being done.
- *Support for a variety of landscape and portrait video aspect ratios* enables 1:1, 4:3 and 16:9 ratios and platform-specific production.
- *Export at different frame rates* (18, 23.976, 24, 25, 29.97, 30, 48, 50, 59.94, 60, 120 and 240), enabling broadcast workflows and matching region-specific camera settings.
- *Export and import project archives that include full original media (or trimmed media for smaller archives)*: excellent post-production feature that enables the project to be completed on another device or platform.
- *Export directly to SanDisk iXpand flash drives and network drives including WD Wireless Pro and the new WD Wireless SSD*: this feature enables selective import and export saving time and space.
- *Export at a variety of resolutions up to 4k*: ideally set up for broadcast workflows.

Kinemaster post-production tools

Kinemaster's advantage over many other apps is its user-friendly UX and it's the only high-end cross-platform app. Fully loaded, the app's quirky audio and video below the main track workflow is the result of it being developed by techos and sound people. *Kinemaster* has always had some issues with working across low-end devices. *Kinemaster* provides a comprehensive list on their site: https://d2hakk7asmds57.cloudfront.net/cdn/v1/doc/KMUG-4_8-20190110-EN.pdf.

We haven't found this an issue and have used the app in workshops with US$160 Android smartphones, and it's worked just fine. *Kinemaster* has an inbuilt analysis program in Settings that will check your device. It's a terrific solution when you need high-end editing on cheap devices, in multi-platform situations.

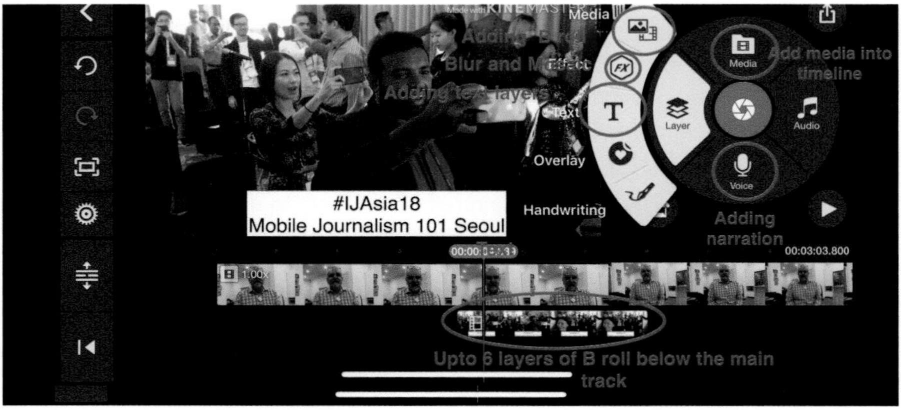

Figure 9.11 ***Kinemaster* UX.**

Ivo Burum

Kinemaster is free to download with a subscription that removes the water mark and adds access to a suite of FX, music and support (US$35/annum). *Kinemaster* is quite intuitive with the following key post-production features:

- ***User-friendly interface*: the interface is large enough to make it easy to see and use.**
- ***FX* enables important mosaic and blur to be added to shots when hiding a feature or a person's identity.**
- ***Full suite of effects*: graphics can be created and manipulated with backgrounds, animated moves, chroma key.**
- ***Audio mixing and ducking*: a fully featured on-board mixing and ducking console.**
- ***Picture grading*: fully featured on-board picture grading.**

I use the above apps because I find them reliable and easy to use. *LumaFusion* is probably the most advanced and its UX takes a bit of practice because so much is packed into a tight space. I have used *LumaFusion* on an iPad and the extra screen real estate makes it feel like a desktop app. There are a number of other powerful edit apps that work on both iOS and Android platforms, such as *Power Director* and *VN* (a relatively new and free app), that offer a variety of impressive story edit and post-production features.

Here is a series of useful specialist post-production apps that I use:

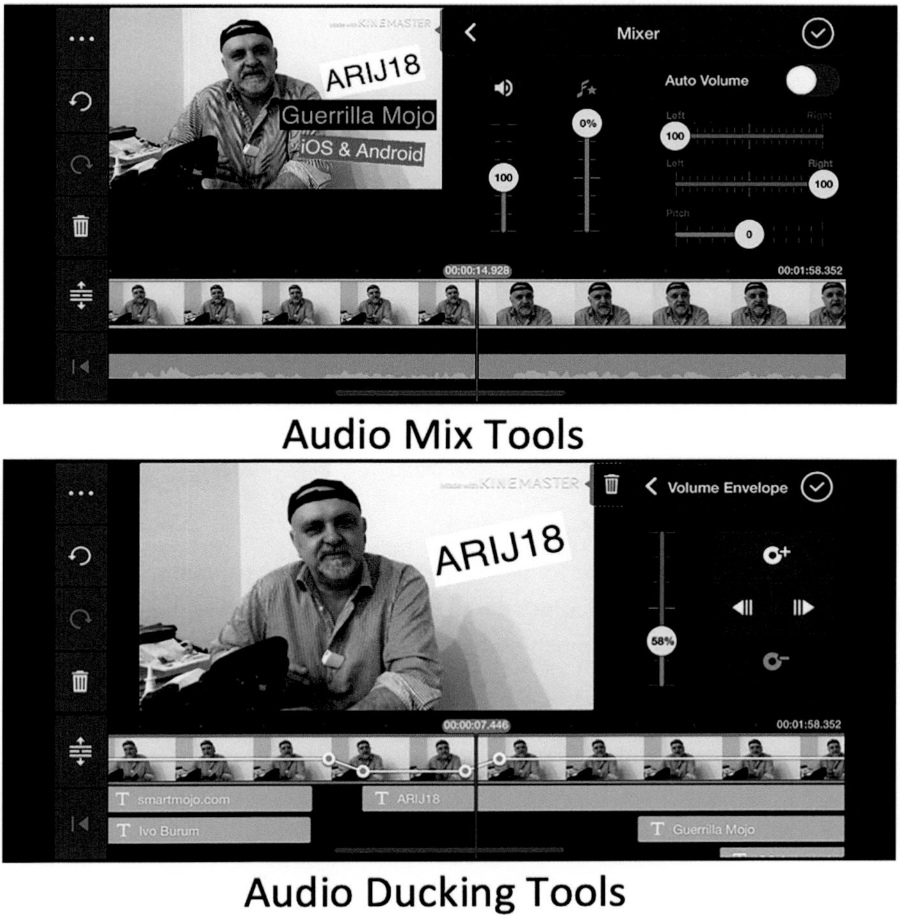

Figure 9.12 ***Kinemaster* mixing and ducking tools.**

Ivo Burum

Video Post-production Apps

- *Video Grade* (iOS): is a fully featured, easy-to-use, video color grading app for iOS that also works with live photos. The best Android video grading app is in *Kinemaster.*

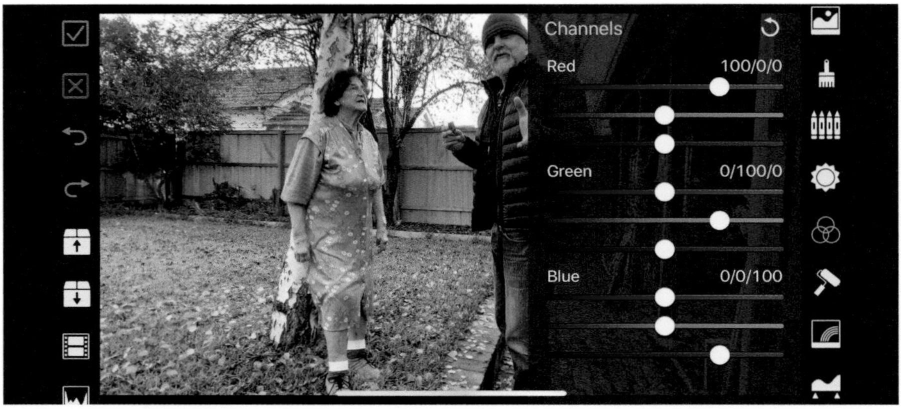

Figure 9.13 Video grading app.

Ivo Burum

- *Vont* (iOS): is one of my favorite text and graphics apps to create text with backgrounds, curved text, graphics for taps and presses, arrows, time code in and out, text animation and much more.

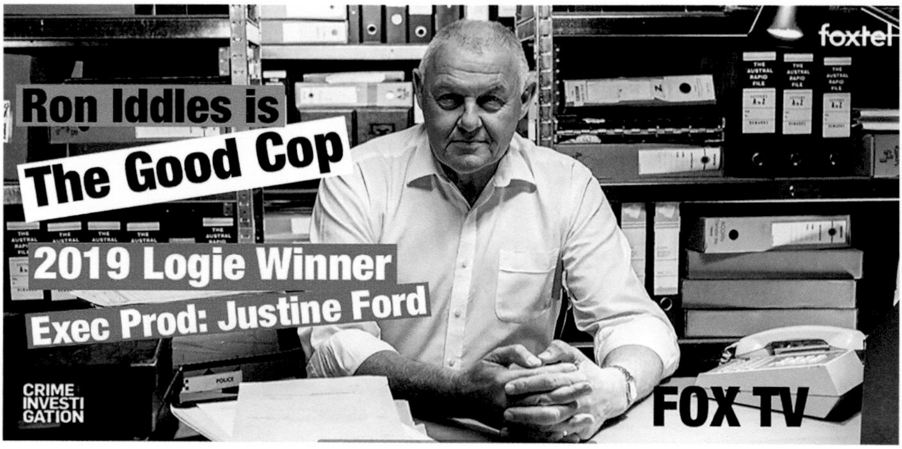

Figure 9.14 *Vont* video graphics app.

Ivo Burum

- *Phonto* (iOS/Android): does exactly what *Vont* does but on stills.
- *Alight Motion* (iOS/Android): is a powerful motion graphics and animation app used to produce multiple layers of graphics, video and audio, visual effects and color correction, keyframe animation available for all settings and much more. Exciting professional app free to use with watermarks with a number of in-app subscriptions.

Figure 9.15 ***Alight Motion*** **app.**

Courtesy of **Alight Motion**

- *Slo-Pro* (iOS): is a super slo-mo app that records at up to 1000 fps enabling super slow motion.
- *Reverse Vid* (iOS): is an easy-to-use app to reverse video, but some edit apps include this feature.

Audio Post-production Apps

Mostly I record my audio with video and detach it if I need to use it separately. However, when you need to record discreet audio files or do additional audio post-production like creating your own soundtrack, or a multi-track mix, you might find the following useful:

- *Ferrite* (iOS): It is a favorite for recording and editing audio on a single- or multi-track project. If you're a teacher, students will warm to it quickly and the free version is all they need. It's by Wooji Juice, whose YouTube site contains 20 how-to video tutorials: www.youtube.com/watch?v=w4wM6fC5qHo&list=PLln17yCH-KYDDAvXoMfx_z0gUZJ9hmlBRl&index=2.
- *RecForge Lite* (Android)*:* Is a powerful yet cumbersome audio recording and post-production app and it will take some time getting your head around the UX. It saves a variety of file types including WAV, but the free version only saves MP3 for 3-minute durations. Students love the power, but hate the UX.
- *Audio Evolution Mobile Studio* (iOS/Android): A fully blown digital audio workstation (DAW) set-up that has MIDI interface and allows users to record audio and instruments and compose multi-track mixes for their videos. Here is a video tutorial: www.youtube.com/watch?v=2BePLCxWnDI.
- *n-Track 9* (iOS/Android): A fully blown DAW set-up that allows users to record audio and instruments and compose multi-track mixes for their videos. The best way to learn is to play. At this link, https://ntrack.com/video-tutorials.php#/select-version, you'll find a series of iOS and Android tutorials.
- *Adobe Spark* (iOS/Android): A relatively recent app from Adobe, the world leader in graphics creation and manipulation. Use it to add animated text and graphics to your pictures. Create the composite and import during the post-production phase of your project. Here is a tutorial: www.youtube.com/watch?v=npAvhRfQUt4.

Export

When exporting your finished video be sure to get the format and the resolution right. All the apps mentioned in this chapter enable the user to select a variety of resolutions and export criteria (see p xx). Be sure to check with the media company you're working with for their specific requirements.

You can export your finished story via AirDrop in the iOS space, or you can use WeTransfer, and if time is not an issue your app may talk to Drop Box, Google Drive or numerous other sites. And while these target sites are essential in a live environment, they might be too dependent on your connection and might end up being a little slow.

You can also use Airstash or one of the Sandisk range of transfer devices. These wireless (local) or UDSBC, or lightning, devices enable fast transfer between phones, desktops and newsrooms.

If you require branded company logos and specific titles these can all be imported into the mojo workflow and sometimes created using your smart device, even using Android. In this instance your workflow remains on the smartphone or can be moved across platforms.

Drew McPherson, one of Australia's most experienced post-production editors, has this list of post-production tips.

1. ***Video*: When dealing with video in post-production, keep it simple. Tell the story with the shots. Don't try and overdo it with effects.**
2. ***Audience*: Know your audience. A wide shot of a presenter holding an important object may not be effective when the audience is viewing on a mobile phone.**
3. ***Music*: When dealing with music, have the picture and music work together. Don't just lay a music track underneath. Having the music finish at the right time is always better than just fading out the music.**
4. ***Graphics*: Make sure they are readable on the device the viewer would be using. Drop shadows and graphic backgrounds help with this.**
5. ***Resolution*: Most phones would be playing back in HD (1920 × 1089), so in most cases shooting and editing in 4k can be overkill.**
6. ***Frame rate*: Make sure the set frame rate of the camera matches the editing app. Otherwise stepping motion and out-of-sync audio might result.**
7. ***Audio bit rate*: I would say 48kHz and 16 bit. 24 bit for higher-end audio (not normally used for online).**
8. ***Mixing*: If you're mixing with headphones, try listening to your video using the speaker to hear the difference. Have parts of the mix disappeared through the speakers? Also try listening to the film with your eyes closed.**

9. **_Color correction_: The aim is to flow from one shot to another seamlessly, without any visual jump that would distract the audience and bring them away from engaging in the film. Tip for color grading on a computer: get to know the video scopes. The information they tell you is essential for matching and correcting shots. Tip for color grading on a phone: make sure the brightness of the phone is set to a high level and not on auto as the phone may dim and affect the result.**

In closing, an important post-production question that's often asked is whether you finish on the phone or take a hybrid approach. Some people believe the answer to this conundrum depends on the technology you use. Truer is that it depends on your story. What does your story need? Is it a hot-breaking news story that requires you to finish and publish quickly from location? If so, do you have time for more than a basic edit? Can you add some advanced post-production to the workflow? Will you finish on location, or does your company policy dictate that an in-house editor completes the story using a desktop suite? Your situation, your requirements and the complexity of your story are the determining factors. If it was just about apps it wouldn't be an issue; we can have hundreds on our phones. But it's about the story and the audience, which may or may not require a tech-heavy post-production approach.

Go mojo …

REFERENCES

Bourriaud, N. (2005). *Postproduction: Culture as Screenplay: How Art Reprograms the World.* New York, Lukas & Sternberg.

Fingas, R. (2017). "Patent Licencing on MP3 Format Expires. Apple-preferred AAC Now a 'Defacto Standard'." https://appleinsider.com/articles/17/05/15/patent-licensing-on-mp3-format-expires-apple-preferred-aac-now-a-de-facto-standard.

McPherson, D. (2019). Interview with I. Burum.

Presonus (2019). "Digital Audio Basics: Sample Rate and Bit Depth." www.presonus.com/learn/technical-articles/sample-rate-and-bit-depth.

CHAPTER 10

MOJO IN THE AGE OF SOCIAL MEDIA

SUMMARY

The emergence of network societies has ushered in a new global communications sphere defined by mobile, instant messaging and social media. Accordingly, the notion of a public sphere defined by a nation-state has shifted to one increasingly built around social platforms and global communications. An effective public sphere enables citizens to have a voice, something social media and new technologies potentially facilitate, especially in marginalised communities. In this chapter we use a social media event to explore trends in social interaction and content creation and introduce strategies mojos might use to help their stories get heard above the online noise.

OVERVIEW

One key to any shared community strategy or advantage, whether social, educational or business, is digital and, more specifically, mobile, which according to Ilicco Elia, Head of Mobile at Deloitte, UK, is the key to social media. Without it, he says, social media "is nothing" (2012). Elia believes mobile provides a revolutionary modern-day campfire storytelling experience because "it enables you to take people on an anytime anywhere cross-platform journey that creates the social in social media" (2012). This level of ubiquity means that 7.1 billion citizen users can form social armies that meet on their social campfire platforms.

Radio and TV brought a new immediacy to storytelling and, in particular, news which included live reports. The Internet has changed all this again. In the late 1990s, with print reporters focused on the page and TV on broadcast, the role of the journalist began to shift as people began looking online for their news and other information (Burum 2018, Ardonato 2018). From 2007, when the smartphone became a modern-day communication tool, journalism's one-to-many conversation was flipped. The audience, no longer a passive receiver, was now at the heart of the news flow, and the journalist's role now included curating citizen user-generated content (UGC). The audience were using Twitter to complain, sharing protest footage on YouTube and Instagram, and generating a buzz on Facebook, and journalism was forced to become part of this conversation (Ardonato 2018). But this was not the first time the role of the press was tested like this.

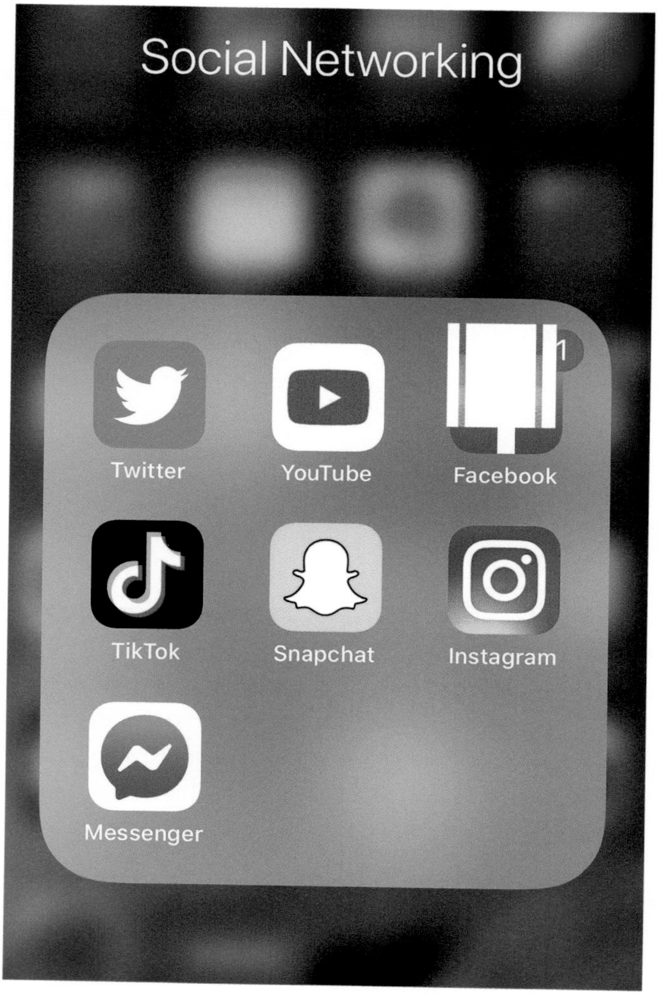

Figure 10.1 **Social media giant Twitter is only twelfth in size.**

Ivo Burum

The press was one of the first institutions affected by the commercialisation of the public sphere in the late nineteenth century, which signaled the sphere's fragmentation (Fraser 1992). Commercial pressures constrained press freedom and forced media to work in a sphere of limited consensus, where the public sphere was shaped by the interests of capitalists who invested in mass media (Kuhn 2011). The result was a decline in effective political journalism, narrowed political debate, and reporting without its independent critical edge.

Journalism professor Jay Rosen states that what is required in any effective public sphere is for the public to be in discussion with itself. The degree to which discussion is of public benefit depends, as Fraser (1992) points out, on the discursive nature of the sphere. Even though the Internet is far more social and inclusive to minority voices than print, television or other broadcast media were just a decade ago, access to new digital media was still marked by severe participation gaps. In 2007, just 33% of people in developing countries were using the Internet, compared to almost 77% in the developed world. Today it's a different story, predominantly because of the ubiquity of smartphones and social penetration (Anderson and Jiang 2018). In 2018, in America, 95% of teens had access to a smartphone. Of these 45% said they are online "almost constantly," mostly accessing YouTube, Instagram and Snapchat. In emerging countries 53% of people have access to smartphones capable of accessing the Internet and social media and apps, and 91% of those access their social media on their smartphones (Silver, Smith et al. 2019).

This reality of a more social content-creation sphere has been embraced by revolutionaries and by broadcasters, including the BBC. In 2012, acknowledging the growing social ecosphere and its global online conversation, new BBC director George Entwistle determined they would include more public service content creation, which may be stories and formats made using mobile and driven by a more socially equitable content-sourcing era (cited in Burum 2018). This chapter investigates how mobile technologies and associated social media skills might be used to create a less culturally homogenised, more diverse and democratic content sphere.

THEORETICAL PERSPECTIVE

Knowing which theory to subscribe to in order to contextualise social media is often a cultural determination; however, a useful approach might be to explore social media from ecological, behaviorist, user and shifting normative perspectives.

Media ecology theory, which is based on a techno-determinist view where technologies drive the type of messages we communicate, is one way to describe our relationship with social media content. A hybridised theory, it posits that the ubiquitous nature of social media connects and influences actions that impact human experience. The resulting chemistry, a relationship between technology and humanity, is an ecological aspect that gives our culture its character (Strate 2004). In this ecosphere old media is subsumed and, in a sense, becomes content for a new media environment, in much the same way that film became content for TV (ibid).

The theory of reasoned action aims to explain the relationship between attitudes and behaviors within human action. It is mainly used to predict how individuals will behave based on pre-existing attitudes and intentions. The success of an information system depends largely on its use value. The theory's exploration of the translation phase in the dialectic between intention and practice is especially useful when investigating attitudes and interaction on social media. The theory posits that attitude is the result of consideration. Ironically, on social media, it is often a lack of consideration that accompanies and catapults interaction. From a mojo perspective, reasoned action can describe a shift in a dialectic between techno-determinism and critical realism, which occurs when user-generated content (UGC) is developed into user-generated stories (UGS). This translation is fundamentally driven by intention which, on social media, is very subjective and often results from impulse and the force of what's been described as collective action. Partially a behavioral response to the hedonics of new technologies (Hassenzahl 2003), these and associated attitudes and praxis develop in apposition to normative media practices.

In one sense, social media developed as a result of technology; in another, it is the product of a normative system of media breaking down. In reality, it is probably a bit of both. Theories of media suggest that "the press takes on the form and coloration of the social and political structures within which it operates" (Siebert, Peterson et al. 1956). This can be positive in many Western liberal democracies, where freedom and cultural diversity prevail, but less so in statist regimes where societal beliefs can be marginalised or dictated by the state or a state-run press. When the dominant media of society is compromised by state control or influenced by corporate imperatives, audiences turn to alternative and often more participatory grass-roots social expressions that can challenge normative theories of media.

Normative media theory, it's argued, has lost its heuristic value in the current digital and social media landscape where a mediatisation of life and society is the new norm. In this space, where interconnectivity has moved from mass communication (one to many) to network societies (many to many), the emphasis is shifting from user to producer (Bruns and

Schmidt 2011, Burum 2018). As the audience becomes a more active participant, they are also a co-producer in today's mediated communication sphere. This interconnectivity results in a highly opinionated and generally less authoritative style of mass communication (Fourie 2017), which is in opposition tonormative practices of media.

One of the fundamental purposes of normative media theory is to act as a ready-reckoner about the level of media freedom, especially in political regimes (Fourie 2017):

- **Level of publication of matters of public concern**
- **Level of reporting allowed on a cross-section of topics**
- **Ability and recognition of a social responsibility to disseminate diverse content**
- **Level of legal, political and financial independence**

In the social media space the above values are tempered by an "acknowledgement of diversity and the recognition of universal human virtue in and through mediated communication" (Fourie 2017). This move away from the kind of control that existed in some levels of media represents a fundamental shift where media's traditional elite has lost some of the social and economic stability required to exercise their control (Pavlik 2008). For example, in the digital age it's presumed there is far less hegemonic voice and greater diversity in media culture. In essence, communication on social media sites is based on a new kind of public who are characterised by hybridisation and fragmentation. They put an emphasis on "the role of civic society, political and cultural minorities ... in which a single idealized Habermasian public sphere with a common normative dimension no longer exists" (Fourie 2017: 114). Notwithstanding this, social media might prove to be a variation rather than a huge shift away from a normative view of media.

A Social History

Initially seen as gossip and kludge, the rising level of UGC has been described as a 24/7 tsunami. With about 500 hours of video being uploaded to YouTube every minute, social media is also big business. Media has responded to this challenge by creating a diversity of outlets and their own social sites, platforms and workflows. The formula is simple: a higher volume of mobile UGC creates more traffic and potentially higher revenues (Newman, Fletcher et al. 2018). It's a model, or algorithm, that has drawn more than 2.6 billion monthly active users to Facebook. Of these, 1.73 billion log on daily and 90% do it using mobile.

Almost seven years ago Facebook revenue from mobile was 14%, today it's 94%. Mobile is a key driver in social media's home–work–play–home net, and news is one of their targets.

As early as 2004, realising that media was converging online, Arthur Sulzberger, publisher of the *New York Times*, announced the importance of having a convergent print–television–online strategy: "Broadband is bringing us all together [combining] all three elements. News is a 24/7 operation, and if you don't have the journalistic muscle in all three [platforms], you can't succeed in broadband" (cited in Quinn and Filak 2005). Seven years later, Rupert Murdoch's decision to split News Corp's publishing business from its film and television assets showed that joining the convergent dots—developing new normative media practices in a digital space—is more complex than Sulzberger had imagined.

This challenge for journalism was set against a backdrop of the new normalisation of digital media and a shift from media ethics, which was the domain of journalists, to a focus on ethical communication across an amorphous series of social networks that connected billions (Fourie 2017). This predominantly mobile ecosphere holds hopes for a revitalisation and expansion of democratic discourse and political engagement (Lasorsa, Lewis et al. 2012). In marginalised areas social media is a means for creating a local voice and can present citizens with opportunities to create and use media as a change agent (Gillmor 2006, Jenkins 2008, Surowiecki 2009).

A Case Study

The Arab Spring provides a context within which to discuss social media's role in creating an alternative and potentially more effective public sphere. It was a revolutionary social moment that's viewed as a success and as a failure (Burum 2018). In 2010, the viral photographs of the battered body of Khaled Said, murdered while in police custody in Alexandria, Egypt, created a social media movement. The Facebook site, *We are all Khaled Said*, built by former Google executive Wael Ghonim, attracted hundreds of thousands of followers and became Egypt's biggest dissident Facebook page. Support for Said rapidly spread across social media and led to international criticism of the Egyptian government.

A few months later, on December 17, Mohamod Bouazizi, an unlicensed fruit vendor from Tunisia, was trading without a permit in the local square when a council inspector "confiscated his scales, slapped him twice, spat on him and insulted his father" (Salt 2011). Deprived of his income and shamed in public, Bouazizi went home, grabbed a can of petrol, returned to the square and set himself on fire. His cousin Ali filmed it on a mobile and posted it on Facebook and Bouazizi's act of self-immolation, in Tunisia, set off three months of horizontal uprisings that helped initiate the overthrow of governments in Tunisia, Egypt, Libya and Yemen.

The Arab Spring lit a social media match under the cinders of years of repression. Statist regimes like Mubarak's devalued the public sphere to a point where media was so repressed that even the Arab bourgeoisie could not "gain enough economic weight to challenge the state" (Dodge 2012). What occurred over those months had Middle East scholar Jeremy Salt saying there is "nothing in the history of the Middle East that stands as a precedent for this eruption of the human spirit" (Salt 2011).

It is argued that deposing the regime in Egypt would not have been possible without social media or mobile penetration because in Egypt reporters could be jailed for up to five years for criticising government (Ghonim 2012). With government owning interests in newspapers and arresting reporters for reasons of national security, social media became a horizontal valve used to bypass censored communication structures (Mason 2012). This new anatomy of mobile protest, an attempt to reclaim a public sphere, is described as a "2.0 revolution" (Lawson 2012). Citizens turned to mobile and social media to create "horizontal links using new technology" (Mason 2012: 301) on the social platforms. On 25 January 2011, on the day of uprisings in Tahrir Square, @FawazRashed tweeted, "We use Facebook to schedule the protests, Twitter to coordinate, and YouTube to tell the world" (Rashed 2011). Facebook decoys were used "to enable the real demonstrations organized via word-of-mouth" (Stein 2012). All this in a region where 65% of people weren't connected to the Internet. This arguably turned the streets into "parliaments, negotiating tables and battlegrounds" (El-Ghobashy 2012: 23) that ignited and galvanised a collective action, which citizens had possibly been preparing since the Damascus spring.[1]

The great paradox in journalism, as Hirst (2012) points out, is that news often happens when the press is absent—at least it did in an analog culture. Possibly the regime's great mistake in the Middle East was that it miscalculated the volume and speed with which mobile technologies and social platforms generate instant viral content streams. In a socially converging world the press can virtually aggregate, scrape and curate citizen witness UGC—mobile pictures and raw video—from the scene, in a curatorial process of meaning making and economic realism, to generate their stories. That's exactly what happened in the

Arab Spring. Social media was a first-stage momentum that broke the "barrier of fear" (ibid), which is probably the revolution's real legacy. The media's attempt to normalise Springer social media content, and the protesters' willingness to press and publish, showcased the use value of UGC as a short-term wake-up agent.

The world watched the Springers' social media revolution, but only 18 months later we were left asking what went wrong (Shihab-Eldin 2012). The revolution might have occurred, but as Eric Goldstein from Human Rights Watch points out, "the laws that Mubarak used to put journalists in prison to control the media are [were] still there" (cited in Dutton 2012) and Egyptians found "themselves living under an even more tyrannical and authoritarian military dictatorship" (ibid). If this was the result of a social media revolution, then we can assume the outcome was a few tweets short of a complete narrative.

While the Internet is one of the defining opportunities of our time, its use as a revolutionary crowd-sourcing tool (Shirky 2008, Surowiecki 2009), or as a means of auditing the crowd (Sabadello 2012), is determined by its level of accessibility and the freedom of the prevailing public sphere. The danger with any patchwork movement that joins horizontally, through social media, such as the Arab Spring, is that it can lack the long-term structures required for sustainability. Consequently, it risks losing its shared revolutionary focus. This is compounded when the technologically horizontal social media world takes on various asymmetrical characteristics (Goode 2009). One of these is the curatorial gatewatching practices of media editors who rank and use social media UGC in the order of its network use value and imperatives. Philosopher Susan Buck-Morse observes in her analysis of 9/11 that the speed with which the images of 9/11 were linked to one image—the American flag and "the nation under attack" (2001)—can reduce alternative online social media messaging to a flattened singular frame. This happened in 2011, when millions of Springer tweets and UGC were subsumed by media and homogenised into one strand captioned "the Arab Spring revolution."

This is a form of gatewatching, where media scrapes social platforms like they once watched the wires, before curating, repackaging, editorialising and subsuming the raw UGC and tweets. This can be a positive; for example, during the Arab Spring, Al Jazeera aggregated revolutionary social media content and delivered it to its television viewers, many of whom did not have access to the Internet. Geir Ruud, CBO of NTB, Norway's digital wire service, believes gatewatching is part of media's filtration role: "there are no filters in social media … they don't edit stuff, that's our role and our future" (2012). Ruud believes journalism could have played this vertical curatorial, verification, or gatewatching role much more during the Arab Spring.

Once UGC is edited by professionals into their stories and into the vertical structures of news operations, it changes form, is editorialised and risks, as Buck-Morse observes, losing its diverse character as it succumbs to the vertical content structures of a publishing process. The potential to maintain the potency of local messaging is possibly diminished when raw UGC is uploaded and used as formless B roll,[2] but it's increased when UGC becomes UGS at source. This is supported by data that shows a high loss ratio of non-structured UGC after events like the Arab Spring (SalahEldeen and Nelson 2012).

Transforming raw UGC into more complete UGS at source does a number of things:

- **It begins a curatorial chain at source which is a first step in creating a more diverse content ecosphere.**
- **It begins an intellectual archival process that encourages creators to think more about their content in social, cultural and economic terms (Lasswell 1948).**
- **It encourages creators to seek out what's been described as online clustering (Newman and Park 2003) around what Wenger (2001) calls functional and supportive communities of practice—which is one reason why people gravitate to social media sites.**

User-generated story creation requires and enables something Jürgen Habermas refers to as "willful control over technical practice." This conscious process can occur when raw citizen witness moments (UGC) are transformed into citizen journalism, or UGS. This more complete form becomes increasingly valuable as digital media transitions to Web TV and more developed behind-the-firewall content.

Sustained democracy, fundamental to any civil society, requires freedom of expression and the protection of an effective public sphere supported by a free press. Without this, it can be argued, revolutions like the Arab Spring only pave the way for another repressive state (Mansour 2013). Once reporters have soaked up the ambient journalism of revolution and moved on, one question remains: How can new, more social and mobile media be used to do more than initiate revolutionary moments, which, as Sabadello suggests, "is the 'sexy' part that media usually focuses on" (2012). Indeed, how can it be used to build civil society with heterogeneous visions of a democratic public sphere? User-generated story potentially does this by developing cultural and social capital, the key ingredients for building grassroots social media into more inclusive global communications. This is the purview of mojos, and one of the focuses of this book.

PRACTICAL APPLICATION

Mojos will create social media content whether they like it or not because it's difficult to speak about mobile and not include social, or vice versa. Whether you are a social junky, or a mobile journalist who's creating content and making it public, the emphasis should be on objectivity and maintaining a high quality of work. As upload rates of UGC soar, the journalist as fact checker is more important than ever. Also important is that citizens learn the skills to enable a politicised use of smart devices to create high-quality publications on social platforms. Hence, in this section we explore audience as producer, mobile strategies in news and corporate environments, brand building on social for mobile, writing for social media and mobile, social production, and distribution.

Social, the People's Platform

In 2006, New York University professor of journalism Jay Rosen published in his blog, *PressThink*, the "citizens formerly known as audience" trope. Telling are Rosen's (1999) concerns about the socialisation of media: "Were we making something happen, because we decided it was good … [and] … did public journalism work? How would we know if it did?" I know that we invited the public to be involved in TV program production, but I don't know that we ever invited them online; we didn't need to. Yes, the public has a means to speak, but what are they doing with the opportunity?

The current medium is social, and mobile is its primary access point delivering what Vincent Mosco calls the "promise of the sublime" (2004). However, it's only once past the sublime belief that technology will fix society that people begin to consider the social institutions required to ensure the most democratic use of the technology. Post the Arab Spring, futurist Howard Rheingold shifted from his 2002 position of technological optimism, where he believed it was enough to be part of the switched-on social smart mob, to one of critical realism (2002), which suggests digital media will only further our social and political agendas if we learn to exert control over it. Are we there?

Journalism with a Social Twist

In the print days news happened everywhere and all the time, yet it felt like it happened at 3pm, when the evening edition landed on the pavement. TV and radio were a more spontaneous and faster delivery system, where breaking news cut into existing programming and daily bulletins were broadcast at set times. The Internet changed the news game, providing an almost instantaneous global reach and mobiles enabled citizens to access all areas, from anywhere and at any time. This was no longer a one-way conversation, it was many to many, and the audience was, as Rosen's blogger wrote, no longer passive. Hence in the age of social and mobile, news is characterised by accessibility and interactivity that develops as a two-way conversation, often before and after the original story is published. Is this citizen journalism?

The term "citizen journalism" is used to describe everything from the coverage of the Arab Spring, to the first footage of the Hudson River plane crash, and the crown jewel of American citizen journalism—the famous Zapruder film (Gant 2007). Gillmor (2010) is in no doubt that Zapruder's film about Kennedy's assassination is an act of citizen journalism. However, the film was shot by a man watching a parade, who at best can be described as an accidental citizen witness. Zapruder's film, the result of being in the right spot at the right time—a citizen witness moment—became newsworthy because Kennedy was shot. Is this journalism, or does journalism require an act of constructed reporting that structures raw content into a narrative for public benefit? While mobile technology makes us all potential Zapruders, does it make us all citizen journalists, or mojos?

Where does the journalistic process begin? Would it have made a difference if Zapruder shot establishing shots of the scene, B roll and vox pops after the assassination? Did he need to structure the raw content, in either an edit or a blog for it to become journalism? Who was the journalist in the first reports of the Hudson River plane crash? Was it the citizen who recorded the first accidental shots because he was in the right place at the right time and posted these online? Did the citizen on the ferry who tweeted what is said to be the first picture of the downed plane need to tweet more than "There's a plane in the

Hudson" and "I'm on the ferry going to pick up the people. Crazy." (Beaumont 2009)? Perhaps the news agency that integrated and voiced those early smartphone images into bulletins, or the social platforms that put the news-like forms around this newsworthy moment made it journalism. Social media is challenging traditional journalism offerings in a process that both blurs the relationship between consumers and professional producers of media and begins to normalise that relationship.

Normalising Social Journalism

Traditionally, many journalists remained faceless because "a journalist's (often secret) network of sources has always been one of his/her most important professional assets" (Deuze 2007). The little black book was an important part of their strategy for remaining impartial. Social media exposes processes, and corrections are highlighted in real time so sources like Twitter become part of the evolving story. This requires a degree of normalisation and renegotiation of journalism's boundaries and an adjustment of approaches to evolving social media practices. The result is online news content that includes a greater amount of UGC and, occasionally, a degree of citizen journalism.

A study of the use of social media in the US presidential elections of 2012 suggested that journalists were mapping old norms onto new technology, while also challenging them. Research demonstrated evidence of tension between journalists, their audiences, their sources and their employers, as these groups sought control over newly important social media spaces (Molyneux and Mourão 2019). Journalists at "more elite" papers, TV and cable, where they had status, were less inclined than counterparts working for less "elite" news outlets, to relinquish gatekeeping roles by sharing their work and stage with other social media news gatherers and commentators (Lasorsa, Lewis et al. 2012). Over time, though, technology has proven more flexible than the profession. As social media platforms added new features and forms of interaction, they became indispensable to journalists who needed to learn social media skills to keep up with the 24-hour news cycle (Molyneux and Mourão 2019).

It's argued that today, in the case of Twitter, journalists are mixing journalistic practices with the norms and practices of social media communities. But as Tandoc and Vos (2016) note, there may be less normalisation (mapping traditional journalistic norms onto new social media tools) and more reworking norms and routines to better suit the new content environments. Either way, Twitter, and social media generally, has become indispensable for journalists, making them more transparent, with growing audience loyalty. Being retweeted by the right followers is seen as enhancing a journalist's social capital in the professional online arena. Conversely, branding may be problematic by inviting criticism from other traditional journalists, guided by anonymity and neutrality.

Social media is a necessary story incubator. However, the trend to subscription suggests audiences are looking for more than what social media currently has to offer. Free online content drives users to a premium layer behind the firewall that requires more developed content that subscribers want to pay for and that advertisers will invest in. This layer will require journalists who are skilled in producing multimedia and, more specifically, UGS, even user-generated programs (UGP).

SOCIAL MEDIA PLATFORMS

Social media is a set of platforms and tools that mojos need to use effectively to maximise story traction and visibility—even production. There are at least 200 major active social media sites. Even though we talk about Twitter a lot, in size it is only twelfth on the list of the top 20 social media networks (Quora.com 2019). On top is Facebook, with 2.6 billion active users, next is YouTube with 1.9 billion and then WhatsApp with 1.5 billion. Here is a brief overview of four of the platforms that mojos use.

Facebook

Facebook is a place to share media and updates with those who follow, or "like" you. In 2019, almost 90% of Facebook's revenue came from mobile and more than 90% of its daily active users logged on using mobile. From a business point of view, clients use Facebook pages to check out business and related events. Facebook offers mojos tools like status updates to help promote stories, activities and products. Seen as a social network, in the Middle East and across the marginalised world Facebook is used extensively to publish news content. It is a fast and effective way for mojos to get their story online. With the addition of "Stories," Facebook has effectively created another more visual "news feed." New filters and effects rely "on the camera so the phone is a more natural home for Stories, but you can post and edit them from your desktop, giving you the chance to create more polished videos" (Svetlik 2019). For mojos, in particular, Facebook Live is an excellent tool for sharing breaking news and events (see Chapter 11).

WhatsApp

Despite having been acquired by Facebook in 2014 for US$19 billion, the WhatsApp instant messaging platform exists as an independent entity. One of WhatsApp's important features is end to end encryption. WhatsApp lets mojos send photos, music, videos, voice memos, animated GIFs and even documents like MS Word or PDF files. In its bid to save Internet bandwidth, WhatsApp uses lossy[3] compression to decrease the size of media files when uploading them to their servers. So when you share a photo, music or a video on WhatsApp, the recipient usually gets a lower-quality version of the original file. The following steps show how to share photos, music and videos on WhatsApp, without losing quality by using the Documents app:

- **Download and install the Documents app from the App Store.**
- **Copy the media file (photo, video or music file) that you want to share on WhatsApp into the Documents app, via Share menu.**
- **Open WhatsApp and select the contact with whom you want to share the file.**
- **Tap on the + icon next to the chat bubble and select Document.**
- **You should see a list of apps that implement the Document Provider extension, where the Documents app should be present. If it's not, tap on "More..." at the bottom of the list and ensure that the toggle next to Documents app is enabled.**
- **Select Documents, and select any WhatsApp compatible file (including photos, music or videos) from its storage.**
- **Once you select the file, tap OK on the confirmation prompt.**

The selected file is now shared with your chosen WhatsApp contact in its original quality, regardless of the smartphone platform.

YouTube

YouTube is the world's top video sharing platform. For mojos it is a quick way of sharing content. Create a YouTube channel, upload video, then embed the link into blog sites or social media. The YouTube algorithm works to promote user's channels by tracking and learning what users engage with. It then suggests user videos in the following ways:

- ***Search*: YouTube analyses how titles, keywords and descriptions match search queries and how often your videos and similar videos are watched.**
- ***Home and suggested videos*: YouTube ranks videos of interest on how they have engaged with like users and offers relevant videos by analysing user activity history.**
- ***Trending*: this is a specific feed of popular videos in a user's country. In this section YouTube considers view count and rate of view growth.**
- ***Subscriptions*: in this page users view the uploaded videos from channels they subscribe to. The algorithm measures view velocity—the speed and number of views a user's video gets immediately after it is uploaded.**

Making money on YouTube depends on engagement, not the number of views. One way for mojos to engage with the public on YouTube, and to stand out from the noise, is to transition from publishing UGC to strong user-generated content (UGS).

Twitter

With 330 million active users, Twitter is excellent for generating quick thoughts and traffic to sites, especially if you incorporate quotes, photos, video and statistics around links that you are tweeting about. Twitter is about curating significant comment to attract follows. One reason Twitter numbers are low compared to other major players is probably because its open forum lends the platform to hate speech and vitriol. In April 2019,

Darren Rovell
@darrenrovell
What's beyond scary here is that Jack Dorsey has no idea what his users want. We don't want to shift to following topics, we've just spent YEARS curating our feed of individuals. I spend an extraordinary amount of time on here. I've never been more concerned with its leadership.

Figure 10.2 **Tweet re Dorsey.**

founder Jack Dorsey revealed plans to make the platform "healthy." Dorsey says that Twitter will move from following people, to following topics. "In the past it's incented a lot of outrage," he said. "It's incented a lot of group harassment" (Fried 2019). Yet Twitter's followers say they want to follow people not topics. "The whole premise behind social media is being able to engage with other people and brands personally. Long-time users have spent years building their connections with industry companies and thought leaders" (Edgecomb 2019).

Dorsey says he's doing it to fight abuse and make the site more meaningful. He's not worried that those changes could mean people will spend less time on Twitter. "If more relevance means less time on the service, that's perfectly fine," he said (cited in Fried 2019).

Instagram

Instagram is a platform used by more than 1 billion people each month with more than 500 million daily active users, making it second only to Facebook in engagement. Once a photo-sharing holiday-type app, today its visceral video and photos make it a branding must-have, especially for the 71% of users under 35 years of age. I particularly like the ability to create and augment composite video and photo slide shows very quickly. See Chapter 2 for process details.

TYPES OF SOCIAL MEDIA CONTENT

Social media visibility and blog traffic is achieved through verbal and non-verbal communication strategies. Verbal communication can be understood when people speak the same language. Often this is synchronous with one speaking first, then the other. Non-verbal communication can have a greater impact on how we think and feel about others (Harman 2015); in fact, the channel is ever present and it is generally asynchronous: you wear clothes, someone reacts; a child cries, someone reacts (Patterson 2009). A study by School of Medicine, University of San Diego,[4] looks at the degree to which emotions—happiness, loneliness, depression—are contagious and can be transferred from one to another online (Coviello, Sohn et al. 2014). Hence, strategies can be employed to tune the types of content when developing your social media presence. Once you've decided on a social media platform, the type of content you consume, or produce, will be determined by the audience you want to impact:

1. ***Infographics*: A 2017 study of 100 million online articles showed that after lists, infographics are the second most-shared social media content. It also showed that long-form content—why, how—gets more shares than short form (Kagan 2017).**
2. ***Interactive content*: Initially content was static one to many, then with Web 2.0 it enabled two-way response, then it became more interactive where the user was asked to participate in the story.**
3. ***Emotional content*: You can get people to "click" a lot easier than to "share." Having the story evoke an emotional response—happiness, sadness—encourages people to "share." People can be 14% more likely to share happy rather than sad emotions. What other emotions are there?**
4. ***Content with images*: Research has shown that Tweets containing images can get 150% more retweets than those without.**
5. ***User-generated content (UGC)*: Often created on a smart device and uploaded in raw form, can be gratuitous or newsworthy.**
6. ***User-generated stories (UGS)*: These are stock in trade for mojos and are an amalgam of all of the above edited in a form designed to evoke emotion, provide information, ask why and make people think.**

Check out Neal Schaffer's site here: https://nealschaffer.com/emotional-role-social-media-sharing/.

CONSIDERATIONS WHEN PRODUCING SOCIAL MEDIA CONTENT

Here are some practical guidelines mojos might consider when working with, or producing for, social media.

1. ***Engagement and identification*: Your own social media content on your blog, or content you upload to other social media sites, needs to be clearly identifiable as yours, so that it can be attributed for editorial and monetary reasons. This is often a question of the availability of resources to create traction for**

your content and brand. Understanding the who, what, when, where, why and how of engagement is critical. Will you engage through your own content or your use of third-party content? Will you engage on your site or "theirs"? This depends on "why" you are engaging.

Engagement for your video and other content also depends on having:

- a clear headline 7–8 words long
- an introductory paragraph of no more than 25 words
- video thumbnails that grab the viewers' attention, which has been shown to attract 32% more comment on Instagram
- Simple statements in active voice

Tip: Once you have an audience you need to keep them. For example, don't make a 30-minute how-to video when a series of 10 3-minute videos might be more engaging.

2. *Researching stories and people*: One of the great advantages of social media is access to more than one-third of the world's population. When I began in television, researching profiles and story ideas took time and involved long phone calls and trips to book, film and radio libraries. Today the Internet's research capabilities and social media's reach makes doing these tasks fast and reasonably cheap.
3. *Editorial impact and ramification:* Understand why your media is unique, where it can best be positioned, how your material will be used on social media and what impact it might have. There's a fine balance between exposure and being ripped off. If you add links to your own blog, make certain of the bone fides of the links. Understand who your audience is and where it's better to upload—your site, with an embedded code into other social media like Twitter, or directly to YouTube from where you embed to your and other blog sites?
4. *Management of content*: What is the social media site's policy on intervention and what protection do they offer your media compared with the legal and ethical protection you have by uploading to your own blog site? Remember that rules are one things and level of restitution is another. If people are posting to your site, make sure that they have the rights to the material they post.
5. *Monetising your social community*: Will you allow branding and advertising on your site and will the social media site's administrators allow your advertising/branding? If you allow advertising on your site, how it's worded is important.

Large media organisations have branding, advertising and labeling policies. Who manages this for your site?

6. *There are only virtual friends in social media*: More friends make you feel like you've won something. But be careful who you allow on the site. Do you check profiles? Are they happy to agree to your rules of social engagement?
7. *Underage social media users*: Generally speaking, anyone under the age of 13 is considered a child. Is your site child friendly and is the content you are uploading to other sites breaking their minimum age rules?
8. *Here for the long haul*: If you are running your own site, will you be around tomorrow? One of the reasons people gravitate to large social media sites is their sense of permanence, which is strange in such a transient space.
9. *Verification on social media*: Verifying who you are protects your followers and indicates your bone fides and that the account is legitimate. In a world full of fake news, the little blue or grey verification badge and checkmark helps people know they are dealing with a person that has been vouched for.

   On Twitter this is represented by a blue check box to the right of the person's name or ID. Here's what you'll need for verification on Twitter:

- Profile photo
- Cover photo
- Use your real name on your profile
- Include your web- or blog site etc.
- Use a confirmed email address and phone number
- Have a public account
- Fill out the verification form and provide required documents

Facebook say that select people, media, entertainment and government pages may be eligible for verification, with a blue checkmark next to the name. Here is a link to their verification form: www.facebook.com/help/contact/342509036134712.

Instagram will verify you if you are a public figure, celebrity, or huge brand. Go to your Profile/Settings/Request Verification.

YouTube classifies verified YouTube names or YouTube accounts with a grey check mark. Your account is generally verified once you create your account when you supply a mobile number and get a verification code via text. Verification enables upload of videos that are longer than 15 minutes and to appeal copyright infringements.

Check out this blog for more information on verification on social media: www.socialreport.com/insights/article/360018984211-How-to-Get-Verified-on-All-Social-Networks-in-2019.

With the rise of fake news especially on social media, it's important to know how to pick the real from the fake.

10. *Fake social media news*: At its most fundamental, fake news is information that is not true. The Ethical Journalism Network[5] defines it like this: "Fake news is information deliberately fabricated and published with the intention to deceive and mislead others into believing falsehoods or doubting verifiable facts." The major point here is intent. Propaganda is all about intent, so is it fake news? Were Leni Riefenstahl's propaganda films about the Nazis a form of fake news? Is it fake news when you lie, or is it just lying?

One of the anomalies of an Internet populated by people who are, as journalism professor Jay Rosen says, no longer just the audience, is that users can have differing perspectives on any one news event. The same story might be produced differently by a number of people, including professional journalists. How we judge whether a story is a deliberate misrepresentation is not always immediately obvious (see Chapter 12). Has the knowledge in the story been objectively represented, or is it a subjective representation, and what difference does that make to the veracity of the story?

Possibly the best advice I've heard regarding fake news is from Gregory Favre, a long-time editor in Sacramento and Chicago. He says, "Do not print an iota beyond what you know" (Dean 2019). Favre is saying use your journalism skills to verify and to determine what is true. This works except when we explain the "why" of a story. Often this explanation is based on a subjective interpretation of available facts, where analysis may differ between correspondents, either professional, citizen or student. This is often the case in conflict reporting where reports from opposing sides can have differing perspective on the same event. Is this fake news or is it a subjective interpretation and ownership of available data (see Chapter 12)?

It's vital to know how to separate the real from the fake, something all mojos can learn:

- Develop a critical mindset: temper emotional responses to stories with a critical eye based on previous knowledge and new information. Be skeptical of content that you are not familiar with. Ask "why" has this story been written and why am I watching it?

- Check the source: using the Internet, check facts in every case. Who told you about the story and the sources, and what is their reputation? There are a number of sites that verify stories, such as Faktisk in Norway. Faktisk, established by *VG*, NRK, *Dag Bladet* and TV2, check and republish stories with correct facts. During the 2017 Norwegian elections, fixed stories got more readers than the fake ones. In only days, Kristoffer Egeberg, editor of Faktisk, said, "We became an actual factor in the election very quickly, where people came to us, politicians started correcting themselves ... this was quite exciting to see" (Funke 2017).
- See who else is reporting the story and examine the evidence: check the evidence and if other reputable providers who you know have, run the story.
- Look for fake images: The power of mobile phones cameras and edit apps enables users to create excellent fake photographs. Can you tell the difference, do you know what to look for? Sites like Google Reverse Image Search help you identify images similar to the image you are checking. Check out https://support.google.com/websearch/answer/1325808?hl=en for the process.
- Check that it "sounds right": If it's too good to be true it probably is.

Author and newspaper executive Jack Fuller has suggested that journalists need to show "modesty in their judgment" about what they know (Dean 2019). In essence, journalists and citizen journalists, including mojos, need to show "humility" and keep an open and enquiring mind. This is another reason why we need to move beyond UGC to UGS that are finished at source, so we know where the information comes from and who produced the piece. Journalists often describe the essence of their work as finding and presenting "the facts" and also "the truth about the facts." In *The Elements of Journalism*, Kovach and Rosentiel describe it as getting the "right facts," and this, they suggest, is based on three core concepts (Dean 2019):

- Transparency means show your work so readers can decide for themselves why they should believe it—avoid omission, tell the audience what you know, reveal the sources.
- Humility means journalists need to stay open-minded, especially about what they don't know.
- Originality is achieved by publishing your own work where you can verify sources.

For information on fake news, see www.mindtools.com/pages/article/fake-news.htm.

ANALYTICS ON SOCIAL MEDIA

Analytics have been a feature of sports reporting for years and now also in social media, especially around online engagement. Analytics can refer to overall performance, or social media content types, or audiences. In essence, analytics track data to provide a picture of conversion decisions—what happens when someone enters your site or page. Three common analytical tools that help provide your social media road map are:

- ***Google Analytics*** **is a robust platform that probably offers the most data and more conversion tracking.**
- ***Facebook Analytics*** **is currently great at tracking user journeys through multiple sources, "omnichannel" and details around engagement with brand across demographic and behavior. Facebook has a media section, www.facebook.com/facebookmedia/, a powerful suite of tools that journalists find useful.**
- ***Twitter Analytics*** **is very specific to your Twitter handle and shows top tweets, top followers, mentions and impressions.**

Maybe start by exploring each and look at some blogs or podcasts like *Perpetual Traffic* at www.digitalmarketer.com/podcast/perpetual-traffic/, which describe various aspects of analytic tools.

In summary, pictures will often form the basis of much social media traffic. Don't believe everything you see, watch, or hear. It's after all in a journalist's nature to be skeptical. You can use a number of tools to help find pictures and in some cases determine if they are factual:

- **Twitter advanced search—check out this link: https://buffer.com/library/twitter-advanced-search**
- **TweetDeck—excellent management and advanced search features—check out this link: https://help.twitter.com/en/using-twitter/advanced-tweetdeck-features**
- **Geofeedia—intelligence platform that links social media posts with locations**

- **NewsWhip—tracks the spread of content after publication and predicts impact**
- **Reddit—is over 1,000,000 communities each offering comment on different topic posts**
- **Google advanced search—is a powerful tool that enables users to drill down into search criteria**
- **Google Reverse Image Search—checks images you can drag and drop, paste in a URL, or if using Chrome right-click the image and look for more information**
- **Facebook search—use keywords and phrases to search**
- **Banjo Live-time Intelligence—is a platform that uses AI to understand what is happening live online**

In all cases try and track down the source to ask them about the media—describe it, when they shot it, what equipment was used and whether they can provide permission. Organisations like the BBC have terrific information on using social media and checking the veracity of media.

In conclusion, convergence has ushered in a new global communication sphere largely influenced and disseminated by mobile and social media. The traditional power that the journalistic field once had (Bourdieu 2005) has been partly eroded by a new set of rules for working within and between subfields of journalism that now includes social media. Accordingly, the notion of a public sphere as a space for debate is shifting from the nation-state to a global sphere increasingly built around social communication networks with their own specific gatewatching practices—for example, Google's banning of the film *The Innocence of Muslims*, the Chinese government instituting their great firewall, or the Gutnik defamation case that tested globalisation of legal principals and cyber law (see Chapter 12).

However, it is not only about being able to speak, and almost anyone can do that, but about having the power to be heard above the online noise. Understanding how to capitalise on this shift was part of my motivation for investigating how mobile technologies and skills can infuse our public sphere with less homogenised and more democratic, culturally diverse content. The Arab Spring showed that freedom of speech is the most basic of human rights and a cornerstone of democracy. It also showed that even though new technologies enable citizens to have a voice, it takes more than one mobile tweet on social media to achieve sustainable change, which requires a sustained, more diverse politicised content creation sphere. And that's what this book addresses.

Go mojo ...

NOTES

1 Damascus Spring was a period of intense political and social debate in Syria which started after the death of President Hafiz al-Asad in June 2000.
2 B roll is overlay or cover shots used to highlight aspects of an interview grab or cover jump cuts. It is essential when compressing and expanding sequences.
3 Lossy compression reduces file size by permanently eliminating especially redundant information.
4 https://journals.plos.org/plosone/article?id=10.1371/journal.pone.0090315.
5 Ethical Journalism Network https://earthjournalism.net.

REFERENCES

Anderson, M. and J. Jiang (2018). "Teens, Social Media & Technology 2018." Pew Research Center.

Ardonato, A. (2018). *Mobile and Social Media Journalism: A Practical Guide.* Thousand Oaks CA, Sage.

Beaumont, C. (2009). "New York Plane Crash: Twitter Breaks the News, Again." *The Telegraph*, 16 January. www.telegraph.co.uk/technology/twitter/4269765/New-York-plane-crash-Twitter-breaks-the-news-again.html.

Bourdieu, P. (2005). "The Political Field, The Social Science Field and the Journalistic Field." In R. Benson and E. Neveu (eds.), *Bourdieu and the Journalistic Field.* Malden, Polity Press.

Bruns, A. and J.-H. Schmidt (2011). "Produsage: A Closer Look at Continuing Developments." *New Review of Hypermedia and Multimedia*, **17**(1): 3–7.

Buck-Morss, S. (2001). "A Global Public Sphere?" *Radical Philosophy* (December): 10–19.

Burum, I. (2018). *Democratising Journalism through Mobile Media*. Abingdon, Routledge.

Coviello L. et al. (2014). "Detecting Emotional Contagion in Massive Social Networks." *PLoS ONE* **9**(3).

Dean, W. (2019). "Journalism as a Discipline of Verification." www.americanpressinstitute.org/journalism-essentials/verification-accuracy/journalism-discipline-verification/.

Deuze, M. (2007). *Media Work.* Cambridge UK; Malden MA, Polity.

Dodge, T. (2012). "From the 'Arab Awakening' to the Arab Spring; the Postcolonial State in the Middle East." In N. D. Kitchen, *After the Arab Spring Power Shift in the Middle East.* London, London School of Economics.

Dutton, J. (2012). "Was the Revolution Lost in Tunisia and Egypt?" Al Jazeera, 5 September. www.aljazeera.com/programmes/insidestory/2012/09/201295847298587 32.html.

Edgecomb, C. (2019). "How Jack Dorsey Plans to Turn Twitter Into More of a Community." www.impactbnd.com/blog/how-jack-dorsey-plans-to-turn-twitter-into-more-of-a-community.

El-Ghobashy, M. (2012). "The Praxis of the Egyptian Revolution." In J. Sowers and C. Toensing (eds.), *The Journey to Tahrir: Revolution. Protest, and Social Change in Egypt*. London, Verso.

Elia, I. (2012). Interview with I. Burum, London.

Fourie, P. J. (2017). "Normative Media Theory in the Digital Media Landscape: From Media Ethics to Ethical Communication." *Communication* **43**(2): 109–127.

Fraser, N. (1992). "Rethinking the Public Sphere: A Contribution to the Critique of Actually Existing Democracy." In C. Calhoun, *Habermas and the Public Sphere*. Cambridge MA, MIT Press.

Fried, I. (2019). "How Jack Dorsey Plans to Change Twitter." www.axios.com/how-jack-dorsey-plans-to-change-twitter-60f0e69c-808a-429d-93c6-6335ea1a38c3.html?utm_source=twitter&utm_medium=social&utm_campaign=organic&utm_content=1100.

Funke, D. (2017). "Three Months after Launching, Faktisk is Already Among the Most PopularSites in Norway." www.poynter.org/fact-checking/2017/three-months-after-launching-faktisk-is-already-among-the-most-popular-sites-in-norway/.

Gant, S. (2007). *We're All Journalists Now*. New York, Free Press.

Ghonim, W. (2012). *Revolution 2.0: The Power of the People is Greater than the People in Power, a Memoir*. New York, Houghton Mifflin Harcourt Publishing.

Gillmor, D. (2006). *We the Media: Grassroots Journalism By the People, For the People*. Sebastopol CA, O'Reilly Media.

Gillmor, D. (2010). *Mediactive*. San Francisco CA, Mediactive.com.

Goode, L. (2009). "Social News, Citizen Journalism and Democracy." *New Media Society* **11**(8).

Harman, W. (2015). "The Psychology of Communication on Social Media." www.wadeharman.com/the-psychology-of-communication-on-social-media/.

Hassenzahl, M. (2003). "The Thing and I: Understanding the Relationship between User and Product." In M. A. Blythe, K. Overbeeke. A. W. Monk and P. C. Wright (eds.), *Funologoy: From Usability to Enjoyment*. Dordrecht, Springer: 31–42.

Hirst, M. (2012). *One Tweet Does Not a Revolution Make: Technological Determinism, Media and Social Change*. AcademiaEdu. www.academia.edu/1789051/

One_tweet_does_not_a_revolution_make_Technological_determinism_media_and_social_change.

Jenkins, H. (2008). *Convergence Culture: Where Old and New Media Collide*. New York, New York University Press.

Kagan, N. (2017). "How to Create Viral Content: 10 Insights from 100 Million Articles." https://okdork.com/why-content-goes-viral-what-analyzing-100-millions-articles-taught-us/.

Kuhn, R. (2011). "Historical Development of the Media in France." In *The Media in Contemporary France*. Maidenhead: McGraw-Hill Education: 5–8.

Lasorsa, D. et al. (2012). "Normalizing Twitter" *Journalism Studies* **13**(1): 19–36.

Lasswell, H. D. (1948). "The Structure and Function of Communication in Society." In L. Bryson, *The Communication of Ideas: A Series of Addresses.* New York, Harper and Row.

Lawson, G. (2012). "After the Arab Spring: Power Shift in the Middle East?: The Arab Uprisings: Revolution or Protests?" In N. Kitchen, *IDEAS Reports-Special Reports*. London, London School of Economics and Political Science.

Mansour, S. (2013). *On the Divide: Press Freedom at Risk in Egypt.* New York, Committe to Protect Journalists.

Mason, P. (2012). "The New Revolutionaries: Experts in Messing Up Hierarchies."In T. Manhire (ed.), *The Arab Spring: Rebellion, Revolution and a New World Order.* London, Guardian: 280–283.

Molyneux, L. and R. R. Mourão (2019). "Political Journalists' Normalization of Twitter." *Journalism Studies* **20**(2): 248–266.

Mosco, V. (2004). *The Digital Sublime*. Cambridge, MIT Press.

Newman, M. and J. Park (2003). "Why Social Networks are Different from Other Types of Networks." *Physical Review E* **68**(September): 36–122.

Newman, N. et al. (2018). "Reuters Digital News Report." Reuters.

Patterson, M. (2009). "Psychology of Nonverbal Communication and Interpersonal Interaction." *Psychology* **3**: 131–151.

Pavlik, J. (2008). *Media in the Digital Age*. New York, Columbia University Press.

Proptalinksi, E. (2018). "Over 90% of Facebook's Advertising Revenue Now Comes from Mobile." https://venturebeat.com/2018/04/25/over-90-of-facebooks-advertising-revenue-now-comes-from-mobile/.

Quinn, S. and V. F. Filak (2005). *Convergent Journalism: An Introduction*. Boston, Elsevier.

Quora.com (2019) www.quora.com/How-many-social-media-sites-are-there-in-the-world-today.

Rashed, F. (2011). "Twitpoper." http://twitter.com/FawazRashed/status/48882406010257408.
Rheingold, H. (2002). *Smart Mobs*. Cambridge MA, Perseus Books.
Rosen, J. (1999). *What are Journalists For?* New Haven, Yale University Press.
Ruud, G. (2012, 2019). Interview with I. Burum.
Sabadello, M. (2012). "The Role of New Media for the Democratization Processes in the Arab World." In Zsolt Sereghy, Sarah Bunk and B. Preiss (eds.), *The Arab Revolutions: Reflections on the Role of Civil Society, Human Rights and New Media in the Transformation Processes*. Austria, Austrian Study Center for Peace and Conflict Resolution.
SalahEldeen, H. and M. Nelson (2012). "Losing My Revolution: How Many Resources Shared on Social Media Have Been Lost?" In *Proceedings of the Second International Conference on Theory and Practice of Digital Libraries*: 125–137.
Salt, J. (2011). *The Great Arab Revolution*. Melbourne, Arena Printing and Publishing: 111.
Shihab-Eldin, A. (2012). "WTF Happened to Egypt's Revolution?" *Huffington Post.*
Shirky, C. (2008). *Here Comes Everybody: The Power of Organisation Without Organisations*. London, Allen Lane.
Siebert, F. et al. (1956). *Four Theories of the Press*. Chicago, University of Illinois.
Silver, L. et al. (2019). *Mobile Connectivity in Emerging Economies*. Washington DC, Pew Research Center.
Stein, E. (2012). Revolutionary Egypt: Promises or Perils. In N. D. Kitchen, *After the Arab Spring: Power Shift in the Middle East.* London, London School of Economics.
Strate, L. (2004). "A Media Ecology Review." *Communication Research Trends* **23**(2): 48.
Surowiecki, J. (2009). *The Wisdom of Crowds*. London, Abacus.
Svetlik, J. (2019). "Facebook Stories: What Is It and How Does it Work?" https://home.bt.com/tech-gadgets/internet/social-media/facebook-stories-what-is-it-and-how-does-it-work-11364169985164.
Tandoc, E. C. and T. P. Vos (2016). "The Journalist Is Marketing the News: Social Media in the Gatekeeping Process." *Journalism Practice* **10**(8): 950–966.
Wenger, E. (2001). "Supporting Communities of Practice: A Survey of Community-Oriented Technologies." https://pdfs.semanticscholar.org/066c/aaa4903b82a97bcbe574e1455f811ae549f9.pdf?_ga=2.240934659.1276545666.1589114319-582961342.1587321906.

CHAPTER 11

MOBILE STREAMING

SUMMARY

This chapter explores the amazingly visceral world of mobile streaming to social media and proprietary sites. A theoretical and a practical approach describes the nuts and bolts of streaming from your smartphone—everything from planning your live stream, streaming tips, platform options, streaming apps, gear and understanding codecs. Streaming expert, renowned radio producer and reporter, Peter Stewart, author of *The Live Streaming Handbook*, provides expert advice and a Break-out Box of streaming tips.

OVERVIEW

Streaming means sending music or video across the Internet so that the audience can listen to it or watch it in real time, or near enough to real time, more often than not on their smartphones. The media is sent in a continuous stream and is played as it arrives. It's not a completely new concept because we have been watching live music and video on TV for ages; however, in the past we watched one way—a TV network or radio station produced and sent the stream and we watched or listened. Today, anyone with a smartphone or a streaming encoder and access to WiFi or 3G, 4G or 5G can send and interact with streams immediately. There is no file to download, just a continuous stream of data that broadcasters prefer because it's hard for most users to save the content and distribute it illegally.

Social media has made streaming popular. "It's a bit like Facetiming or Skyping all your followers at once" (Stewart 2018). And with a smartphone, you potentially have your own live TV station and your audience literally in the palm of your hand. Face Book Live, YouTube Live and Periscope all offer streaming options and you can stream to specific private sites using apps and/or encoder boxes. It seems that the fear of missing out (FOMO) is driving people to interact with social and with streams. However, what really drives streaming is our love of pictures—as humans, we have evolved to interpret visual information faster than the written word:

- **85% of the US Internet audience watches videos online**
- **Live Internet video will account for 17% of the total video traffic by 2222[1]**
- **In just one second, more video will move across the Internet than you could watch in almost two years of doing nothing else**

- **Embedded videos on websites can increase traffic by up to 55%**
- **Mentioning the word "video" in the subject line of an email can increase open rates by 19%[2]**
- **Users spend 40 minutes a day,[3] on average, watching YouTube on mobile devices**

Streaming expert Peter Stewart (2018) believes statistics like the above suggest that video is here to stay and hence the use of video is now a pre-eminent tool in most marketing campaigns. Facebook has more than 2.6 billion followers and 92% of these log on daily, more than 80% of them do this using their mobile. This rise in video and live streaming is partly due to accessibility of technology. Stewart attributes this to more effective 3G and 4G technology, cheaper data plans and better and faster technology, which makes live streaming "fast, mobile and accessible." The result is immediate interaction with a global audience in what Stewart says is "unscripted and unpredictable, raw and real, fresh; nothing is better than a right-now, real-time experience" (Stewart 2018). I think Peter's right, but time will tell.

The growth of the social media giants and companies like Netflix that provide over-the-top (OTT) affordable streaming services has led to more development of streaming technologies, policies around geofencing[4] and the legalities of streaming. However, while potentially accessible to almost a third of the world's population, even during lockdowns and pandemics, mobile live streaming can be impacted by technical inconsistencies and diminishing creative and editorial quality that can occur when you go live. Going live with no second take has always required more planning and thought, yet as Stewart observes, we often see unfocused and unstructured content that risks being boring. The *New York Times* wrote: "many live videos are either plagued by technical malfunctions, feel contrived, drone on too long, ignore audience questions or are simply boring" (Spayd 2016). If it can be inconsistent and boring, why is live streaming so popular?

THEORETICAL PERSPECTIVE

There are basically two ways that we've received TV: through broadcasters (free to air or cable) or through an Internet streaming service (IPTV or OTT services like Netflix). Broadcast is defined by a single-node source, where Internet arrives via the same client server model that delivers email and the Web. Given this, in this current post-convergent media landscape, we need to ask whether the term "broadcasting" is still relevant. Notwithstanding the redefinition of the term, the appearance of OTT suggests some cross-breeding is still going on—we still have series and formats and genres. As happened with the printing press, the telephone and even writing, new technology will subsume the old. Producing TV, as Raymond Williams argued, is a combination of many different inventions, or as McLuhan might argue, the sum of many evolving mediums (1964). What are the characteristics of streams?

Historically, public broadcasting has been an essential medium for informing the public. Yet its practice of narrowcasting is in a way problematic to its discursive responsibility in the public sphere. "Critics suggest that the narrowcasting inherent in personalization exists in tension to public service broadcasting's (PSB) enduring commitments" (Kant 2014). Streaming's accessibility and its algorithmic personalisation may provide a more utilitarian and egalitarian means of information flow. If informing people is essential in a democracy and in any healthy public sphere, then you might conclude that the accessibility of YouTube and Facebook streams make them a far more effective information mode than any previous or current PSB system. In essence, they have arrived as competitors to PSB (Hills and Michalis 2000), challenging PSB's role as narrowcast news providers and competing for the public's leisure time (Kant 2014). The public's leisure time provides access to their hip pocket.

Kant (2014) argues that the global access that Web 2.0 provides these platforms to potentially enable them to consume and produce shared cultural resources is a double-edged sword. Facebook's old mission was "to make the world more open and connected" (Johnson 2017). Is the world closer together? YouTube claims their repository of online user-generated video content provides audiences with what they call "a forum for people to connect, inform, and inspire across the globe" (cited in Kant 2014). These promises have been problematic as the sites, which champion a form of participatory egalitarianism, are actually commercial ventures that connect and stream audiences, according to taste and interest, for monetary gain.[5]

The social media giants are enabled in their endeavors because they have redefined broadcasts from one to many, to streams that are many to many, and which suggest a more egalitarian mode of information transfer. New terms heralded the move from analog to digital, and the flick of a switch potentially transformed audiences to budding producers of content (Rosen 2006, Bruns 2010). Streaming extended that potential, but in a strange way is devoid of personalisation—which is derived also through style, skill and format—while increasing the feel of the personal.

When Facebook switched on Live it was an invitation to stream raw and personal and it was, in some respects, a test for their personalisation algorithms that rely on "cookies, java scripts, and IP addresses, to track the consumption patterns and browsing habits of platform users in order to deliver individually tailored content" (Kant 2014). The free Web services that social media giants offer are not free at all; they are supported by monetisation models that include data mining and enable the individual personalisation needed to retain users as customers. A variety of commercial opportunities associated with streaming are discussed in Peter Stewart's *The Live Streaming Handbook*.

Diversity is having a choice of what to watch and when, and also being able to produce content and upload or stream it. The relationship with social media, Internet and apps has meant that streaming services are at times replacing broadcast as a mode of watching TV. Almost 6 in every 10 Americans aged 18–29 watch their TV via streaming services and almost 25% of Americans are always online thanks to mobile connectivity (Perrin and Jiang 2014). "Among mobile internet users—the 83% of Americans who use the internet at least occasionally using a smartphone, tablet or other mobile device—89% go online daily and 31% go online almost constantly" (ibid). It's not only young people who are using mobile to access streams on the net. In 2017, 45% of US adults often got their news streamed to their mobile device. "Nearly two-thirds (65%) of US adults who get news on both mobile and desktop prefer mobile" (Mitchell and Barthel 2017). Many of these mobile users set real-time alerts for breaking news, and large numbers stream TV and their mobile screen simultaneously for news and social chatter (Perrin and Jiang 2014). Jay Manuel from Periscope believes that live streaming "seamlessly bridge(s) the gap between TV and social media. Having the opportunity to communicate with viewers in real time changes the game" (cited in Hacki 2015).

The relationship or, as Manuel calls it, "the game," between broadcast and streaming came to a head in 2012 when NBC, who had the US rights to the London Olympics, chose to tape and delay the US telecast. Being a broadcaster, NBC could create a geofence and control the play-out even to the extent that it included five ad breaks in the first 30 minutes of the telecast. They had to recoup their US$1.2 billion license fee somehow. Moments like these can set a whole audience against a broadcaster. In the above example, viewers turned to VPN services to change the "IP address" of their computer from the US to the UK, enabling access to the BBC's Internet stream of the Olympics (Burroughs and Rugg 2014). This stream was comparatively ad free and contained numerous segments that NBC had excluded from their broadcast.

This commercial battle is still raging, and companies like Netflix are re-contextualising streaming as both a cultural and technological practice (Burroughs and Rugg 2014). The traditional industrial models of broadcast frameworks that are based on the concept of a nation-state are being subsumed by the Internet and a streaming culture perpetuated by global smartphone penetration. Technological innovation in streaming, previously not possible because of bandwidth and hardware limitations, is being driven by new capacity, faster smartphones, 4G connectivity and social media adoption. It's enabled nearly three billion smartphone users to receive streams and to stream their own content from almost anywhere. This has led to a recalibration between content suppliers and audiences who are, in essence, a more modern streaming version of what Axel Bruns (2010) called "produsers"—where flow becomes increasingly channeled through the networked individual. This subsequently leads to media industries beginning to adapt and mesh analog viewership with digital streaming. As the streaming ecosphere begins to grow, it becomes increasingly important to know how to produce dynamic streams, and that's what we'll discuss next.

PRACTICAL PERSPECTIVE

The quality of any live stream depends on your connection speed, which often depends on how you stream: ethernet, WiFi, 4G and even a bonded combination where all these methods are used simultaneously (see p xx). But there is another critical factor: planning. Going live should not be an excuse for publishing content that is unfocused. Why are you streaming? Is it to increase your brand's reach beyond TV and into social media to target or catch potential customers where they are (Hacki 2015)? Content that's boring or long-winded won't catch anyone long term and would often be better if recorded and edited. Deciding why you are streaming, whether it's an immersive experience to an unfolding event and worth sharing, or a how-to explanation, are important considerations. There's no second take on "live"; so you have to be ready to think and react fast and, ironically, that takes planning and skill, even in a live-stream situation.

My first mobile streaming experience was using Facebook Live. It was terrible. I said "hi," I was nervous, and I really had nothing to say that couldn't be said in an edited video. But I was going live, something that in TV required an OB[6] truck and an army of people, and it cost a bomb. Here I was, albeit without much thought, going live from my mobile and reaching my global audience. So, what should I have done?

Streaming Plan

It is important to have a streaming plan—to stream or not to stream? Is my content something that needs to be streamed live—a "now" event that's immersive with lots of social chat and a global theme? What's so special about what I'm streaming that it works better live?

To determine this, you might need to have evolved your streaming strategy or a content plan, not unlike that which is required for any TV program or news article. The following points are a good start:

- **What is your aim for your stream—do you want to generate more followers, sell something, let the local community know about an event, and how will going live do that?**
- **How will your live stream complement your overall media strategy—will it support a bigger plan, or is it a one-off injection of energy and information?**
- **Make sure your audience is ready and prepared for the live stream:**
  - **Know the demographic**
  - **Understand the type of audience and their media habits**
  - **Understand the opposition—by analysing their streams and strategies**
  - **Be clear about why you are targeting them—a learning experience, for entertainment, or for public service**

The above might sound like a commercial strategy and you might be saying, "I'm not a business," but the same steps apply for any story and any streaming opportunity[7]—ask why am I doing it, for whom and how. Let me explain.

What to Stream?

Giving your viewers a "sneak peek" to satisfy expectations of voyeurism in a "reality TV" world:

- ***Personal*: Introspective immersive content makes viewers feel like they are part of your select group, gaining access to a closed world. We often used DV cameras in TV to achieve this feel. They were raw and often unedited, and it felt like the personal comments were being broadcast live.**
- ***Exclusive event*: You're letting your friends, customers and prospective clients feel as though they are there and involved. You are having a real-time conversation with them and giving them an authentic experience that others not taking the stream won't get. We used this in TV to provide the audience a glimpse of the making of a series, or a red-carpet event, a rock concert or sports.**
- ***How-to*: Live streaming a demonstration is not new and is used in news a lot. What is now possible is for 3 billion people to stream about their own expertise. The better you are at what you stream the bigger your audience, potentially. Novelty will hook an audience, but expertise and a structured stream will keep them and have them come back. Your own vulnerability and transparency will also be tested, so be ready to expose your strengths and minimise vulnerabilities.**

There are 50 million active content creators on YouTube generating 5 billion videos each day. Choosing what to stream about is a personal and a business decision, but looking at what type of video content was trending on YouTube in 2020 is staggering, with product reviews at number one, followed by how-to videos. What will you stream?

"Being constantly connected has trained us to expect immediacy and relevance in moments of intent—the I-want-to-know, I-want-to-go, I-want-to-do and I-want-to-buy moments," reports Google. "These micro-moments are the new battlegrounds for people's hearts, minds, and dollars" (Gesenhues 2015). They are some of the key identifiers when deciding what to stream.

Stewart (2018) says that streaming helps "humanise your brand." It gives the audience an access-all-areas pass and a front-row seat that makes them feel special. So whether you are live-streaming to increase business, or to provide information to your church or motorcycle groups, or your friends, or just answering an "I-want-moment," make the experience great. In streaming, like all forms of storytelling, maintaining a consistent quality is the next measure that your audience will come to depend on. If, as Josue Valles suggests, "you focus on solving your audience's problems, they'll come back again and again—you'll create a loyal community."

Developing a Plan for your Stream

In Chapter 3 I described SCRAP, a story development tool. My approach to the steps you need to follow to achieve your live streaming strategy is similar:

- ***Story*—what is it and how best will you tell it using your live strategy?**
- ***Characters*—why and who will you interview and are you ready with the right questions?**
- ***Structure*—does your approach for your live stream have a clear beginning, middle and end?**
- ***Actuality*—do you have the rights to stream all that you are recording; are you ready for a two-way chat, and how will you handle your interviewees and your own questions?**
- ***Production*—are you prepared for the weather, is connection speed fast, do you have the right equipment, and do you know how to use it to capture the moment you are streaming live?**

Tip: Stream something interesting that benefits from being live, something that you are an expert on, or an interview with an expert. Above all, do your homework.

Yes, it's live and that's what makes it fun and exciting, but making it sing creatively and editorially, with lots of take-home, will have your audience coming back. How do you do that? Well, if you are fronting the stream, you need to be as interesting as the content. Hence you will need to:

- **Speak well and at the right pace. Generally that's at three words a second, but above all you need to be yourself.**

- **Know your subject matter and know why you are streaming, with relevant questions. If you need notes, use them, and make it obvious you are referring to notes.**
- **Have your interviewees lined up or close by if you are walking and talking (see Chapter 6).**
- **Try and stay on track, which is sometimes difficult if you are monitoring and responding to live comments that ask for certain information. Sometimes, if comments are too tangential, you can tell your audience that you'll address all comments in an info sheet. This requires planning.**
- **Have all your prepared packages ready and accessible so that the throw is as seamless as possible.**
- **Be technically proficient: the pictures need to be framed and lit well (see Chapter 4), and given it's live and on a mobile and probably being operated by the person on camera (the mojo), it will take some skill and planning.**

If in doubt do a dry run. Test the stream by sending a stream to yourself. Even after all your planning, if you still think that it might all be too hard, ask a friend to help and share the tasks. Peter Stewart says, if the idea of live video scares you, or you can't show a scene because of privacy (at the scene of a pile up) or technical reasons (poor connectivity), then consider using the "audio only" live stream feature on Periscope which will post your stream out on your Twitter account. I reckon, plan it, find a reason and a structure, use video and audio and have a go.

Practice makes perfect, especially when you are live in front of billions. With more than 500 hours of video being uploaded to YouTube every minute, if your video is to stand out, it needs to be different and slicker, with a strong story. Here's a good performance trick to settle the nerves and get you thinking one step ahead, which is important when live streaming.

Tip: When you are walking or driving down the street and come to a red light, stop, look around at what's happening, quickly think of something to say that describes the intersection and the situation, then say it as if you are live and before the light turns green. At the next red light fix the mistakes you made at the previous attempt.

Here is Peter Stewart's terrific Break-out Box of tips for better live streaming:

1. *Plan and Promote.* Think where to go, what to show, what to say and how to end. Then take a still image of your location and put that on social media together with a message about when and where you will go live and what people will see.
2. *Prepare Your Camera.* Clean the lens; turn on "do not disturb"; check the power, signal and storage. Hold your phone horizontally, have the sun behind you, and frame up a great opening image to immediately engage the viewer.
3. *Starting Your Stream.* Introduce, welcome and explain. Tell people who you are, what you will show and what they will learn.
4. *Remember the Audio.* If you are showing what you can see (usually more interesting that a view of your face), then you (the cameraperson) will be behind the phone and possibly off-mic (check how many inbuilt mics your phone has). You will benefit from an external mic that can always be best placed to pick up your commentary or an interview with a guest, whatever direction the camera is facing.
5. *Steady Shots.* Play to the strengths of live video: show things that are moving, or move yourself—but no wild pans or too much walking without a stabiliser.
6. *Stream for the Edit.* Remember the Five-Shot Rule—show close-ups of hands, get down low for another perspective and so on. Don't just keep everything at eye-height. This will help you at Step 17.
7. *Ways to Engage.* It's *live* video, so encourage viewers to react by text or emoji and then thank them by name for doing so. Answer their questions as appropriate.
8. *Repeat Step 3.* There will always be a churn of people joining the stream, so briefly explain what's happening.
9. *Be Like a DJ.* As a radio presenter will throw ahead "after the break ..." to keep people listening, you need to encourage people to keep watching. So tease what's coming up.
10. *Share the Love.* Ask viewers to follow, like and share the video with their own network.

11. *Legals.* Be aware of issues surrounding the law and ethics: are you allowed to be streaming on this land or at this event? Do people mind being on live video? Do they know that it's live? At a breaking news event, be careful not to be too graphic or intrude on privacy or grief. Don't show police positions at a siege. Consider that a "rescue attempt" may go wrong and you may end up live-streaming a death. Consider possible slander or offensive language used by guests, or by trolling commenters on-screen.
12. *Timing is Everything.* Stream for around 10–20 minutes, depending on the evolving story.
13. *At the End.* Thank viewers for watching, have a "call to action" (perhaps promote another live stream, your website, on-air coverage), encourage them to share the video, and say goodbye.
14. *Save the Video.* When you have finished the live stream, accept the prompt to save the video to your device. Then either on your phone or on a desktop, you can edit the stream into a shorter package (using the different types of shots you gathered in Step 6).
15. *Repeat!* If you are at the scene of a developing story, and there's time and something to show, repeat the above on your second most-popular social media live-streaming channel. You will have a different audience there who will share to a different community.
16. *Be Creative and Engaging.* A live stream may be a "breaking story" at a factory fire, but it could be a news conference, or a walk of the route that a missing person last took, or of sunrise on the longest day, or a drone's-eye view of an old village, or as basic as a live explainer on a breaking story from your newsroom desk. The key is remembering it is live (something happening now), it is video (so show something moving or move yourself), and it is interactive (so ask and answer questions).

Analysing your Live Stream

Measuring success is important, and metrics will enable any ongoing stream to be fine-tuned. In TV the most important metric was the number of viewers who watched the show and we called that "ratings." Commercial networks live or die as a result of these independent reports and even public broadcasters are driven by viewing numbers. In the digital age the measure of program or story reach needs to be made across platforms.

When tracking viewership for your stream consider these three metrics:

- ***Total views*—the total number of viewers who tune into your video content while it's live and after it's recorded for on-demand playback**
- ***Total live views*—the total number of viewers who tune into some portion of the stream while it's live**
- ***Concurrent live views*—the maximum number of viewers watching at once at any given point in your broadcast**

Depending on the type of content you are streaming, Stewart (2018) believes the following metrics can also be used to determine a measure of success:

- ***Maximum concurrent viewership*—focus on organically trending the topic on the platform, cross-promotion and producer interaction.**
- ***Highest engagement numbers*—you will want a content strategy that relies on live audience decision-making, continual development of the story arc, and built-in "wow" factors.**
- ***Longest retention time or watch minutes*—concentrate on recapping to new joiners, great forward promotion, and "what will happen" moments, such as experiments.**

Knowing your audience and having the right streaming strategy is essential to get strong results. The final important elements are your streaming tools (apps, decoder boxes and phones) and your knowledge of technical aspects of streaming, and that's what we discuss next.

Choosing the Right Streaming Tools

You can download many streaming apps that work with smartphones. In this section I'll look at only a few to describe the differences that can exist between them.

The first are social media streaming apps, whose popularity is having a growing impact on normalising live streaming video on mobile.

- ***Facebook Live*** **is a powerful tool that's relatively simple to use, can accommodate two-person live chat and can be scheduled using "Pages" in Facebook, through a "Post" alerting your "Friends" in advance, and promoted on social media like "Twitter." Facebook has an excellent Facebook Streaming Guide.[8] Facebook is a social networking site so Live has a strong community feel about it that suggests users are "Friends" you converse or chat with.**
- ***Twitter Go Live/Periscope*** **is not unlike its parent Twitter in that it is used to provide updates around, for example, breaking news or business. Periscope offers a large suite of settings and 360 video.**
- ***YouTube Live*** **is an easy-access streaming tool with great video features, as you would expect from a Google company, with YouTube DNA. YouTube Live offers easy-to-publish either into Camera Roll or Live. It has a well-organised Live library and users can monetise their streams. On the downside, comments fly past very quickly.**

Some key differences between the above social streaming options are that Facebook Live and YouTube Live offer archiving features. Periscope streams are deleted after 24 hours, but users can elect to save them. Facebook Live viewers are anonymous until the end of the stream, whereas Periscope provides a name when a viewer joins. Knowing this helps revise the style of streams to target the audience. YouTube and Periscope allow unlisted or public streams and Facebook enables split-screen two-person chat.

Other streaming apps worth considering are:

- ***LiveAir Solo*** **was developed by Teradek,[9] and it enables users to stream live, archive packages on your phone, and roll packages, graphics and overlays stored on the phone, into the stream. The app enables users to send the stream to social media and to proprietary sites.**
- ***Switcher Studio*****[10] creates and streams professional multi-camera productions using iPhones and iPads (up to 9 connected devices). Supports screen sharing, seamlessly integrates with FCPX, graphics, and enables streaming to Facebook Live, Periscope Producer, YouTube Live and RTMP sites.**

- ***Wirecast Go* captures a number of input devices and has a layers feature, a replay facility, and streams to YouTube or RTMP servers.**

Staying with mobile apps, using Facebook and *YouTube Live* or *Live Air Solo* is simply a matter of following comprehensive how-to videos online. Stewart has extensive guides to the various streaming features of the above platforms in *The Live-Streaming Handbook: How to Create Live Video for Social Media on your Phone and Desktop.*

Switcher Studio which requires a monthly or annual subscription is a little more complex but excellent.

Switcher Studio enables users to record multiple smartphones to one central smartphone and cut the feed, while recording isolated streams from individual cameras. In the past this required a studio and multi-cam set-up and outside it was an outside broadcast (OB). These are very expensive state-of-the art recording and streaming alternatives. Today, depending on the job, you can do similar with a bunch of smartphones using *Switcher Studio.*

Switcher Studio is free for 14 days, then it's US$25/month. Up to nine separate smartphones can be slaved and edited in a live multi-cam feed. A comprehensive overview of *Switcher Studio* is available at http://switcherstudio.com.

Other streaming options are streaming encoders, like those produced by Teradek. These can include reasonably expensive bonded boxes that utilise multiple sending options simultaneously: 4G dongles, WiFi, Ethernet. They split the signal to minimise its size and bond the individual parts together at the receiving end. This means that smaller parts of the signal can be sent faster via each dongle through much smaller online pipes. These streams can be sent to multiple destinations simultaneously, so all platforms receive the stream simultaneously. You can use your own cameras with these options:

- **Laptop webcam**
- **Professional video camera or DSLR**
- **Desktop streaming software like the various forms of OBS (Open Broadcast Software)**

Using Open Broadcast Software (OBS) (https://obsproject.com), OBS Studio is a free desk-based open-source cross-platform streaming and recording program built with Qt and maintained by the OBS Project. There are versions for Windows, macOS and Linux distributions.

Tip: Check the latency on whatever streaming method and device you use.

Technical Terms

Understanding the streaming language is crucial. Following are a number of technical terms explained:

- *Codecs* When working with video and audio, and especially when streaming, it's important to understand a little about how codecs work. Codecs encode (compress) a signal at the transmitting (sending) end and decode (decompress) it at the receiving end. A video codec is a compression algorithm designed to reduce the file size while retaining as much quality as possible. Finding this balance between quality—we want shot integrity to be as high as possible—and size—the smaller the file the faster the stream—is the job of codecs.

  Codecs are powerful digital formulas for delivering quality and speed that are wrapped in formats, which are like containers holding the data that has been compressed using codecs. Examples of formats are QuickTime, Windows Media and MPEG4.
- *Bandwidth* is the viewer's connection speed to the Internet. To a large extent bandwidth controls the viewer's ability to retrieve and play (stream) video smoothly over the Internet.
- *Data rate* refers to the size of video files and is measured in bits and specifically Kbps (kilobits per second). For example, a stream at 1000Kbps means that every second 1000 kilobits of data can be transferred.
- *Resolution* is a measure of the width and the height of the frame—the aspect ratio. It refers to the number of pixels. For examples 1920 × 1080 is referred to as HD1 and means that horizontally there are 190 pixels and vertically 1080. When we upload a video story or stream a live event, we need to be mindful of the resolution; too high and it may not stream, too low and it can look grainy.

Delivering video over the Web is an essential part of the mojo workflow and often means trading image quality for lower resolution/bit rates that are easier to send/upload. See Chapter 9 for more detail on audio and video codecs, frame rate and aspect ratio.

In closing, streaming is all about being able to broadcast to a global audience—your audience. Cut-through and ongoing traction requires some thought, having something to say, having the right person to say it to, telling it clearly and succinctly, and using equipment that reduces lag between when we send and when someone receives the stream. If you are not enjoying someone else's stream, you might decide to produce your own.

Go mojo …

NOTES

1 www.cisco.com/c/en/us/solutions/collateral/service-provider/visual-networking-index-vni/white-paper-c11-741490.html.
2 www.walkaroundvideos.com/blog/2016/11/video-in-the-subject-line-increases-open-and-click-through-rates.
3 https://optinmonster.com/video-marketing-statistics-what-you-must-know/.
4 Geofencing is a location-based service in which an app or other software uses GPS, RFID, WiFi or cellular data to trigger a preprogrammed action when a mobile device enters or exits a virtual boundary.
5 See Kant 2014 for a more detailed description.
6 Outside Broadcast (OB) truck.
7 See Peter Stewart's *The Live Streaming Handbook* for extended strategy.
8 There are numerous terrific Facebook Live streaming guides online. Here's a link to the basics: www.facebook.com/help/1534561009906955?helpref=faq_content.
9 Live Air Solo http://teradek.com/pages/liveair-solo.
10 Switcher Studio https://switcherstudio.com/.

REFERENCES

Bruns, A. (2010). "Exploring the Pro-Am Interface between Production and Produsage." Paper presented at The Internet Turning 40: The Never-Ending Novelty of New Media Research, Hong Kong.

Burroughs, B. and A. Rugg (2014). "Extending the Broadcast: Streaming Culture and the Problems of Digital Geographies." *Journal of Broadcasting & Electronic Media* **58**(3).

Gesenhues, A. (2015). "YouTube 'How To' Video Searches Up 70%, with Over 100 Million Hours Watched in 2015." https://searchengineland.com/youtube-how-to-searches-up-70-yoy-with-over-100m-hours-of-how-to-videos-watched-in-2015-220773.

Hacki, C. (2015). "Is Mobile Live Streaming the Missing Link Between TV and Social Media?" www.huffingtonpost.com/cathy-hackl/is-mobile-live-streaming-_b_8153282.html.

Hills, J. and M. Michalis (2000). "The Internet: A Challenge to Public Service Broadcasting?" *International Communication Gazette* **62**(6): 477–493.

Johnson, K. (2017). "Facebook Gives Up on Making the World More Open and Connected, Now Wants to Bring the World Closer Together." https://venturebeat.com/2017/06/22/facebook-gives-up-on-making-the-world-more-open-and-connected-now-wants-to-bring-the-world-closer-together/.

Kant, T. (2014). "Giving the 'Viewers' a Voice? Situating the Individual in Relation to Personalization, Narrowcasting, and Public Service Broadcasting." *Journal of Broadcasting & Electronic Media* **58**(3): 381–399.

McLuhan, M. (1964). *Understanding Media: The Extension of Man*. New York, Penguin.

Mitchell, A. and M. Barthel (2017). "Interest in National News Increases Sharply Among Democrats." www.journalism.org/2017/05/10/interest-in-national-news-increases-sharply-among-democrats/#use-of-mobile-devices-for-news-continues-to-grow.

Perrin, A. and J. Jiang (2014). "About a Quarter of U.S. Adults Say They are 'Almost Constantly' Online." www.pewresearch.org/fact-tank/2018/03/14/about-a-quarter-of-americans-report-going-online-almost-constantly/.

Rosen, J. (2006). "The People Formerly Known as the Audience." *PressThink* http://archive.pressthink.org/2006/06/27/ppl_frmr.html.

Spayd, L. (2016). "Facebook Live: Too Much, Too Soon." *New York Times*. www.nytimes.com/2016/08/21/public-editor/facebook-live-too-much-too-soon.html.

Stewart, P. (2018). *The Live Streaming Handbook: How to Create Live Video for Social Media on your Phone and Desktop*. New York, Routledge.

CHAPTER 12

ETHICAL MOJO

SUMMARY

The speed of the 24/7 information clickstream has shone a spotlight on a growing need to practice ethical journalism. With content spreading across social media like wildfire, working ethically has never been more important. In this chapter we explore principles of ethical journalism and how mojos can be more ethical in their dealings with the public and representation of information. We introduce a set of guidelines for ethical journalism: accuracy and truth, compassion, humanity, conflict of interest and accountability. I speak with Aidan White, founder and former director of the Ethical Journalism Network, who provides a Break-out Box.

OVERVIEW

The practice of being ethical in journalism and the notion of public and free speech have been intertwined since the public's right to speak was first defended in England in the seventeenth century. Yet the concept of "journalism ethics," has been described as an oxymoron, like "military intelligence" (Smith 2008). Ethics in journalism is seen by some as a list of rules to play by, others say being "too ethical" produces lazy journalism, while others see ethics in journalism as a PR exercise (ibid). What is it for you?

Just as other professionals who work in an area of public trust have codes they abide by, journalists have obligations that define their responsibilities in the public sphere (ibid):

- **Be undaunted in their pursuit of informing the public and unhampered by conflicting interests—difficult to do in a business.**
- **Treat the audience and news makers (who could be the audience) with fairness and respect—difficult in an era where news is scraped.**
- **Promote democracy and support a healthy public sphere and act as watchdog over the actions of government, especially in statist regimes.**

If the above principles are journalistic ideals, then why are journalists so often held in disdain? In 2012, a poll that established nurses as the most trusted workers rated newspaper journalists at 22 out of 30. The *News of The World* phone-hacking scandal, which saw journalists more as puppets acting for corporate owners and deceiving the public, didn't help. Employees of the Murdoch-owned paper were accused of phone hacking (even the phones of the royals and of murdered schoolgirl Milly Dowler, relatives of deceased British servicemen and victims of the London bombings) and police bribery. In July 2011, after 168 years of publication, the *News of the World* stopped its presses and closed its doors. With journalism being tainted by these dodgy practices, spin-doctoring and fake news, questions about journalism ethics became front and center and led to the Leveson inquiry into the culture, practises and ethics of the British press.

Now that the public has taken to social media and the Internet to comment on the news, and in some cases to participate as producers in the news cycle, the issue of ethical reporting is even more relevant. If, in the eyes of the public, journalists had issues being ethical, how will the public hold their own to account and to the same ethical standards that journalists are judged by? In an Internet that is almost impossible to patrol, the genie may already be out of the bottle and we are left wondering who is watching the news watchers.

While ethics is not about media law, it is difficult to ignore the "dialectical relationship between law and ethics," an intersect Patching and Hirst (2013) call the ethico-legal paradox—the confusion that arises when legal and moral obligations of a journalist conflict. The nexus is often hard to distinguish, and journalists can be jailed when not revealing their sources, which they refuse to do on ethical grounds.

Doctors bury their mistakes. Lawyers jail theirs. Journalists often publish theirs (Pearson and Polden 2011). Journalism's indiscretions can impact many, very quickly. Pearson finds that the high public profile of journalism makes the study of law and ethics imperative for journalists on at least three counts: public responsibility that gives them license to publish; self-protection through the law and ethical behavior to avoid defamation and copyright issues; and professionalism and knowledge of the law that sets them apart from the online publishing public. One issue is that as journalism redefines itself on a series of online platforms, it's competing with new players, new ways of delivering the news and a new set of standards. In their search for new revenue streams, the danger is that the professionalism of journalism will become even more subservient to its business masters. This has resulted in the public questioning journalism's ethics and ability to fulfil its role as the public's watchdog—which is arguably journalism's main role in society.

THEORETICAL PERSPECTIVE

Journalists are often asked to defend press freedom and the relevance of the media. Once clearly seen as embodying the principles of the Fourth Estate,[1] the press has struggled over the past decade to reposition itself in a new global media ecosphere. In 1859, philosopher John Mill wrote, "The time, it is to be hoped, is gone by, when any defense would be necessary of 'the liberty of the press' as one of the securities against corrupt and tyrannical government." There has never been a greater need to restate these ideals than in the new millennium, where the business of media is no longer owned solely by the traditional oligarchs, but by new money who has a new set of social rules, principles, ethics and moral standards.

Ethics and morality are key conundrums for social media platforms. In one sense morality in its base form is a social construct. It's about how we act with each other, and there are a number of theories or approaches to being moral or ethical. In the first instance, being virtuous is about reflection and determining to live a life ethically to a set of, for example, Socratic standards. On the other hand, consequentialists believe the end result is what matters, finding a balance between good and bad as their guiding principle. Deontologists might take a Kantian or Lockean approach and dissect reason using ethical principles. Underlying each of the principles at the heart of ethical journalism is a social contract to provide all citizens with a voice, which can only happen if we have a free press.

The dialectic between free speech and the ruling voice goes back to 399BC when Socrates was sentenced to death for raising his voice against the government. The Socratic experience sits as a cornerstone of the study of free speech and ethics. When Socrates asked his archetypal ethics question, "What does it mean to be moral?", he was proposing an idea, or thesis. His subsequent follow-up questions, which exposed the weaknesses in the answer, set up an antithesis, and the result was a synthesis of the original problem. In essence, it's what the press defends, their liberty to investigate and to report freely. Milton's rallying cry echoes still, "Give me the liberty to know, to utter, and to argue freely according to conscience, above all liberties" (Martin and Adam 1994).

However, another way of looking at free speech, rooted in concepts of ethics and morality, is that it's not free at all, but a social obligation or contract we have with ourselves and our neighbors. Plato, a student of Socrates and Aristotle's teacher, added to the ethical conundrum by arguing that ethics and morality were not lists of laws prohibiting enjoyment of life but a guide to help people live good lives (Smith 2008). Plato argued that people are composed of three temperaments: basic drives or needs like food and sex; an assertive and defensive nature; and reason. The balance between these three drivers is appropriate for ethical behavior.

Aristotle developed Plato's doctrine by positing that the right course of action always lies between two extremes. An example of this can be found in the journalist covering the mass graves at Laniste in Bosnia in 2005. I was the only video journalist present at this highly emotional scene, where relatives were digging through the remains of more than 300 bodies. The importance of the event is weighed against the angst caused to families by a journalist being there, or at least that's the perceived ethical question.

One extreme would be for the journalist not to film—but he is the only journalist there. Another view is that since the event is newsworthy, the video journalist should be allowed to film anything. What is an ethical approach? Does the journalist use long lenses and act like a spy, an enemy of the families, recording something that he shouldn't be? Does he seek

Figure 12.1 Laniste graves Bosnia, image from documentary.

Ivo Burum

permission? Does he mingle and use an unobtrusive mobile camera? The "ethical or golden mean" is somewhere between the two extremes. Seeking this balance is what's been called "virtue-based ethics" (Smith 2008). This is always one of the first questions mojos need to answer at any job—to what extent do I go to get the story and how? Ethics plays a part in how we come to "our" answer.

People are, of course, motivated by self-interest, but overcoming societal problems was generally easier when people agreed on what were called social contracts. Philosopher Immanuel Kant believed that keeping your promises—adhering to your social obligations—should not be judged by consequences, rather that the test of morality is whether you try and do the right thing. Living up to a social contract might simply be an act of reasoning between right and wrong. In larger communities, interaction requires policing, so we built a framework that we call government to check if people and laws were moral. Philosopher John Locke was happy to cede authority to government as long as it protected a citizen's natural rights. The role of journalists, who also enter into social contracts when they produce stories, is to act as a watchdog over government and business, to protect those natural rights.

Journalists, like mojos, working alone in the field, are always considering key ethical dilemmas: What ought we to do in a given situation? What is the right action? What is the moral outcome? These questions are balanced against an implied or legislated[2] right of freedom to express views without recrimination in any medium. The right to freedom of expression contained in articles 19 and 20 of the International Covenant on Civil and Political Rights (ICCPR) is limited to protect against vilification, hate speech, the reputation of others and national security. Hence, freedom of speech, as an absolute right, is an ideal that's often limited by law. Locke had a view that freedom of speech should exist, but be limited in its publication. Kant, on the other hand, noted freedom of speech is important to democracy precisely because it results in a "new sociability" and an "interchange of varied points of view," a more participatory social and political dynamic "that constituted the public" (Muhlmann 2010).

Journalists confront these liberties and judge the moral and ethical virtue of the story when they consider the impact that stories have on stakeholders. Yet as Muhlmann (2010) argues, the profession and business of journalism can impose "biased and distorted points of view" compared to those that would freely circulate in a public space "not controlled by the media." This dialectic between journalism's role as the sentinel of free ideals, the provider of an ethical, reasoned and balanced lens through which to view the relationship between society, the state and its corporate masters, is crucial. When this avenue no longer exists, when the public sphere chokes politically, commercially and ethically, and journalists are thrown into jail, citizens resort to other means—revolution and social media—to express their views.

The prevalence of social media, even in liberal democracies, is enabling greater freedom of speech and the proliferation of unethical reports that we call fake news. Currently, in Singapore, a new law limits free speech under the guise of protecting the public against fake news. Seen by journalists and others as a move to clamp down on freedom of speech, the law "requires online media platforms to carry corrections, or remove content the government considers to be false, with penalties including prison terms of up to 10 years, or fines up to S$1m" (Fullerton 2019). These laws potentially work to choke journalism's ability to provide information to enable citizens to make informed choices. Yet the legislators in Singapore say their law is justified because journalists are not the only people who are providing information to the public. "Free speech should not be affected by this bill. We are talking here about falsehoods. We are talking about bots... trolls... fake accounts and so on," says law minister Shanmugam (ibid).

The press as the primary purveyor of truth and ethical reporting has been a contested concept ever since industrialists came to own the presses. Commercial pressures constrained press freedom, forcing it to work in a sphere of limited consensus, where the public sphere was shaped by the interests of capitalist merchants who invested in mass media (Kuhn 2011). The result was a decline in effective political journalism, narrowed political debate around commercial imperatives and reporting without "its independent critical edge" (Benson 2009). This censoring of media by industry or state can lead to repressed media and revolutions like that which occurred in Egypt, Tunisia, Libya and Yemen, where the public sphere was choked by a lack of a free press. New York University journalism professor Jay Rosen says that what is required in an effective public sphere where the public is not dominated is for it "to be in discussion with itself" (1999). While this may be occurring online, the degree to which the discussion is of public benefit depends, as Fraser (1992) points out, on the relevance of the discursive nature of the sphere—which ostensibly is the freedom that the Singapore laws are limiting.

Historically, the lack of a public sphere, or the existence of a heavily mediated one, has led to alternative community or underground communication: the Paris Commune (1871), where workers' rights were championed; the Russian Revolution (1917), where the Bolsheviks deposed the tsars and formed what would later be known as the Soviet Union; the rise of organisations like the Central Australian Aboriginal Media Association (1980) to champion Indigenous rights in Australia; the shadow Kosovo Assembly (1991), where parallel underground Albanian schools, clinics and hospitals existed; and the Moqattam slum city of Cairo (2011), where a lack of food turned the Zabaleen into potential revolutionaries (Mason 2012). Hence, any discussion of the public sphere needs to move beyond a narrow Habermasian view of landowners and capitalists who challenged feudal systems for their own vested interests (Benson 2009). It needs to include all the forms of alternative and community media functioning as a "resource that facilitates cultural citizenship in ways that differentiate it from other media" (Meadows, Forde et al. 2010). It needs to include all the online noise that the Singaporean government is trying to limit.

In summary, one of the problems is that in an Internet of billions, run by social platform giants, ethical self-regulation is a difficult proposition. One of the major obstacles in creating a new concept of journalism stronger than the original is still a dialectic between the ideals of the profession and the business. This clash underpins the growing need for a trained local voice. What is needed, as Merrill (1993) points out, is to be able to separate the "wheat from the chaff" to form "compatible strains of wheat into new but similar hybrids." Merrill suggests that the basic principle of this dialectic is to let opposites clash and wait for the winners to form a new group. This might result in organisational dynamics and rules, but we also need relevant training that includes ethics, in particular during the transformation phase. Mojo praxis uses cultural capital—local knowledge, holistic skills, communication tools and knowledge—to transcend relational positions within this growing subfield of communication called mobile journalism.

Ethical ideologies have always been important in shaping the public sphere and promoting a civic society where citizens articulate their own views in order to influence political institutions. However, to silence one opinion is to silence a truth. In network societies built on social platforms servicing billions of people, post-truth opinion can push fake news as truth, to billions of people in milliseconds. Durkheim argued that the survival of society could only be based on overarching principles such as human rights, democracy, ethics and inclusive citizenship, which requires "an even greater role for an independent and effective media" (Hadland 2008). Bearing witness and writing what's been described as the first draft of history is a journalist's lot and our responsibility. But we'll need more than digital tools; we'll need a moral and ethical compass. This is where citizen journalism, mojos and a neo-journalistic skill set that marries relevant legacy skills with new digital ones, can play a defining role.

PRACTICAL PERSPECTIVE

Ethics in journalism practice requires standards, knowledge of the craft, and an ability to tell the truth. Following is a summary of key ethical considerations facing journalists and especially mojos, who work solo where often the only ethical sounding board is their own moral code.

According to the Ethical Journalism Network (2018), the main ethical principles that must apply to a journalist's and mojo's work, whether working in social media, in print, or on TV are:

- **Accuracy and telling the truth**
- **Independence and doing good journalism**
- **Compassion with an emphasis on humanity**
- **Impartiality and being honest about any conflicts of interest**
- **Accountability for your work, sources and audience**

Aidan White, the founder of the Ethical Journalism Network, says that "Journalists must rebuild public trust by sticking to ethical rules and by being open and honest in the way they work" (2019).

Accuracy and Truth

One of the key aspects of journalism has always been that the public believed what the profession told them. This has changed with the advent of social media and a growing level of misinformation.

Of course, fake news has always been here, often labelled as propaganda. Leni Riefenstahl's[3] films about the Third Reich were propaganda and considered inaccurate, fake in that sense, and hence, highly unethical.

There are generally three types of story—the one you produce with your own content, the one a colleague produces, and the one you and colleagues scrape from the Internet. The first step in each case is to verify that the facts of the story are true. Ask yourself where the material has come from, especially in a story scraped from online media. Are you able to verify the facts at source? The Internet helps and hinders this process. Access to information means we can drill into stories very quickly to get to the source, but with so many users it takes time to verify the veracity of information. White says, "Journalists can separate themselves from the chaos of online communications by being transparent in their reporting, by revealing their sources of information, and by relentlessly checking facts" (2019).

The best advice when planning is to check your facts on the Internet and, if possible, on the ground. No amount of online research will trump on-the-ground verification. Verification continues even during a shoot. When you land on location to record your story, go to the local pub, order a beer, ask a question—verify a fact. Verification continues through out the edit.

One important question about verification is what you do if you can't completely confirm a story. In this case, and knowing that someone else may also publish it, it's important to contextualise the story's unverified state. "If there are doubts about unverified information, try to avoid using it, but if you do, tell the public about why it is not wholly reliable," says White (2019). In some cases, you'll need to fix existing facts and republish. The Norwegian watchdog site Faktisk searches out online mistakes, or intentionally misleading content, fixes it and republishes stories. Commencing two months before the 2017 Norwegian elections, Faktisk very quickly became must-viewing. "In only a matter of days, we went from being nothing before we launched to being something a lot of people spoke about," said Kristoffer Egeberg, editor of Faktisk (Funke 2017). Funded by long-time media competitors, *VG*, *Dag Bladet*, NRK and TV2, Faktisk is now finding that republished stories get more views than the initial incorrect story—showing that ethical reporting can still trump—excuse the pun—what's fake.

"The first casualty in war is truth." Who said this? Should it be attributed to Arthur Ponsonby who said it in *Falsehood in Wartime* (1928) or US Senator Hiram Johnson who said it in a 1918 speech? Or did it originate in the *Idler* magazine from 11 November 1758, which says "among the calamities of war may be jointly numbered the diminution of the love of truth, by the falsehoods which interest dictates, and credulity encourages." Or, the first corroborated quote, "In war, truth is the first casualty," attributed to Greek writer Aeschylus (525BC–456BC). Which is right, or more to the point, which will you cite and why? Being accurate is about contextualising your information. How you do this will determine which definition is accurate and why you're using it.

The other real cost of telling the truth, in particular in conflict regions, is life. The price of telling the truth can get journalists killed—like Marie Colvin, killed in Syria in 2012. Even when there is an overthrow of government, things can get worse. In the first 12 months of Morsi's government in Egypt, from August 2012 to July 2013, the Committee to Protect Journalists documents at least 78 assaults against journalists (Mansour 2013). And it's not getting better. In 2018, journalists Jefferson Lopes from Brazil shot dead in his lounge room, Leslie Anna del Real shot in the head in her restaurant, Musa Abdul Kareem killed in Libya, Ron Hiaasen killed in the newsroom in Maryland, Shujaat Bukhari killed in India, and *Post* correspondent Jamal Khashoggi killed at the Saudi Arabian consulate in Istanbul are just a few of more than 50 journalists murdered that year. Ironically, the media freedom group Reporters Without Borders said that in 2018 the US made it into the top five deadliest countries for journalists that year for the first time, with six journalists dying (*Guardian* 2018).

The New York-based Committee to Protect Journalists reported that the context for the crisis is "complex, and closely tied to changes in technology that have allowed more people to practise journalism even as it has made journalists expendable to the political and criminal groups who once needed the news media to spread their message" (ibid). This suggests a lot of untrained journalists are being slaughtered.

In journalism training we are never placed in harm's way, not intentionally, so in this context we were all untrained. And I didn't really learn about working in conflict situations until I did it on documentary shoots and for *Foreign Correspondent*. One problem today is that so many more people have access to reporting tools. Trained or not trained they take an opportunity as a responsibility to expose the truth. Patrolling this level of storytelling and the safety of the citizens and journalists telling these stories is an impossible task. It's made all the more difficult by a 24/7 content stream that's, as Charles Feldman (2008) points out, as powerful as a tsunami.

In particular, editors will need to decide how to use user-generated content (UGC) and most importantly how to verify it. In fact UGC has been used in newsrooms for years (photographs, letters). However, the growth in smartphones and social media means it is playing a prominent role in real-time news reporting. With declining revenue streams, UGC, actuality footage created by citizens using mobiles, "means you kind of have this central hub of people communicating and sharing information, not only on social media but also obviously talking to one another," said *Denver Post* social media editor Dan Petty. "I can't emphasise enough how proximity in a crisis situation like that is important" (cited in Reid 2013). This could mean turning to established social media sources running local UGC to get the facts. Hard-working journalists who are not able to be in two places at once can often be trumped by citizen UGC. What impact can this have on a journalist's morale? Hence, one of the key roles of the editor is to make certain that all their journalists have a workflow that incorporates UGC, which is seen as an initiative driven by the journalists, who are working on the frontline of verification.

Independence

Because journalists want to remain independent and don't want their sources tainted, they don't reveal sources. Is it also because they don't want to be seen to be using tainted sources, or being influenced by the business of journalism? Either way, when reporting the news, remaining independent of corporate and government structures is one of the pillars of strong journalism.

Aiden White says always ask who wants me to publish the story and why? Ask also, who will benefit from this story being told? If a government or business benefits, is that my role as a journalist? If the public will benefit as well, then is that OK?

With the advent of smartphone technology, freelance journalists can work on the fringe of conflict zones independent of the military. While effective, this is a dangerous way of working. Hence, journalists use the technology to embed with military to gain safe and exclusive access like they got in the Iraq war. We all wondered how much independence journalists had when embedded with US forces. Unique access to the front line was tempered by an uneasy feeling that it was all propaganda for the US. In fact, the Iraq war was based on what's been described as a lie, that Hussein had weapons of mass destruction (WMD). The media supported the lie until the outbreak of the war, at which point they shifted their position. The "terror frame" became the old story and was replaced by a new story where media questioned the reasons for going to war.

Here is a simple checklist adapted from The Ethical Journalism Network and Thompson Foundation (2019) to check story independence:

- **Propaganda—determine if the story is propaganda and, if so, what you'll tell your audience and what fixes you'll make. Indeed, determine whether you'll run it.**

- **Public relations—determine if it is a form of PR and the impact of timely publication.**
- **Public interest/benefit—determine whether the story is in the public interest and what public benefit it has.**

White's advice is, "Tell those who want you to do biased reporting that your commitment to transparency means you'll have to disclose conflicts of interest to the public" (2019).

Compassion

What type of journalist are you? Are you a corporate hound, who needs to make the daily quota of stories to keep your job, which might mean cutting ethical corners? Or are you the type who sees the face behind the story and its impact on community?

Being compassionate is about being fair and balanced, without losing your story edge, or becoming a lazy journalist. For example, dead soldiers wearing Serb uniforms are recorded and broadcast/published and a statement from Serb commanders says it's the work of a Bosnian terror cell. Strong pictures, a statement from a general—what do you do? Accept the statement and the graphic pictures because it's the splash of the day, or investigate and speak with locals? It's a difficult conundrum in a 24/7 news cycle. "Speed is not the friend of truth", says White. "Ethical journalism is thinking journalism, and to report honestly and conscientiously you need time to think." I came across this scene at the Laniste graves in Bosnia—300 plus bodies in two mass graves. It was an important story, but so sad and so criminal. Families were literally digging up their own relatives. I had to slow down so that I could make some quick decisions. Here's my dilemma:

- **I was the only journalist, and this was a hot story. *I asked families and the police and those digging if they wanted this story told.***
- **How do I film this respectfully given families are there? *I get led to the bodies by family, not by authorities.***
- **Do I hold onto the footage for my documentary, or does it go public that day? *I gave the footage away to APTV and we cut a story and published that day. My network was furious.***

What would you have done?

One of the ways journalists can be compassionate is not to roll in with large crews. Working with smart technology enables reporters to remain small and remain unobtrusive. Reporters are often, as Patching and Hirst (2013) describe, "first-responders," often in emotive situations. I found in my work, especially on *Foreign Correspondent* (ABC TV), that working small enabled me to accommodate talent, shift tack, stop, think and alter perspective, and focus accordingly—in essence to be more compassionate. On *Missing Persons Unit* (Nine Network), our crews filmed in very sensitive situations. Here, working solo as a video journalist or as part of a very small crew was an advantage. It enabled journalists to shift their work tempo to a pace that more suited the talent and the story.

On the *Missing Persons Unit case*, after eight days missing, a body "popped" and was fished out of a river. I filmed the retrieval, with permission from police, while the family watched on from a distance restricted by police. Should I have asked the family for permission?

What would you do?

Humanity

Avoid promoting hate speech and think of the consequences of publishing "that" piece. Professional ethics are tied to human values and must be technology agnostic. If journalism is about anything it is about principles that protect values and support ideals that inform and propagate a moral existence.

A lack of humanity in media reporting is often driven by vested interests and represented by fearmongering. In an attention economy where publishers look for cut-through, fear is a valuable tool, drawing people in by appealing to their anxieties. "TV news and radio talk show programming uses auditory cues, linguistic patterns, and segment cliff hangers in order to entice people to stay attentive. Fear is regularly employed because it works" (Boyd 2012). And it's because of these vexatious and "toxic online communications that people are very suspicious about internet sources" says White (2019).

In our networked social societies attention is the economic commodity that's most sought after. That's why the "short is best" mantra is often peddled, as is "if it bleeds it leads"; make it graphic and change it quickly. However, the opposite is probably true (Newman, Fletcher et al. 2018): the current trend toward subscription indicates that the audience is willing to pay for behind-the-pay-wall information that is verified, probably more in-depth, with a higher production value and ethically solid.

In network societies we need to consider the humane principles that should influence decisions about the spread of information. I would argue that three principles should be at the core of journalistic practice:

- **choice of story and how it's reported—is it for public benefit?**
- **avoid reporting fake stories by verifying sources**
- **report in order to increase public knowledge and create a more informed, humane and connected public sphere**

Conflict of Interest

A conflict of interest occurs when someone who is expected to act impartially has a personal stake in an issue (emotional, financial, political). Did the US military have a personal stake in their decision to embed troops? In every case, a conflict of interest is a real problem—even if nobody misbehaves (Jerz 2017). An interesting conundrum. It's a journalist's emotion and passion about a cause or issue that is often a key driver for a story. If this is true, how does a journalist write a neutral fact-based report of an event?

During the 1950s and 1960s, the American Society of Newspaper Editors (ASNE) debated and ultimately abandoned the practice of allowing features syndicates, which sold content to newspapers, to wine and dine editors during their annual convention. Freedom from all obligations except that of fidelity to the public interest is vital (Mellinger 2017). A statement of principles in 1975 determined that "Journalists must avoid impropriety and the appearance of impropriety as well as any conflict of interest or the appearance of conflict. They should neither accept anything nor pursue any activity that might compromise or seem to compromise their integrity" (ibid).

While appearing to be an ethical determination, this challenged libertarian assumptions about the rights of the press, "even the right to attend an after-hours syndicate party" (ibid). In his seminal chapter describing a libertarian framework for the press, Seibert (1956) wrote, "In the place of state supervision, libertarian theory provides for a more informal type of control through the self-righting process and through the free competition in the market place of information, opinions, and entertainment." Later he concluded that libertarianism's "greatest defect has been its failure to provide rigorous standards for the day-to-day operations of the mass media—in short, a stable formula to distinguish between liberty and abuse of liberty" (ibid).

These early deliberations, which led to an awareness of the need for ethical restraint, social responsibility and accountability by the press, divided journalists on definitions of conflict of interest and impartiality. Should a reporter with children in day care be assigned to a story about a new scientific study on the effects of day care on child development? Should an atheist cover a story that involves religion? Should pack-a-day smokers cover health issues? Should pacifists cover wars? These are questions that editors grapple with daily. The ethics of corporate or checkbook journalism adds another layer of questions to the conflict of interest equation.

Accountability

Media accountability is predicated on the simple principle that media should serve the public, something that journalists can only achieve if they enjoy independence from financial and political pressures (Bertrand 2005). Media accountability is sometimes confused with self-regulation, but what is it really, and who are we accountable to?

"While regulation involves only political rulers and while self-regulation involves only the media industry, media accountability involves press, profession and public" (ibid). This suggests a role for a Press Council as an arbiter of accountability in media. An institution established in the UK, the Australian Press Council was founded in 1976. Its principle responsibility is for the administration of an agreed Code of Practice and the investigation of public complaints about editorial content in the media. The second is the defense of press freedom. But defining the role of the Press Council is not an easy task. In the US there is no Press Council, possibly because freedom of the press is enshrined as a founding principle of the nation-state. Instead you have a number of organisations like the Newspaper Association of America, American Press Institute, US Press Association, all with their own agendas, making it difficult to determine effectiveness and a cohesive position on press issues. The last of the smaller NGO-funded organisations like the Washington News Council closed their doors in 2014. Director John Hamer said, "The eruption of online digital news and information made our mission of promoting high standards in journalism much more difficult, if not impossible. How can anyone oversee a cyber-tsunami?" (Silverman 2014).

But even in countries that have Press Councils, scope and powers can differ. The extent of their power is determined by their exact purpose (their charter) and the means (freedom from the state and corporate interference) they have to achieve this (Bertrand 1978). Another issue with Press Councils is the cost of investigation, or more to the point, who pays for it. In general, a Press Council can either wait for a violation of professional ethics to be brought to its attention by the public or discover them by its own means. The latter is an expensive option—like investigative journalism—that generally requires funding from Press Council backers, the media owners, who are the ones generally being investigated. Hence the majority of Press Councils adjudicate complaints and don't chase issues.

Hence, accountability begins at home. Knowing your craft, having the right mindset, being ethical and maintaining independence are steps to being more accountable and the principles all journalists must adhere to. Being accountable as a journalist requires a real attempt to produce balanced stories that communicate meaning and context and that can change lives. The American Press Institute (Jane 2016) spoke with 17 journalists and came up with these seven key traits that journalists who practice accountability journalism exhibit:

- **Exhibit broad curiosity—eagerly adapt to new technologies and platforms**
- **Think about multiple audiences**
- **Work hard to create context for their audiences**
- **Smartly balance their time on story choices and audience interactions**
- **Spend considerable time building relationships with sources, readers**
- **Build connections and teamwork within their own newsrooms**
- **Find their own way and direct their own work**

Freedom of speech is a right that is often abused and when it is, the result can be war and even genocide. In some countries freedom of speech is enshrined in the constitution while others, like Singapore,[4] are legislating to restrict those freedoms. Australia, where recently there were Federal Police raids to seize information from a journalist and media organisations, has the MEAA[5] to remind government that "Journalism is not a crime." Police raided the ABC's Sydney headquarters on Wednesday 5 June 2019 over a 2017 investigative report alleging that Australian soldiers killed unarmed men and children. Another search at the home of newspaper journalist Annika Smethurst related to her 2018 report about a government plan to spy on Australian citizens. Acting Commissioner Neil Gaughan said the searches related to stories where top-secret government information had been published. In a statement ABC Managing Director David Anderson said the police raid "raises legitimate concerns over freedom of the press" (Savage 2019).

Press freedom in Australia is not constitutionally guaranteed. In the state of Victoria, press freedom is explicitly protected under the Charter of Human Rights and Responsibilities. However, a series of legislative changes in recent years have the potential to curb press freedom in Australia:

- **2011, Evidence Amendment Act protects the identity of journalists' sources and extends this protection to the sources of bloggers, citizen journalists, independent media organisations, and anyone "active in the publication of news in any medium." However, the Evidence Amendment Act can only be applied in federal cases.**
- **2014, Parliament approved the National Security Legislation Amendment Act, which introduced a 5–10-year prison sentence for any person who discloses information relating to "special" intelligence operations.**
- **2014, Parliament introduced the Freedom of Information Amendment Bill designed to cut government funding for freedom of information services.**
- **2014, Parliament announced plans to cut approximately A$250 million (US$190 million) of funding to the ABC.**
- **2015, Parliament passed telecommunications legislation that requires Internet and mobile phone providers to store user metadata for two years.**
- **2015, Australian government continued to restrict media coverage at immigration detention centers.**
- **2018, the Foreign Interference Bill imposes 15-year prison terms on people leaking classified information including trade secrets.**

In closing, our profession needs a code of ethics, probably even in the US. In Australia our code was formally tabled in 1994. Each member of the Australian Journalists' Association is bound by its rules to observe this Code of Ethics in her/his employment:

- **To report and interpret news with a scrupulous honesty.**
- **Not to suppress essential facts nor distort the truth by omission or wrong or improper emphasis.**

- **To respect all confidences received by him in the course of his calling.**
- **To observe at all times the fraternal obligations arising from his membership of the Association and not on any occasion to take unfair or improper advantage of a fellow member of the Association.**
- **Not to allow his personal interests to influence him in the discharge of his duties, nor to accept or offer any present, gift or consideration, or benefit or advantage of whatsoever kind that may have the effect of so benefiting him.**
- **To use only fair and honest means to obtain news, pictures and documents.**
- **Always to reveal his identity as a representative of the press before obtaining any personal interview for the purpose of using it for publication.**
- **To do his utmost to maintain full confidence in the integrity and dignity of the calling of a journalist.**

A mobile journalist's primary aim is to gather news and information. In doing their jobs mojos will need to maintain trust. A mojo and any journalist will only be trusted if their stories are verified, balanced and ethical. White says, "If there are doubts about unverified information, try to avoid using it, but if you do, tell the public about why it is not wholly reliable."

James Curran (1991) argues that citizens need "a democratic media to enable them to contribute to public debate and have an input in the framing of public policy." Without this, society will resort to extreme revolutionary measures, like the Arab Spring. In expressing their right to speak, Aidan White (2019) believes mojos and all journalists should consider the following ethical standards:

- **Being ethical is not a lifestyle choice for journalists. Our livelihood depends on providing accurate, reliable and trustworthy information.**
- **We will not deliver stories that people will trust if we make propaganda for politicians or sweet-talk for corporate advertisers and sponsors.**
- **Tell those who want you to do biased reporting that your commitment to transparency means you'll have to disclose conflicts of interest to the public.**
- **Do them a favor by encouraging them to develop real stories that are truthful, interesting and that may also get their message across.**
- **Ethical journalists always think before they publish. They ask themselves, "Is this picture or video necessary to tell the story? Who might suffer if this is published?"**

- **Remember, journalism will always be slower than social media and online players who don't care about the harm or damage they may cause.**
- **Considered and thoughtful journalism may arrive later than the stream of confusion that comes from social media, but it's always what people are waiting for—information they know they can trust.**

One of the main purposes of training citizens and journalists to mojo is a real desire to democratise a storytelling skill set—to create a common digital language across spheres of communication—so that smart technologies can potentially help citizens speak more freely in their own voice.

Citizen mojos trained with multimedia skills, working across network societies, producing quality alternative journalism, can potentially counteract the gatekeeping practices of large media by enabling a global public sphere with a more diverse politicised frame. For mojo to be regarded as a game changer, mojos must focus on ethical journalism principles which are guided and indeed limited by laws such as privacy, defamation and copyright, and that's what we discuss next.

Go mojo ...

NOTES

1 The term "Fourth Estate" refers to the press and news media both in the explicit capacity of advocacy and implicit ability to frame political issues. It wields significant indirect social influence, in particular over the other estates Lord Spiritual (clergy), Lord Temporal (hereditary peers) and House of Commons.
2 US Declaration of Independence, US Constitution, Bill of Rights and the 1st Amendment that enshrines the right to free speech.
3 The last surviving member of Hitler's inner circle, Reifenstahl produced *Triumph of the Will* and *Olympia*, considered Third Reich propaganda.
4 The 'Protection from Online Falsehoods and Manipulation Bill' enables government to force corrections and impose fines on media and social media for what it deems fake news.
5 The Australian Media Entertainment and Arts Alliance.

REFERENCES

Benson, R. (2009). "Shaping the Public Sphere: Habermas and Beyond." *The American Sociologist* **40** (Fall): 175–192.

Bertrand, C.-J. (1978). "Press Councils Around The World: Unraveling a Definitional Dilemma." *Journalism Quarterly* **55**(2): 241–250.

Bertrand, C.-J. (2005). "Media Accountability." *Pacific Journalism Review* **11**(2): 5–16.

Boyd, D. (2012). "The Ethics of Fear and How it Undermines an Informed Citizenry." www.poynter.org/reporting-editing/2012/fear-undermines-an-informed-citizenry-as-media-struggles-with-attention-economy/.

Curran, J. (1991). "Rethinking the Media and the Public Sphere." In C. Sparks and P. S. Dahlgren (eds.), *Communication and Citizenship: Journalism and the Public Sphere*. London, Routledge.

Feldman, C. (2008). *No Time To Think: The Menace of Media Speed*. New York, Continumum International Publishing.

Fraser, N. (1992). "Rethinking the Public Sphere: A Contribution to the Critique of Actually Existing Democracy." In C. Calhoun (ed.), *Habermas and The Public Sphere*. Cambridge MA, MIT Press.

Fullerton, J. (2019). "Singapore to Introduce Anti-fake News Law, Allowing Removal of Articles." *Guardian*. www.theguardian.com/world/2019/apr/01/singapore-to-introduce-anti-fake-news-law-allowing-removal-of-articles.

Funke, D. (2017). "Three Months After Launching, Faktisk is Already Among the Most Popular Sites in Norway." www.poynter.org/fact-checking/2017/three-months-after-launching-faktisk-is-already-among-the-most-popular-sites-in-norway/.

Guardian (2018). "Journalist Death Toll: Retaliation Killings Nearly Double in 2018." *Guardian*. www.theguardian.com/media/2018/dec/19/journalists-death-toll-nearly-doubles-in-2018.

Hadland, A. (2008). "Shooting the Messenger: Mediating the Public and the Role of the Media in South Africa's Xenophobic Violence." CORDESRIA. Cameroun, Democracy and Governance Reserach Institute.

Jane, E. (2016). "7 Characteristics of Effective Accountability Journalists." www.americanpressinstitute.org/publications/reports/white-papers/characteristics-effective-accountability-journalists/.

Jerz, D. (2017). "Conflict of Interest: How Journalists Avoid It." https://jerz.setonhill.edu/writing/journalism1/conflict-of-interest/.

Kuhn, R. (2011). "Historical Development of the Media in France." In *The Media in Contemporary France*. Maidenhead: McGraw-Hill Education: 5–8.

Mansour, S. (2013). *On the Divide: Press Freedom at Risk in Egypt*. New York, Committee to Protect Journalists.

Martin, R. and S. Adam (1994). *A Sourcebook of Canadian Media Law*. Ottawa ON, Carlton University Press.

Mason, P. (2012). *Why it's Kicking off Everywhere: The New Global Revolutions*. London and New York, Verso.

Meadows, M. et al. (2010). "Making Spaces: Community Media and Formation of the Democratic Public Sphere in Australia." In C. Rodriguez, D. Kidd and L. Stein (eds.), *Making our Media: Global Initiatives Toward a Democratic Public Sphere*. Kreswell NJ, Hampton Press: 163–181.

Mellinger, G. (2017). "Conflicts of Interest in Journalism: Debating a Post-Hutchins Ethical Self-Consciousness." *American Journalism* **34**(4): 386–406.

Merrill, J. (1993). *The Dialectic in Journalism*. Baton Rouge LA, Louisiana State University Press.

Muhlmann, G. (2010). *Journalism for Democracy*. Malden, Polity Press.

Newman, N. et al. (2018). "Reuters Digital News Report." Reuters.

Patching, R. and M. Hirst (2013). *Journalism Ethics:Arguments and Cases for the 21st Century*. London, Routledge.

Pearson, M. and M. Polden (2011). *The Journalist's Guide to Media Law*. Crows Nest NSW, Allen and Unwin.

Reid, A. (2013). "How Newsrooms Manage UGC in Breaking News Situations." www.journalism.co.uk/news/how-newsrooms-manage-ugc-in-breaking-news-situations/s2/a553185/.

Rosen, J. (1999). *What are Journalists For?* New Haven, Yale University Press.

Savage, J. (2019). "Australia Media Raids: Police Do Not Rule Out Prosecuting Journalists." BBC News. www.bbc.co.uk/news/world-australia-48537377.

Siebert, F. et al. (1956). *Four Theories of the Press*. Chicago, University of Illinois Press.

Silverman, C. (2014). "Last Press Council in U.S. will Close Next Month." www.poynter.org/reporting-editing/2014/last-press-council-in-u-s-will-close-next-month/.

Smith, R. F. (2008). *Ethics in Journalism*. Malden MA; Oxford, Blackwell.

White, A. (2019). Interviewed by I. Burum by email.

CHAPTER 13

DEFAMATION AND COPYRIGHT

SUMMARY

Laws that impact mobile journalism are a country-specific conundrum. However, issues of privacy, defamation and copyright that impact all journalists become exponentially relevant in a globalised, media-rich online landscape. In this chapter I take an Australian POV to describe principles of defamation and copyright law that apply to journalists. Many of these principles will apply globally; however, you should always check the information provided against your country's specific laws before you act.

OVERVIEW

Defamation law is designed to protect a person's reputation. If a publication or a speech makes the reader, viewer or listener think less of someone, that person is said to have been defamed. Defamation law is of particular interest to journalists who publish material about people. It's especially of concern to mojos, who often publish video quickly from location.

Since 2006 Australia has had uniform defamation laws designed to protect a person's reputation. Reputation is, however, a mysterious concept, and while based on a perceived view that we have of ourselves, it relates more to a social view that we have of each other, or that we feel society should have of us. A defamation suit is measured against quantifiable damage to a good name, the context of the defamatory publication and how it impacts the plaintiff in a broader community context.

The concept of reputation can be regarded as something that the marketplace might define as intangible property, not unlike good will (Post 1986), which, like a form of property, defamation law seeks to protect. The problem here is that each society can view this context differently and this artificially inflates or reduces the value of reputation, which in my career has been directly tied to my marquee value—my earning power in the industry.

So, when protecting reputation, we protect a form of property that can be quantified in the marketplace. The courts see this property as something earned, that you have worked for, using your strength, your brains, or your looks. It has what Marx might call "use value," which can be traded on. This concept of reputation as property presupposes "that individuals are connected to each other through the institution of the market," hence "a mere injury to the feelings without actual deterioration of person or property, cannot form an independent and substantive ground of proceeding" (ibid). In this definition, pecuniary loss is the basis for bringing a defamation action.

Reputation is also seen as a form of honor where a person "identifies with the normative characteristics of a particular social role and in return personally receives from others the regard and estimation that society accords to that role" (Post 1986). This reputation is not earned but claimed, and unlike reputation as property, where individuals are equal in the marketplace, honor presupposes that people are not equal and they enjoy status without deference to work. Protection means that defamation law must acknowledge and reaffirm status of social roles.

Finally, reputation is also seen as dignified. Society uses the law of defamation to protect dignity and maintain civility. Unlike reputation as property, dignity is not earned, rather it is essential in every human being (ibid) and cannot be restored through monetary damages·

THEORETICAL PERSPECTIVE

The globalisation of defamation is a real issue in the digital age where stories travel across borders in milliseconds. The law of defamation was rooted in the community in which the person dwelt and had a reputation, but with decisions like *Dow Jones & Co., Inc. v. Gutnick,*[1] defamation plaintiffs have the ability to involve long-distance defendants in court cases (Weaver and Partlett 2008).

The case resulted from an article written in the United States and uploaded from there onto the Internet. The article contained allegations about Melbourne businessman Joseph Gutnick, which he claimed were defamatory. He was able to prove that five copies of the print edition were read in Victoria. The Internet version had 550,000 subscribers, of which 1,700 had Victoria credit cards. He sued under Victoria law, claiming this was where his reputation had been damaged.

The defendants argued strongly that the case should be heard in the United States, where the article was written (and where it is more difficult for a defamation action to succeed because of a constitutional guarantee of a free press). The High Court agreed with Mr Gutnick and ruled that in deciding where the offending material had been "published," the court will look to where the offending material was received—not where it originated from. You can read the High Court's judgment in this case at www.austlii.edu.au/cgi-bin/disp.pl/au/cases/cth/high%5fct/2002/56.html?query=title+%28+%22gutnick%22+%29.

Historically, in defamation cases, the courts became the forum for protection when other methods of redress, like self-help, didn't work. Locally, church and state competed, finally fixing liability for defamation in common law, where it was seen as a tort. For a long time, in defamation cases plaintiff's prevailed so publishers were cautious about publication. "Some newspapers (especially in London) would, for example, hire 'night barristers' to read over proposed copy and help advise them regarding potential liabilities. Books on political and public figures in Australia would likewise be vetted by London barristers for potential libels"[2] (ibid).

However, just as the printing press changed the speed and the distribution of print, the Internet has globalised information flow and hence the potential scope for bringing defamation action. With international audiences, the media is today more susceptible than ever to defamation action. But with free speech being a catch-cry and smartphones enabling it to occur anytime and across borders, now more than ever a balance between reputational protection and free speech sits at the core of defamation. In a clash of values, reputational protection was given greater weight than freedom of expression.[3] As a result, at common law, defamation defendants were usually forced to bear the burden of proving that their statements were true, and generally had only a limited range of defenses at their disposal (ibid).

The common law tradition began to give way in 1964 when the United States Supreme Court rendered its landmark decision in *New York Times Co. v. Sullivan.*[4] The court "articulated broad constitutional protections for expression and limited the ability of public officials to recover for defamation," having first to prove that the defendant published the statement with actual malice (Weaver and Partlett 2008). "In other words, a plaintiff must show that the defendant 'knew' that the allegedly defamatory statement was untrue or acted with 'reckless disregard,' as to whether it was true or false" (ibid). This shifted the burden of proof from defendant to plaintiff.

The next shift away from a "malice standard" came in deliberations such as *Rosenbloom v. Metromedia, Inc.*[5] where the court suggested that the existence of constitutional protections should turn on whether the publication is related to the "public interest" (ibid), one test being the level of state interest and level of private or public concern. Through this early period of US change in defamation law, commonwealth countries maintained a common law view that defamation is a necessary protection. More recently this has begun to shift in favor of freedom of expression (ibid) (see *Lang v. Australian Broadcasting Corporation*[6] and its reliance on qualified privilege as a defense).[7] When UK courts stressed that flexibility is to be accorded to responsible journalism, they noted the "public importance, seriousness, urgency, overall tone and whether it included the claimant's position—as well as matters about the information's source, such as what steps had been taken to verify it"[8] (ibid).

Australia, the UK, New Zealand and the US have taken different approaches (constitutional and common law) to defamation laws, and while in Australia and New Zealand defamation laws are slow to provide space for free speech, the stated principle in each case involved an extension of free speech protections to defamatory speech (ibid). Having said this, if a defamation plaintiff decides to sue in the United States rather than in his home country, he will find a dramatically different and, in many respects, unfamiliar and hostile environment for the litigation. *Dow Jones & Co,. Inc. v. Gutnick*[9] determined that the plaintiff was able to show that even though Dow Jones published in the US, every download of the offending article in Australia was a publication constituting a cause for action. Not able to rely on a First Amendment defense,[10] this case had far-reaching implications on who could bring defamation action.

As speech technology and smartphones have become more democratised and the Internet more affordable and accessible, one-way information flow is now two way. Unlike the advent of the printing press in 1436, which provided content to a mass market, affordable technologies means that those who have an ability to reach a global audience now include the audience (Rosen 2006).

As the Internet of things becomes more an Internet for all people, it might help homogenise defamation laws and create global standards to account for new cross-jurisdictional communications. It's either this step or having potential defendants curbing their publication to account for the most restrictive of regimes in which the material will be downloaded. Plaintiffs will need to realise that while everyone using smartphones and the Internet is a potential publisher, not everyone publishing potentially defamatory content on the Internet will have deep pockets. And because of the speed and proliferation of online content, stopping or curbing the spread and the damage may prove difficult. From a defamation perspective, this makes trans-jurisdictional defamation suits more problematic (Weaver and Partlett 2008).

One of the great benefits of democratising mobile skills, including ethics and basic legal principles, is that citizens become more practiced at what can or can't be said, and augmenting or editing free speech becomes a learned and local determination, rather than a restrictive law.

Next is a practical primer for defamation and an overview of the fundamentals of copyright.

PRACTICAL PERSPECTIVE

Defamation

Following are a series of answers to basic questions regarding defamation that I am always asked. As a practical guide I use Pearson and Polden's *The Journalist's Guide to Media Law* (2011) because it's easy to understand. You'll find more comprehensive information about these in the above book.

What is defamation? In short, defamation is the publication of false or vilifying material that harms an individual's (the plaintiff) reputation. It is a civil wrong that allows a plaintiff to sue those who are responsible (the defendant). Anyone who participates, authorises or repeats the defamatory material can be sued.

Who can sue? In Australia any living person (there are exceptions where the estate of the deceased can sue) or entity, except a corporation or government body, can bring an action for defamation. Who can sue in your country?

Are there different types of defamation? Common law recognises two forms of defamation: slander is a false or defamatory statement that's spoken and in a transient form; libel is a false or defamatory statement that's published. In both instances, the statement causes injury to a person's reputation (see p xx). One mistake a journalist can make is publishing material that's driven by their moral outrage that doesn't meet a legal defense.

Defamation matter: Defamation can occur in the following circumstances:

- **printed matters communicated in magazines, papers and other periodicals**
- **television, radio, Internet and other forms of electronic communication**
- **a letter or note**

- **a picture, gesture or something spoken**
- **any other thing that by some means is communicated to a person**

In each of the above circumstances something might be seen to be defamatory if it conveys a defamatory imputation; it is obvious that it refers to the plaintiff; and it is published to at least one other person besides the plaintiff and defendant.[11]

The plaintiff's case is often based on the degree of damage to reputation caused by the publication of libelous or slanderous material. In this case the verdict and reward rely on three considerations:

- ***Consolation*: The plaintiff was able to prove that physical, mental or personal distress occurred due to the publication; for example, illness, humiliation, lowering of self-esteem.**
- ***Reparation*: The plaintiff demonstrated that harm was done to their personal and (if relevant) business reputation by providing evidence that financial loss or a downturn in business occurred due to the defamatory publication.**
- ***Vindication*: Looks at the attitude of others toward the plaintiff before and after the defamation occurred. Was the defendant shunned after publication?**

Mitigating damages: A damaged reputation remains damaged. A defendant may try to mitigate damages by:

1. **Apologising to the plaintiff for the defamatory publication**
2. **Publishing a correction of the defamatory matter**

Or, if the plaintiff has:

3. **Already recovered damages for defamation**
4. **Received, or agreed to receive, compensation**

Myths about Defamation: In the Australian context there are a number of myths surrounding defamation that Pearson and Polden (2011) identify:

1. **Myth: Defamation laws serve to restore a person's damaged reputation.**

Reality: Once damaged, a reputation is rarely restored, and damages are monetary and a way of compensating for this fact.

2. **Myth: Defamation makes a mockery of press freedom.**
   Reality: Press freedom relies in part on practicing good journalism and this means staying within the bounds of defamation law.
3. **Myth: Journalists don't get sued for defamation, only their publications do.**
   Reality: Not true.
4. **Myth: I'm protected if I quote someone else making a defamatory statement.**
   Reality: Not true, but there are some situations, such as reporting from Parliament, that are protected by "qualified privilege." Check in your jurisdiction.
5. **Myth: I'm safe if I give both sides of the story.**
   Reality: Not True.
6. **Myth: Accidents happen, and it was an honest mistake.**
   Reality: Ignorance is no defense.
7. **Myth: It's okay to publish the truth.**
   Reality: Being able to prove the truth is often difficult and most important.
8. **Myth: Poor people don't sue.**
   Reality: While legal aid in Australia is not available to bring defamation action, there are lawyers who will work on a no-win no-fee basis.

Defamation period: The new laws in Australia prescribe that there is a 12-month window from the date of publication for the plaintiff to lodge a claim of defamation, unless the plaintiff can convince the court that it was not reasonable to do so. In this case it can be extended to three years. Check in your country.

The Internet of bad news travels fast: Earlier we discussed the *Dow Jones v. Gutnick* case where, in a landmark decision about the impact of regional and physical location on restricting actionable publications, the High Court of Australia found in favor of Gutnick.

Tip: Because a person claiming to be defamed will sit on their reputation, the way to avoid defamation is to make sure that the information you have is correct and, importantly, that you can prove it's true. Getting the right permission helps, as does giving the person you are commenting about the right of reply.

Finally, it's important to check and understand your country's defamation laws and see a professional before you publish. Bearing this advice in mind, here is a simple defamation checklist:

- **is the statement true and importantly can you prove that it is?**
- **does it discredit someone?**
- **is it published (it will be in the case of mojo stories)?**
- **does it identify the person?**
- **has the journalist been negligent, or deliberately tried to defame someone?**

In an era of post-truth comment it's easy to slip—everyone is doing it—so it's important to think before you speak and write—what is it I'm saying, why and what's the impact? This is where defamation defense begins and ends.

Copyright

After diversity one of the most important reasons I shoot my own material is copyright. Owning copyright enables me to leverage my skills, contacts and equipment into a sustainable production model. One of the first things I tell mojo trainees and students is don't delete your footage, because that unique shot on the Amazon River, among the ruins of Aleppo, travelling on the Nile, or that moment with a homeless child, is worth money. You may also need it when you produce an update on your story, or when your story needs verification.

This section introduces a number of concepts around copyright. Once again it is seen from an Australian perspective, but I have referenced US laws and kept it general, so that much will apply to your mojo world. When dealing with copyright it is always important to seek professional advice before acting.

What is copyright? Copyright encourages creative expression by providing authors of a work with exclusive rights to make and sell copies of their works, to create derivatives, and the right to perform or display their works publicly. Copyright is a form of intellectual property embodied in Australian law in the provisions of the Copyright Act 1968 (Cth). In the US, where copyright is governed by the 1976 Copyright Act (enacted in 1978), it also sits in the intellectual property bucket; in the UK copyright law is governed by the Copyright, Designs and Patents Act 1988 and, as in Australia, registration is not required but vested immediately to the author of:

- **literary works**
- **dramatic works**
- **musical works**
- **artistic works and other subject matter such as:**
    - **films**
    - **sound recordings**
    - **broadcasts**
    - **published editions**

It is important to understand that in Australia, the US and the UK copyright protects the skill and labor involved in a particular expression of ideas in a physical medium (the work or the expression of the idea), not the information or ideas as such.

Who owns the copyright on your work? By Australian, US and UK law the author does, or more correctly, the authors do. If you went on an internship, which is not deemed as employment, and wrote an article, Australian copyright law gives you rights in that material. However, if your supervisor rewrote portions of that article, they too could claim copyright in that work. So, protecting your original work is critical.

Copyright for hire: In general, the copyright owner is the author/creator/maker of the work in question. However, a work created in the context of employment, or as it's referred to in the US, works made for hire, is generally owned by the employer. A work created by a contractor is owned by the contractor; however, it is possible to vary these provisions by agreement.

What am I protecting? Copyright is a protection of an expression of a thought—not the idea. The Australian Copyright Act is a bundle of exclusive rights in relation to the work or material in question. They include the rights:

- **to copy or reproduce the work**
- **to make an adaptation of it**

- **to publish it**
- **to perform it in public**
- **to broadcast it to the public**

When can we use material without permission? In Australia there are a number of exceptions that allow copyright-protected material to be used in certain ways without permission. These include Fair Dealing for the purpose of:

- ***Research or study*—does not constitute a breach of copyright if the purpose is for research or study; if the work could not otherwise be obtained in time at a reasonable commercial price; if the impact of its use under fair dealings on the value of the work, the amount used (10% or a single chapter) is seen as reasonable.**
- ***Criticism or review*—does not constitute an infringement of the copyright in the work if it is for the purpose of criticism or review of that or of another work, and a sufficient acknowledgment of title and author of the work is made. Criticism and review involve making a judgment of the material or of the underlying ideas. It may be strongly expressed, humorous, and need not be balanced as long as it's a genuine review and the material is used for making comparison or making a point.**
- ***Parody or satire*—under fair dealings a copyrighted work can be used for the purpose of parody or satire.**
- ***Reporting the news*—if it is for the purpose of, or is associated with, the reporting of news in a newspaper, magazine or similar periodical, cinema or electronic, and a sufficient acknowledgment of title and author of the work is made, it is fair dealings.**
- ***Reproduction for judicial proceedings or legal advice*—if it is for the purpose of the giving of professional advice by:**
    - **a legal practitioner**
    - **a person registered as a patent attorney**
    - **a person registered as a trademarks attorney**

In Australia, educational institutions can hold and use copyrighted material as long as it is for a prescribed course and is included in the collection of the school library. The specific circumstances of how using copyright-protected material without permission in an online environment will determine whether or not fair dealing applies.

Copyright in social media, websites and blogs: Protects material commonly appearing on websites, blogs, social media platforms and cloud-based services. A complete website, blog or social media platform is not protected by copyright, but its individual components are; for example:

- **The written articles and photographs on a blog, Facebook or Twitter post will each be separately protected.**
- **The text, musical works and sound recordings on a band's website will each be separately protected.**
- **Text, video and images on a museum's website will each be separately protected.**

Using content created by others in websites, blogs or social media platforms: If you are using material created by others (third-party material) in a website, blog or social media platform:

- **Be sure that you actually have permission when using copyright-protected material created by others**
- **Keep records of any permissions you obtain**
- **Check the various copyright licenses that social media sites allow**

Express permission: In some instances, the copyright owner has already granted express permission for anyone to use the material in certain ways. For example, YouTube and Facebook have express permissions, or general licenses, like those promoted by Creative Commons (CC) that are especially useful for people not intending to generate income from CC usage. This will require attribution of source and creator.

Creative Commons is a not-for-profit that is building a globally accessible library of knowledge by providing CC licenses that give a free, standardised way to grant copyright permissions and ensure proper attribution in creative and academic works, and allow others to copy, distribute and make use of those works.

When using CC, creators choose a set of conditions they wish to apply to their work. The examples below are copied from https://creativecommons.org/use-remix/cc-licenses/Conditions:

> ***Attribution (by)*: CC licenses require that others who use your work in any way give you credit the way you request, but not in a way that suggests you**

endorse them or their use. If they want to use your work without giving you credit or for endorsement purposes, they must get your permission first.

ShareAlike (sa): **Others can copy, distribute, display, perform, and modify your work as long as they distribute any modified work on the same terms. If they want to distribute modified works under other terms, they must get your permission first.**

NonCommercial (nc): **Others can copy, distribute, display, perform and (unless you have chosen NoDerivatives) modify and use your work for any purpose other than commercially, for which they must get your permission first.**

NoDerivatives (nd): **You let others copy, distribute, display and perform only original copies of your work. If they want to modify your work, they must get your permission first.**

At https://creativecommons.org/use-remix/cc-licenses/ you'll find the six express licenses that are based on the above conditions. When working with social media, check their licences and what the terms are before use—always.

Implied permission: In some cases, such as commissioning someone to write a story or shoot a video, you may have an implied permission (a license) even though the owner has not formally granted a license. Because determining the scope of implied permission can be difficult, it is preferable to get express permission quantifying uses, in writing.

How long does copyright last? In Australia from 1 January 2019 the following apply:

- **Works (literary, dramatic or musical)—70 years after the author's death**
- **Works with unknown author—70 years after making, or 70 years after first made public (if within 50 years of making)**
- **Sound and film recording—70 years after making, or 70 years after first made public (if within 50 years of making)**

In the US, for works created on or after 1 January 1978, copyright in general lasts the life of the author plus 70 years; for anonymous works, pseudonymous works, and works made for hire, the copyright endures for a term of 95 years from the year of its first publication, or a term of 120 years from the year of its creation, whichever expires first. A detailed explanation can be found at this link: www.copyright.gov/title17/title17.pdf.

The public domain: Once copyright expires it is often referred to as being in the "public domain." Different countries' laws about copyright mean that the same content may be out of copyright in one country but still protected in another. For example, under Australian law, copyright has expired in a photograph taken before 1 January 1955, yet it could still be protected under US law. In this case, there is no issue with uploading that picture within Australia and offering access to persons located in Australia but not the US. This poses a potential risk of action if the material is used online (see *Dow Jones v. Gutnick*).

Moral rights

Creators of copyright material have the following rights:

- **to be attributed when their work is used**
- **not to have their work falsely attributed to someone else, nor to have the altered work attributed as if it were unaltered**
- **not to have the work treated in a manner that would prejudice the creator's honor or reputation**

In some cases, you may be able to defend yourself against a claim by arguing it was reasonable not to attribute a creator, or to treat the work in a way that could prejudice the creator's honor or reputation. However, in most cases it is preferable to get the creator to consent to the way you want to use his or her material.

Defamation and copyright are essential concepts for mojos to grasp, not only so that we stay out of trouble, but because understanding copyright, in particular, has its own rewards. I generally try and publish content that I know and can prove is true and attribute regularly. Everyone can make a mistake especially when it comes to copyright. Checking the laws in your country, asking a professional and checking again, is most important and rectifying mistakes as quickly as possible is essential.

In conclusion, I've spent years dealing with copyright issues and have tried very hard to attribute all uses of material. This is the least we can do to make sure that struggling musicians, writers and filmmakers get their dues. The brief overview in this chapter is an introduction to copyright. Defamation is also an interesting concept. Over my time I have never been sued for defamation; I had been threatened, or at least the program I was producing had, but never sued. That either means I never do hard stories, or that I am careful. I'd like to think it's because I know the law and, when needed, seek expert advice before publishing.

My tip for dealing with copyright and defamation is to seek legal advice when in doubt and before publishing.

Go mojo ...

NOTES

1 *Dow Jones & Co., Inc. v. Gutnick* was an Internet defamation case. The 28 October 2000 edition of Barron's Online, published by Dow Jones, contained an article entitled "Unholy Gains" in which several references were made to the respondent, Joseph Gutnick, who contended that part of the article defamed him. Gutnick brought the suit in Australia because the Internet version of the magazine had 1,700 Australian-based credit cards. All seven High Court justices decided that Gutnick had the right to sue for defamation at his primary residence and the place he was best known. The High Court decided that defamation occurred as soon as a third party read the publication and thought less of the individual who was defamed.

2 Paul Barry's *The Rise and Fall of Kerry Packer* was vetted like this.

3 See *Gertz v. Welch*, 418 U.S. 323 (1974); see also Russell L. Weaver, Andrew Kenyon, Clive C. P. Walker and David F. Partlett, *The Right to Speak III: Defamation, Reputation & Free Speech* 4–15 (2006) (hereafter *The Right to Speak III*). On the definition of reputation, see Lawrence McNamara, *Reputation and Defamation* (2008), arguing that reputation is a community's moral judgment.

4 *New York Times Co. v. Sullivan*, 376 U.S. 254 (1964), was a landmark decision where the US Supreme Court ruled that protections in the 1st Amendment to the US Constitution restrict the ability of American public officials to sue for defamation.

5 403 U.S. 29 (1971).

6 *Lange v. Australian Broadcasting Corporation* is a High Court of Australia case that upheld the existence of an implied freedom of political communication in the Australian Constitution. However, that did not itself provide a defense to a defamation action. The High Court extended the defense of qualified privilege to be compatible with the freedom of political communication. The High Court found that ABC had defamed Lange.

7 (1997) 189 C.L.R. 520, 521 (Austl.).

8 *The Right to Speak III*, supra, at 103.

9 (2002) 210 C.L.R. 575 (Austl.).

10 Enables freedom of speech, a free press and the rights of people to protest and to petition the government for a redress of grievances.

11 See Pearson and Polden (2001) *The Journalists Guide to Media Law* for a comprehensive description of each.

REFERENCES

Pearson, M. and M. Polden (2011). *The Journalist's Guide to Media Law.* Crows Nest NSW, Allen and Unwin.

Post, R. C. (1986). "The Social Foundations of Defamation Law: Reputation and the Constitution." *Californian Law Review* **74**(3): 691–742.

Rosen, J. (2006). "The People Formerly Known as the Audience." *PressThink* http://archive.pressthink.org/2006/06/27/ppl_frmr.html.

Weaver, R. and D. Partlett (2008). "The Globalization of Defamation." https://law.anu.edu.au/sites/all/files/partlett_paper.doc.

CHAPTER 14

TRAINING: A COMMON PEDAGOGICAL BRIDGE

SUMMARY

The aim of this chapter is to introduce a discussion around pedagogy for transforming mobile user-generated content (UGC) to a more autonomous and complete subfield of mobile journalism that I call user-generated story (UGS). This chapter shifts the lens from a techno-determinist view to the importance of digital storytelling skills and reflectivity. In essence, it attempts to bring some order to the complex mobile space. This chapter, which discusses issues related to mojo training, distinguishes between the various forms of mojo training; investigates a multimedia storytelling view, specifically at secondary school; discusses how mojo might be introduced into the tertiary journalism curriculum; summarises a pedagogical approach and an evaluation scaffold; and introduces various ethical issues that need further consideration.

OVERVIEW

Currently mojo training is very popular across spheres of communication where it is taught as short training workshops to journalists and executives, as longer developed courses to people in the marginalised world, and as part of university curricula. It is being taught by broadcast technicians, radio, print and TV journalists, academics, and television producers. In some cases, mojo is being taught by people with no video, journalism or communications experience. In these cases, it is often taught as a very flat, single-planar form. Hildegunn Soldal, the former online editor of the *Guardian*, suggests that we might need a mini-disruption in mobile for it to reach its true potential:

> I definitely believe we need to tell stories in a way that works on a mobile phone—but using the right tools/effects to tell that particular story in the best way. Some stories are more visual, some need graphics, audio, photographs, some work best as a written story—but more and more I think we can blend them to keep the audience engaged in the story. And with the help of technology we can also allow the user to choose the most convenient format for them at any time.
>
> (Soldal 2019)

In essence we need to shift the focus away from mobile tools and focus on story, audience and platform to help determine the level of integration between tools and the story format. As Soldal says, "We need to start with the question 'What's the best way to tell this story?'"

McLuhan's (1964) well-known trope about communications in the twentieth century, "the medium is the message," suggests that the "personal and social consequences of any medium … of any extension of our selves—result from the new scale that is introduced into our affairs by each extension of ourselves, or by any new technology" (1964). Mobile technologies are, in a sense, an extension of ourselves. They are changing the way we communicate and the power balance between what Bourdieu (2005) described as fields of communication. Notwithstanding this shift, unless mojo trainers include people trained in journalism and especially video production, we might, as Soldal suggests, need a disruption.

One of our tasks as educators is to find core training models and curricula to enable a common digital language (CDL) across three spheres of communication—in schools, community and the workplace. The commonality of this philosophy was espoused by cultural critic Raymond Williams (2000) more than half a century ago when he said that we need "a common education, that will give our society its cohesion and prevent it disintegrating into a series of specialist departments." Yet it's the specialist, or niche, nature of the Web, and its accessibility via mobile, that's one of its great draw cards. A key consideration for educators is whether digital cultural values are aligned to technology, skill sets, culture or a combination of all three?

PRACTICAL PERSPECTIVE

Mediums and their Messages

Practitioners working in a converging digital landscape need to know how to work across screens, platforms and fields. For example, a print journalist may have decided not to use shorthand and never again to record audio-only interviews now that he/she is using a smart device that makes recording pictures and stripping audio a breeze. Stylistically and editorially, certain elements are required to manifestly decode or embellish a desired message when it's produced as a video story across a variety of screens and platforms. In radio, voice and pauses told a story, but in video we also like to see supplementary B roll[1] to heighten story dynamics. Hence, it's important that trainers understand the various levels of digital media literacy. It's therefore critical that any discussion around the translation of literacies in the convergent space begins by addressing the trainer's own understanding of digital video literacies, mediums, styles, workflows, platforms and digital options.

Meyrowitz (1998) describes three media literacy concepts impacting challenge-based mobile video training and praxis:

- ***Content literacy*** **is an ability to analyse a mediated text or other kinds of messages, ideas and behaviors that move between mediums—structure, who the creators are, economic and political influence—and is a key to understanding the mediated nature of content. How institutional and commercial forces impact the same story differ between its radio report and its TV report, and across TV genres such as news and current affairs and general production.**

  This focus on media content is an aspect of communication that's not specific to media practitioners. Moreover, one could argue that for democracy to function every citizen needs to know about content literacy—how to analyse media and its political economy and how to create countervailing messaging.
- ***Media as language or grammar*** **suggests that media has its own language and grammar that varies across mediums. For example, one person can't sing a melody and harmony at the same time, unless it is in a multi-track audio recording. Hence the need to understand how visual and audio languages and associated production variables within each medium are typically used to attempt to shape perception. Because grammar alters depending on the medium, when educators or practitioners first begin working with video, invariably there are new languages to learn. Understanding media grammar means being able to manipulate its elements to affect message content and meaning.**
- ***Media literacy*****: This is understanding the functions (technological) of a medium both on a micro and a macro level and how it's impacted by its environment and how each shapes key aspects of communication at a singular and a social level. The list below by Meyrowitz (1998) identifies sample characteristics that can be used to distinguish one medium from another (e.g., radio vs television). For example:**
  - **Type of sensory information (visual, oral, olfactory)**

- **The form of information within each sense (picture vs written word, clicks vs voice)**
- **Uni-directional vs bi-directional vs multi-directional (radio vs telephone vs online)**
- **Simultaneous vs sequential (multi-response vs in turn)**
- **Nature of dissemination (one to one vs one to many vs many to many)**

It's in media literacy, in particular, that I find a level of digital "trainer skill lag" (TSL), a situation where some teachers might lack the requisite digital knowledge to be able to develop and train beyond a flat and limited representation of the language.

Production variables can be manipulated within each medium to alter perception of message content (the list in Fig 14.1 has been developed from Meyrowitz, with Online/Web added):

Table 14.1 Type of production variables that can alter message meaning

Print media	Stills photography	Radio and audio	Video, TV and film	Online/Web
Size and shape of the type face, it's style and color and how its laid up in line, paragraph and page form.	Size of the frame and the positioning of the subject, in a black and white or color representation, either grainy or high-resolution, with particular focal depth.	The level of ancillary or multi-track audio, music, special FX and perspective.	The use of interviewees, stand-ups, narration, B roll, special FX, style of editing and the fine line between objectivity and subjectivity that impacts multi-planar story construction.	Transformation of audio and video elements across platforms and screens can take on varied perspectives.

Cultural and institutional forces tend to encourage particular uses of grammar and can restrict one's ability to manipulate them in media productions. Here are additional examples of how visual variables can operate in a video, TV or movie, and in a mojo context:

- **Shots sizes alter perceptions of reality in both factual and fiction sequences and play on our sense of interpersonal space that shifts culturally. For example, close-ups simulate intimate personal responses to key characters and moments. Highlighting a character's reaction to their own violent act in close-up** presents a specific view of that character at that point in the sequence/program. In drama and factual shows, in particular, the use of framing acts as a form of writing that embellishes natural story drama without making it look like it's been embellished. Gaye Tuchman (1978) calls this an "aura of representation." For example, mojos choosing not to shoot themselves in close-up for a less dramatic and a wider, possibly more objective frame.

- Camera angles are another tool to convey position—low angle (camera below subject) equals power, level is peer to peer, and high angle suggests a diminutive or weak person.
- Lens choice plays with our perception of background and foreground, with long lenses compressing the two and leaving the viewer with a sense of claustrophobia and impending impact.
- Handheld or sticks is part of a relational grammar that impacts the interpersonal and the dynamic feel of a sequence/program and is often shot on wide lens and close to the action.
- Editing choice further impacts the viewer's belief sensors. If you are making a documentary and you follow a cop to a door, where she knocks, having the next shot as an interior of the person opening the door breaks the reality spell—our camera is out not in—and can only happen in drama. Editing grammar helps settle perceptions of allegiance and style while playing a key role in the manipulation of a public's perception of the sequence/program. Media grammar literacy should also involve awareness of the impact of not as easily "seen" sound-track elements.

The Convergent Space

Teaching convergent media, including mobile journalism, requires an appreciation of the above characteristics that inform a set of questions about what media is and how it functions to deliver messages. Moreover, the holistic skills and increased level of cultural and social capital required to produce complete mobile stories—to transform user-generated content (UGC) to effective user-generated stories (UGS)—begins an intellectual archival process, described as the Lasswell process, where we ask who says what to whom, in what channel, with what effect. This deeper thought process encourages creators to think more about their content in cultural, social, economic and politicised terms. In a digital context, this can encourage what's been described as online clustering by like-minded individuals

(Newman and Park 2003) around what Wenger (2001) calls functional and supportive communities of practice.

This level of thought about what, why and where to publish can help shape what Barbara Gentikow (2007) calls a nation's cultural canon. This cultural thought process potentially gives rise to eudemonic pursuits such as increased civic mindfulness. This identity-forming shift begins once we move from the early sublime stage of artifact evolution, where we are awestruck by hedonic functionality, to the more banal stage, when artifacts shift from being "sources of utopian visions," to "forces for social and economic change" (Mosco 2004). Henry Jenkins (2008) believes this shift first occurs in the brain of the individual through what he coins convergence talk, which he says is the time taken to discover, agree and settle on change. This shift begins even with raw UGC, which has its own use value, something Archer (2007) calls "self-talk." One role of the teacher in delivering a mobile curriculum might be to focus praxis beyond the initial user experience, to more eudemonic community-minded pursuits, where UGC is developed into civic-minded UGS.

A Case for Spinning UGC into UGS

It's important to begin defining mojo potential in the early stages of the tech adoption. Boczkowski (2004) points out that much of what becomes unique or revolutionary about new technology usually develops at the outset of its use—during the sublime stage; hence it's imperative we begin the attitudinal shift from passive receivers to proactive consumers as early as possible after technology adoption.

One way of achieving this is for education to embrace the challenge of a multi-planar video storytelling language. As this becomes more relational across spheres of communication, the growing level of video literacy opens up new opportunities for media research and pedagogy. These opportunities result in new levels of praxis and outcome. In the process, citizens, students and digitally trained journalists become interlocutors or "force-fields ... reacting to one another" (Benson and Neveu 2005). The mojo skill set is a binding agent for connecting creative fibers—raw UGC—in a relational narrative that maintains the uniqueness of each participating voice. As the narrative, or self-talk that exalts UGC to the lofty heights of citizen journalism grows, it becomes self-supporting non-productive folklore. And like any unresolved narrative—like the Arab Spring rioters' use of smartphones to galvanise society into a life-changing revolution—it can fail to fulfill its long-term function, in this case,

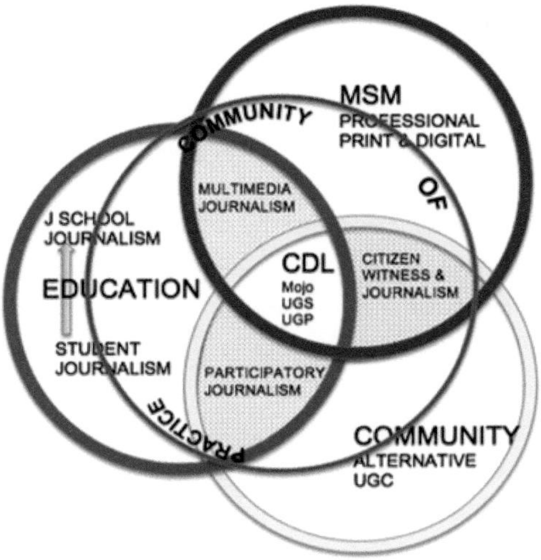

Figure 14.1 **Spheres of communication.**

Ivo Burum

to be a sustained voice with the resonance of powerful citizen journalism.[2] Without story skills and associated structures (news, social media, Web TV, proprietary sites) the fibers float online in fragmented, unwoven, unfulfilled forms. A common digital language (CDL) can help join UGC fibers into diverse user-generated stories (UGS), which can be produced locally by professional, student or citizen journalists.

Joining the Dots—Building Social Communities of Practice

Training creates a successful marriage between skills and technology. It enables mojos to perform tasks—research, produce and publish—that result in output. Each task, like each individual UGC fiber, becomes more complex and involved as mojo narratives develop from research through production (filming, editing) to publication. This transformative phase generates a more digitally aware user, with greater literacy and increased self-confidence. As users begin to recognise each other's content creation signals (their online UGS), they begin uniting (weaving) in concert in niche online virtual communities of practice, or network societies (Wenger 2007, Castells 2008). Through these online societies galvanised by a growing narrative, citizens potentially gain new forms of social power and ways to organise themselves. These clusters potentially create a new diverse field of collective cross-spherical journalism designed to promote a greater level of democracy, something that didn't always occur with the Arab Spring, where media used citizen UGC to wrap and color their own stories.[3]

One of the few times UGC was structured by citizens in the Arab Spring was on Wael Ghonim's Facebook page, *We are all Khaled Said* (2010). While Hirst (2012) is right, one tweet does not a revolution make, a lot of them can form story chains. Ghonim collated the social media noise into his Facebook page to give it form. The page galvanised Springers, showing them that they were not alone and had a collective ownership in the outcome and the story of the Arab Spring that he published using their UGC. This galvanising effect potentially occurs when citizens learn to weave their own UGC into more complete thought-out UGS narratives. They potentially begin to transform anonymous network societies into democratic communities of practice who have a more engaged eudemonic voice.

Mojo: Transforming Behavioral Aspects within Media and Communication Pedagogy

The mojo described in this book was first developed from self-shot[4] local journalism workshops that the author ran in an inner-city school. Storytelling was used as an intervention to help students engage with each other, the curriculum and their community. Students of all ages are drawn to the opportunity to engage in local storytelling because it provides an opportunity to speak out, like the Arab Springers did, to protect what they viewed as their collective interest.

As identified by Clark and Monserrate (2011), the idea that storytelling can redress alienation tendencies is consistent with emergent concepts of self-actualised and engaged citizenship among students of all ages who practice journalism (Burum 2012, 2018). Clark and Monserrate posit that "participation in the culture of high school journalism can provide young people with opportunities to develop the skills and experiences necessary for civic engagement, including the experience of collective decision-making" (2011: 417).

These pedagogies are also grounded in behavioral psychology and educational developmental theories such as the Positive Development Model (PDM). Small and Memmo (2004)

Table 14.2 PDM assets and mojo intersect

Asset	Impact of mojo
Helping youth achieve their full potential is the best way to prevent them from experiencing problems.	Mojo builds literacy and holistic multi-media skills, which develop confidence that increases potential.
Youth need support and opportunities to succeed.	Mojo training provides core teamwork skills that enable mojos to recognise and work with support networks to achieve short-term and sustainable goals and individual skills that support personal growth.
Communities need to mobilise and build capacity to support the positive development of youth.	Mojo promotes community journalism practices and principles that politicise engagement and increase local capacity for civic-minded engagement.
Youth should not be viewed as problems to be fixed but as partners who are cultivated and developed.	Mojo advocates local and hyperlocal working models, where mojos, community and local media integrate through shared skills and goals.

described a broad set of individual attributes and PDM assets that impact youth. Burum (2018) describes how mojo training intersects with these assets in Table 14.2.

Built around specific developmental assets, or building blocks, PDM assets reflect internal and external qualities that can be aligned with mojo imperatives:

- **Support development—Mojo praxis encourages development of the individual and their role as a team member. This leads to a greater appreciation of their role in family and community.**
- **Empowerment shifts—As mojos begin to appreciate their individual worth and communal values, new opportunities emerge for engagement with local services.**
- **Boundaries and expectations shift—Production, organisational and editorial mojo skills help establish an understanding of the need for structures in society, at home and at school.**
- **Constructive use of time—Mojo praxis requires and encourages time management skills.**
- **Commitment to learning—Published mojo stories lead to positive reinforcement and generate a thirst for further learning.**

- **Social competencies—Successful mojo praxis requires planning interviews, filming, editing and publishing, which involve weaving school and community relationships to form a basis for mojo interaction.**
- **Positive identity—Overall mojo praxis leads to greater self-esteem as mojos receive recognition and connect with family and community and plan for the future.**

A Case for Mojo in Journalism Education

Teaching journalism as a silo model may not be viable. In large universities, like big corporations, making this cultural and curricular shift can often be difficult. In 2020, at La Trobe university in Australia, media industries students get a varied introduction to video and mobile storytelling. In the first year they form groups to produce stories and package these into TV programs; in the second year they do a mobile storytelling unit where they dig deep into story, mobile skills and the digital ecosphere; in the third year they combine that training into a thematically driven, more-developed set of stories and programs using a variety of tools. At the core of all this exists a storytelling culture.

One of the advantages we are seeing with mobile training is that it offers a personal experience. Each student works at their own pace as they immerse themselves into a holistic mobile skill set that's required in journalism. But many university journalism lecturers still have issues seeing mobile as a legitimate teaching tool when, in fact, mobile is much more; it's our new digital pen.

What should journalism schools teach their students? At Reynolds in Missouri, the priority is more scientific economic journalism research. Since 2013, Columbia University has been graduating double-degree majors in computer science and journalism. At Munk, in Toronto, subject experts are recruited to become journalists in their own disciplines. The Poynter Institute is researching distance learning, and Rosental Alves, at the University of Texas, is training across international borders. And in Melbourne our media industries program, which includes a mobile storytelling subject, explores the future shape of our media industry.

Raju Narisetti, Professor of Professional Practice at Columbia Journalism School, believes a first step to deciding what to teach lies in redefining the news business and how news organisations develop the experience around content (2018). Key to this is understanding the relationship between converging technologies and content. Geir Ruud, CBO of NTB, the Norwegian wire service, says education needs to play a pivotal role in transforming journalists' perceptions and business practices from analog to digital, and desk to hand-held. He believes there's still a role for the traditional journalist if the traditional journalist is not too traditional. Ruud believes "journalists should start with social media training on day one of the academy ... if you want to be a carpenter you get a hammer and nail on day one, start training" (cited in Burum 2018). And that's a perfect fit for mojo, says Ruud. "Getting the thing done and delivered that's what mojo does ... most days you can make 3 stories a day, or 13 if you work for our website. Give them a computer and an iPhone and see if they can float" (ibid).

Journalism education, the bridge to Ruud's practical approach, teaches students to search for answers and seek to develop and promote pathways to truth and civic-minded citizens, or at least it should. The mojo training advocated in this book takes a neo-journalistic, or market-driven approach. Elements of legacy and multimedia journalism are used to form a skill set that includes the analytical and turnaround skills required in the 24-hour news cycle and story skills needed to work on longer-form storytelling. There are four essential components to the new journalism and communication curriculum:

- **Digital skills—Mojo provides skills that enable journalists to shoot video, record audio, write, edit and to publish across social platforms and devices from a mobile.**
- **Journalistic integrity—Enabling community and student mojos to publish early in their training instills an early appreciation of a need to get it right and to keep it balanced.**
- **Knowing the business of journalism—the more journalists begin to work independently, the greater their need to understand their business, audience and market.**
- **The ability to research, verify and write—are key journalistic skills that will always be relevant. Strong research and writing necessitate literacy, inquiry, verification, skepticism, knowledge of ethics and legal implications.**

Roger Patching's (1996) journalism training conundrum, "900 into 300 won't go," indicated there were three times as many journalism graduates as there were jobs in journalism. Desktop publishing gives "many graduates the opportunity to produce boutique publications" (1996: 60). Similarly, mobile skills provide an opportunity to produce UGS and UGP. These story and program-making skills potentially alter Patching's equation by creating more job opportunities for journalism students, who are now also trained to produce long-form programs for Web TV and over-the-top (OTT) digital broadcast portals.[5]

Evaluating Change: Mojo as a Transformative Pedagogical Tool for Twenty-first-century Learning

This pedagogical approach for mojo training is an experiential learning or challenge-based methodology that involves increasing knowledge by interacting with opportunities (tasks). There are a number of approaches that I use:

- ***Constructivist*—where meaning comes through cultural and social or engaged capital, from habitus to social and field engagement.**
- ***Reflective*—inquiry approach that mojo supports and that enables an ongoing evaluation of the curriculum.**
- ***Integrative*—where students connect with community and learn real-world problem-solving approaches.**
- ***Collaborative*—video development, production and reflection by fellow students using mobiles facilitate online collaboration beyond the classroom structure and immediate augmentation of work and teaching.**

The challenge-based nature of mojo work leads to inquiry where students drill down into the project to identify truth and production imperatives. As is common in challenge-based learning, organic milestones need to be met before moving to the next phase of story development. These milestones mirror standard story production pathways and unlock the next phase of the learning process.

Harvard Professor Ruben Puentedura believes we need to rewrite our definitions of communications, especially the relationship between technology and learning. Puentedura suggests that because we live in a mobile world, we should not be thinking about "a computer in fixed location 'A' at school and a computer in fixed location 'B' at home" (2013). We should be thinking about "what can a student do at all locations between school and home [and] how do we go from traditional learning places to a continuum of learning spaces so that the entire world becomes a place of learning for the students" (2013). Indeed, this is a mobile-first philosophy.

Past research on technological approaches to education such as Bloom's taxonomy (Fig 14.2) developed in 1956, transitioned pedagogical scaffolds and concepts of learning from behaviorist models to those that are more constructivist in nature. Today, Bloom's taxonomy has a number of identified shortcomings, including that evaluation occurs at the top of its scaffold.

Evaluation	▲	Use knowledge and learning to make judgment about the value of thing or product
Synthesis	│	Structure information in new way to propose alternative solutions
Analysis	│	Break information into segments to better understand possibilities and support thesis
Application	│	Apply used knowledge in a learned or new context
Comprehension	│	Grasp the meaning of information, materials and/or facts
Knowledge	│	Recall facts or remember previously learned information

Figure 14.2 **Bloom's taxonomy.**

Ivo Burum

If, as Bloom says, evaluation is a judgment based on criteria either "determined by the student, or those which are given to him" (Bloom and Krathwohl 1984), it follows that evaluation could occur at every stage of the learning scaffold as new information is received. An alternative delivery model I use is called SAMR (substitution, augmentation, modification and redefinition). Developed by Puentedura, SAMR explains how technology and practices such as mojo can be integrated into classrooms. The use value of technology at each stage of the SAMR scaffold alters and either enhances or transforms the task. SAMR suits the multi-planar nature of mojo and most task-oriented visual-type work.

Figure 14.3 describes the various developmental stages of the SAMR model:

***Substitution*: Technology acts as a substitute without functional change, for example, using a word processor to write a script instead of a pen. Mojo provides a story construct around which to discover the impact of the technology.**

***Augmentation*: Technology acts to augment the task, resulting in functional improvement—searchable word tool, spell checker, font enhancement or**

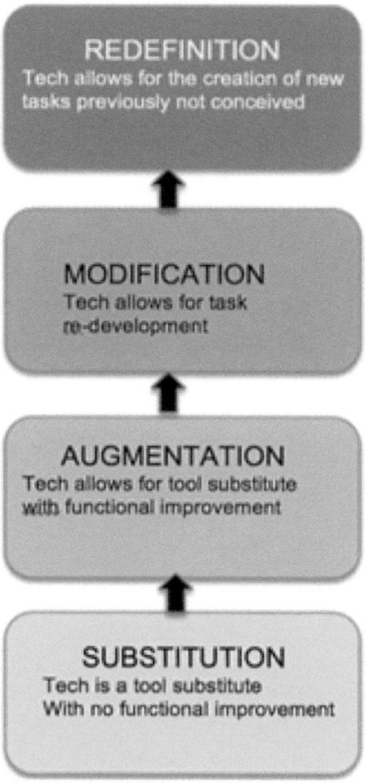

Figure 14.3 **Developmental stages of the SAMR model.**

Ivo Burum

format to write and develop the script. Mojo provides research parameters with technology enabling searchable characters in a script commenced at the substitution stage.

In the next, and first stage of the transformation phase, mojo acts as an educational tool for enhancing classroom experience, literacy levels and to build student confidence.

***Modification*: Technology modifies and transforms the task—visualisation of the script with a storyboard in a form that can be rearranged on the page, with associated audio grabs of readings, video and data mind maps of links to themes, plot settings and character, which can be presented via a Word document, spreadsheet, or PowerPoint. The task is modified from a flat individual local task to one that can be viewed online and modified by others.**

Redefinition: **Technology enables the creation of previously inconceivable tasks. Mojo skills transform a written story, or script, into a digital UGS ready for immediate global exposure, online publication between schools and other communities to provide real-time feedback and perspective.**

Clark and Monserrate found that school-based journalism models can transform a student's perspective "beyond peer groups to some form of collective identity" (2011). Constanza-Chock (2011) contends that a eudemonic conscience can only be achieved through a search for identity and a desire to belong to a broader world that encompasses school, home and community (2011). One of the by-products of authorising student views—primary, secondary and tertiary—through mobile journalism studies is that students find their own civic identity. As mojo helps young people become more expressive, it potentially begins a new dialectic between curriculum and the community, theory and praxis, and alternative and more mainstream perceptions of the role of the media in community and education.

Moreover, it's anticipated that students will carry their civic-minded attitude from the school community and campus into adult life. In some cases, this may involve transitioning through tertiary journalism studies, where students will modify their attitudes about participatory citizen journalism to accord with professional fields. This type of classroom approach, which authorises agency and the individual student voice, works to encourage a discursive reflectivity about family and community and potentially empowers students "as knowledgeable participants in learning conversations" (Bishop, Berryman et al. 2009).

In closing, it is clear that media is facing manifold issues as it continues its convergence from print to digital publishing and beyond. As described by Deuze (2012), journalists should be living a "media life extreme" because, like the rest of us, their personal and work life "takes place in media" and today we "can only imagine a life outside of media." Journalists say they are not afraid of convergence but are worried about not having enough time to do the job right. The 24-hour news cycle requires journalists to do more, much more quickly. Hence, finding enough time for upskilling is always difficult. However, multimedia skills are key for journalists, and the lack of these potentially creates new divisions between professionals and non-professionals who may have these skills.

One issue is that historically many print journalists remained faceless, and their closed network of sources has always been an important part of their strategy for remaining impartial. Working with social media exposes journalism processes and sources. Corrections are highlighted in real time so that sources like Twitter become part of the evolving story. Social media has tipped that on its head. Journalists are now more transparent and create their own personal relations and audience loyalty by interacting and being visible. This creates a shifting state of media work and a blurring of the lines between producer and consumer (Hedman and Djerf-Pierre 2013). Moreover, growth in trained citizen journalists increases the possibility that journalists can be trumped by more complete representations of news events produced by citizens.

The training that's offered to students is also offered to journalists to help them across their own epistemic divide. This training and associated literacies form a common digital language (CDL) across spheres of communication. This CDL is crucial to enable alternative journalism to be produced in the community to a professional standard, while still retaining its alternative weight. Vizibee's Neha Manaktala believes "mobile is where our starting point is and where the audience is as well" (in Reid 2013). As Professor Puentedura (2013) observed, mobile is the conduit in the home–work–play–home continuum—the bridge between audiences. As Head of Deloitte Mobile, Ilico Elia reminds us "mobile is the social in social media," the campfire of old, made digital. A common mobile language will enable a more politicised global campfire conversation. Mojo training provides competencies that enable even alternative journalists to question the role of journalism, to discern between Lippmann's spoon-fed view and Dewey's more reflexive purpose for it (Lippmann 2008).

Creating a CDL bridge between community, school and the professional media sphere can help make sense of society by facilitating a dialogue for change. The form of training, the level of trainer expertise and the delivery and publishing models are key considerations so that institutionalisation of practices doesn't shape the space in ways that underestimate mobile's full potential.

NOTES

1 B roll is footage used to visually describe a situation, a point made in an interview and to cover narration.

2 See Chapter 10.

3 See CNN's use of iReport UGC to color their reporters' stories; see the use of UGC in the plane on the Hudson River story and the Boston bombing.

4 Self-shot is a term I use to define early experiments in UGC.

5 Over-the-top (OTT) content describes broadband delivery of video and audio (Netflix, Now TV) without a multiple-system operator being involved in the control or distribution.

REFERENCES

Archer, M. (2007). *Making Our Way Through the World.* New York, Cambridge University Press.

Benson, R. and E. Neveu (2005). *Bourdieu and the Journalistic Field.* Cambridge, Polity Press.

Bishop, R. et al. (2009). "Te Kotahitanga: Addressing Educational Disparities Facing Māori Students in New Zealand." *Teaching and Teacher Education* **25**(5): 734–742.

Bloom, B. and D. Krathwohl (1984). *Taxonomy of Educational Objectives, The Classification of Educational Goals, Handbook I: Cognitive Domain.* New York, Longman.

Boczkowski, P. (2004). *Digitizing the News: Innovation in Online Newspapers.* Cambridge, MA, MIT Press.

Bourdieu, P. (2005). "The Political Field, The Social Science Field and the Journalistic Field." In R. Benson and E. Neveu (eds.), *Bourdieu and the Journalistic Field.* Malden, Polity Press.

Burum, I. (2012). "Using Mobile Media to Create a More Diverse Public Sphere in Marginalised Communities: How to Mojo." *International Journal of Community Diversity* **12**(1): 11–22.

Burum, I. (2018). *Democratising Journalism Through Mobile Media.* Abingdon, Routledge.

Castells, M. (2008). "The New Public Sphere: Global Civil Society, Communication Networks, and Global Governance." *The Annals of the American Academy of Political and Social Sciences* **616**(78): 78–91.

Clark, L. S. and R. Monserrate (2011). " High School Journalism and the Making of Young Citizens." *Journalism* **12**(4): 417–432.

Constanza-Chock, S. (2011). "Digital Popular Communication Lessons on Information and Communication Technologies for Social Change from the Immigrant Rights Movement." New York, Wiley Online Library: 33.

Deuze, M. (2012). *Media Life.* Cambridge UK, Polity Press.

Dewey, J. (2012). *The Public and its Problems.* Edited and introduced by M. Rogers. Pennsylvania, Penn State University.

Forde, S. (2011). *Challenging the News: The Journalism of Alternative and Community Media*. Basingstoke, Palgrave Macmillan.

Gentikow, B. (2007). "The Role of Media in Developing Literacies and Cultural Techniques." *Nordic Journal of Digital Literacies* **2**: 78–96.

Hedman, U. and M. Djerf-Pierre (2013). "The Social Journalist: Embracing the Social Media Life or Creating a New Digital Divide?" *Digital Journalsim* **1**(3): 1–18.

Hirst, M. (2012). *One Tweet Does Not a Revolution Make: Technological Determinism, Media and Social Change*. AcademiaEdu. www.academia.edu/1789051/One_tweet_does_not_a_revolution_make_Technological_determinism_media_and_social_change.

Jenkins, H. (2008). *Convergence Culture: Where Old and New Media Collide*. New York, New York University Press.

Lippmann, W. (2008). *Liberty and The News*. Princeton, Princeton University Press.

McLuhan, M. (1964). *Understanding Media: The Extension of Man*. New York, Penguin.

Meyrowitz, J. (1998). "Multiple Media Literacies." *Journal of Communication* **48**(1): 96–108.

Mosco, V. (2004). *The Digital Sublime*. Cambridge MA, MIT Press.

Narisetti, R. (2018). Keynote speech at the session titled "New Media Landscape: Content Fit for the 21st Century" at Inspirefest 2018. www.youtube.com/watch?v=DfakdXk5EXs.

Newman, M. and J. Park (2003). "Why Social Networks are Different from Other Types of Networks." *Physical Review E* **64**: 36–122.

Patching, R. (1996). "900 into 300 Won't Go:Are Australia's Journalism Courses Producing Too Many Graduates?" *Australian Journalism Review* **18**(1): 53–64.

Puentedura, R. (2013). "Technology In Education: A Brief Introduction." www.youtube.com/watch?v=rMazGEAiZ9c.

Reid, A. (2013). "How Newsrooms Manage UGC in Breaking News Situations." www.journalism.co.uk/news/how-newsrooms-manage-ugc-in-breaking-news-situations/s2/a553185/.

Ruud, G. (2016). Interview with I. Burum.

Small, S. and M. Memmo (2004). "Contemporary Models of Youth Development and Problem Prevention: Toward an Integration of Terms, Concepts and Models." *Family Relations* **53**(1): 3–11.

Soldal, H. (2019). Interview with I. Burum.

Tuchman, G. (1978). *Making News: A Study in the Construction of Reality*. New York, Free Press.

Wenger, E. (2001). "Supporting Communities of Practice: A Survey of Community-Oriented Technologies." Self-published report. www.ewenger.com/tech.

Wenger, E. (2007). "Communities of Practice: A Brief Introduction." In *Communities of Practice.* Cambridge UK, Cambridge University Press.

Williams, R. (2000). "Culture is Ordinary." In B. Levinson (ed.) *Schooling the Symbolic Animal: Social and Cultural Dimensions of Education.* Lanham, MD, Rowman and Littlefield Publishers: 31–35.

APPENDIX

RESOURCES

Here is a short list of mojo resources that may help hone your expert skills.

BOOKS

MOJO: The Mobile Journalism Handbook: How to Make Broadcast Videos with an iPhone or iPad by Ivo Burum and Stephen Quinn (Focal Press 2015), ISBN: 9781138824904. This was the first book written on mobile journalism praxis and basic theory and is one of Routledge's most-sold media books. www.amazon.co.uk/MOJO-Mobile-Journalism-Handbook-Broadcast/dp/1138824909

Democratising Journalism through Mobile Media by Ivo Burum (Routledge 2016, 2018) part of the Routledge Journalism series. www.amazon.co.uk/s?k=democratising+journalism+through&i=stripbooks&ref=nb_sb_noss

Mobile Storytelling: A Journalist's Guide to the Smartphone Galaxy by Wytse Vellinga and Björn Staschen (Kindle ebook, March 2018). www.amazon.co.uk/dp/B07BMH43X1

The Live-Streaming Handbook: How to Create Live Video for Social Media on Your Phone and Desktop by Peter Stewart (Routledge 2017), ISBN: 9781138630055. www.routledge.com/The-Live-Streaming-Handbook-How-to-create-live-video-for-social-media/Stewart/p/book/9781138630055

Smartphone Video Storytelling by Robb Montgomery (Routledge 2018). www.taylorfrancis.com/books/9781315206288

BLOGS AND WEBSITES

BBC Academy is a journalism education blog from the BBC that covers all aspects of journalism. www.bbc.co.uk/blogs/academy

Mobile Storytelling, a blog by Dutch television journalist and mobile journalism trainer Wytse Vellinga, is an excellent practical resource. http://mobile-storytelling.com

SmartFilming is a blog in German by mobile journalist Florian Reichart. Florian's "blog roll" provides links to more than a dozen mobile journalism blogs around the world, many of which are in English. https://smartfilming.blog

Smartphone Film Pro is a blog managed by video journalist Neil Sheppard. One of the best sources of free information about apps, equipment and techniques. www.smartphonefilmpro.com

Smartmojo is a blog written by the author of this book, Ivo Burum, that provides tests, how-to videos and other mojo training information. http://smartmojo.com

Journalist's Toolbox is a vast online resource for journalism in general. It has an excellent subsection on mobile journalism, which is regularly updated and includes links to websites, blogs, online guides and news stories. www.journaliststoolbox.org/

Mojo-Manual by Corine Podger is an excellent online mojo resource. http://www.mojo-manual.org

Mojo Workin', written by the author of this book, Ivo Burum, is a series of articles on gijn.org that answer many questions about mojo. E.g. https://gijn.org/2018/06/04/mojo-workin-developing-and-producing-on-a-smart-phone-part-1/

Global Investigative Journalism Network (GIJN) at gijn.org is one of the most comprehensive resources and everything digital journalism. https://helpdesk.gijn.org/support/home

ARIJ Resources. The Arab Reporters for Investigative Journalism has a number of mojo tip sheets in Arabic and English. https://en.arij.net

IJNET. New mobile journalism guide has free resources for reporters and newsrooms. https://ijnet.org/en/story/new-mobile-journalism-guide-has-free-resources-reporters-newsrooms

sraquinn.org by Stephen Quinn contains information and many useful tips on creating and teaching mojo. https://sraquinn.org

The Mobile Side is a blog by Francesco Facchini in English and Italian. www.themobileside.com

Titanium Media by Glen Mulcahy https://titanium-media.com/blog and his old blog which is great, tvvj.wordpress.com

Philip Bromwell https://vimeo.com/philipbromwell

MOJO TRAINERS

Neal Augenstein (@AugensteinWTOP), radio reporter at WTOP. Mojo trainer: https://iphonereporting.com

Ivo Burum (@citizenmojo) global trainer and university lecturer. Mojo trainer: https://smartmojo.com and YouTube Ivo Burum www.youtube.com/channel/UCbzXc_2w8MusLgal2w2fS_Q

Marc Blank-Settle (@marcsettle). Mojo trainer: BBC Academy: bbc.co.uk

Glen Mulcahy (@GlenBMulcahy), founder of Mojofest. Mojo trainer: https://titanium-media.com/blog and his old blog which is great, tvvj.wordpress.com (English)

Stephen Quinn (@sraquinn) is a journalist, wine author and mojo trainer. Stephen has written more than 20 journalism books. https://sraquinn.org/mojo/

Corrine Podger (@corinepodger) works and trains across the digital space. http://www.mojo-manual.org

Björn Staschen (@BjoernSta), NDR journalist: bjoernsta.de (German/English)

Peter Stewart @TweeterStewart, live-streaming trainer and radio broadcaster

Wytse Vellinga (@WytseVellinga), journalist and mojo trainer: mobielejournalistiek.wordpress.com (Netherlands)

Nick Garnett (@nicholasgarnett), BBC reporter: nickgarnett.co.uk (English)

Robb Montgomery (@robbmontgomery), mojo trainer: robbmontgomery.com

Martin Shakeshaft (@m_shakeshaft), video journalist, mojo trainer: martinshakeshaft.com (English)

Philip Bromwell (@philipbromwell) https://vimeo.com/philipbromwell

GLOSSARY

4k 4k will have a resolution of at least 3840 × 2160. The result is a picture with about 8.3 million pixels, about four times that of HDTV.

1080p 1080p is a high-definition video format with a resolution of 1920 × 1080 pixels. The "p" stands for progressive scan, which means that each video frame is transmitted as a whole in a single sweep.

360p The majority of YouTube and Hulu videos are/were displayed in 360p. It is generally referred to as 640 (horizontal) × 360 (vertical).

720p It means the image has 720 lines of "vertical resolution," the entire image is 1280 × 720 pixels (approx. 920,000 pixels in total).

A roll The primary editorial media content in digital video and film editing.

Actuality Content from the scene that doesn't have to be set up, such as police doing their job at an accident (sent from location or packaged later). In some countries it also refers to packages containing the voice(s) of the newsmaker(s), as well as of the reporter.

Ad lib Improvised, unrehearsed and spontaneous comments.

Algorithm A very specific instruction written for a computer to enable them to undertake predefined tasks.

Anchor The key narrator of a newscast or other program.

Archive As a noun, an archive is the media that has been stored in a retrievable format.

Artificial Intelligence (AI) AI exists when software can make decisions outside the data strategy and rules set by humans, to form new solutions.

Aspect ratio The ratio of width to height for an image or screen. The North American "analog" television standard (used until late 2010) used the almost square 4:3 (1.33 wide by 1 high) ratio. Since digital and HDTV receivers, picture ratios widened to 16 × 9. Now with multi-platform, multi-screen devices aspect ratios are even more relevant.

Autocue The computer or app that shows the script to the presenter in front of the camera lens. Script is usually only three or four words wide, so the reader's eyes don't travel too far when reading the script on air.

AVID A professional non-linear edit system.

B roll Supplementary or backup material. B roll is used to cover narration, jump cuts, and to introduce and highlight aspects of an interview.

Back-announce Where the presenter returns after a taped item or studio interview and adds extra facts, either a last-minute update, a reiteration of a major point, or something the journo forgot to put in the script.

Bandwidth Measured in bits per second, bandwidth describes connection/exchange speeds to the World Wide Web.

Bit rate Speed at which bit positions are transmitted, normally expressed in bits per second.

Broadband Communications channels that are capable of carrying a wide range of frequencies—broadcast television, cable television, microwave and satellite are examples of broadband technologies.

Broadcasting The one-way dissemination of any form of radio-electric communications utilising pre-assigned radio frequencies intended to be received by the public.

Bug A colorful graphic that appears either as a watermark or 100% on a screen to identify the network or journalist.

Burnt-in time code A time code is made visible or "burned in" to a dub. A dub with a burnt-in time code can be used to choose the exact location of a shot or soundbite in advance of or during an edit.

Cable The term cable (television) networks describes the means used to distribute TV and radio broadcasts by means of broadband cables and denotes networks outside the traditional free-to-air group.

Camera person An operator of a camera either in a studio or in the field.

Character generator A studio device for electronically projecting text across a television screen. Feature on high-end mobile edit and specialist graphics apps.

Chief of Staff The CoS will assess stories, assign early reporters and crews and act as a sounding board for story planning and editing.

Chroma key In TV it is an electronic matting process of inserting one image over a background. Used very commonly with weather readers. Feature on high-end mobile edit apps.

Close-up (CU) A tight video shot, generally of the face and neck, used to capture emotion and facial detail.

Closed question A question that results in a *yes* or *no* answer. Not recommended unless you want a *yes* or *no* reply.

Codec Computer algorithm that is used to compress the size of audio, video and image files to enable faster streaming and publication. Examples of codec: Video = H.265, H.264, MPEG-4, MPEG-2. Audio = AAC, MP3, Vorbis.

Color correction The changing of color shadings in a video picture. Feature on high-end mobile edit and specialist apps.

Compression The application of any of several techniques that reduce the amount of video or audio information required to represent that information in data transmission. This method reduces the required bandwidth.

Continuity (filmmaking) The maintenance of continuous action and self-consistent detail in and between the various scenes of a film, TV broadcast or online video publication.

Copyright Protects the author's right in published or unpublished original work (for the duration of its author's life plus 70 years) from unauthorised duplication without license, due credit and compensation. A copyright protects the work not the idea.

Cost per click System where an advertiser pays an agreed amount for each click someone makes on a link leading to their web site.

Crawl Information put across the bottom of the screen as a newsflash.

Credit Opening credits are shown at the beginning of a show/movie after the production logos and list the most important members of the production. Closing credits come at the end of a show and list all the cast and crew involved in the production.

Current affairs An in-depth exploration of the news: current cultural, political and social events of importance at the present time. Often the reason for producing current affairs stories is to understand the *why* of an event.

Cut A form of an edit (when a shot is cut for length) that butts against another edit. It's also how we refer to an edit of a scene of a show e.g. the 1st cut, the 2nd cut etc.

Data-driven journalism A term in use since 2009 to describe a journalistic process based on filtering large data sets to use in a story.

Day editor The person who dictates what stories the reporters will do (in consultation with the Chief of Staff and the Network Editor) and approves the script after rewriting.

Dead air A video term for silence where there should be sound, perhaps resulting from a gap in audio between edits.

Defamation Any false communication, either written (libel) or spoken (slander), that harms a person's reputation; decreases the respect, regard, or confidence in which a person is held.

Digital media Any type of information in digital form including computer-generated text, graphics and animations, as well as photographs, animation, sound and video.

Editor The person who edits video shots together to form scenes and programs. It can also be a person in charge of a television strand.

ENG Electronic news gathering, mostly but not solely associated with crews working with Betacam cameras.

EPG Electronic program guide.

Executive Producer Has editorial, managerial and creative responsibility for a program and can also be the series writer.

Extra wide shot (EWS) Used to establish location; sometimes incorrectly referred to as an extra-long shot.

Eyeline The screen direction that the talent is looking at, either from the right side of the camera to the left or vice versa.

Ferrite Advanced audio recording and edit app.

Field Producer A person who works outside the headquarters studio—in the field—to supervise the production of programs or segments. In a magazine program, this person often directs the program.

Floor Manager The director's representative on the TV studio floor. The studio control room (namely the director) addresses the crew and talent through the FM.

Format An established system standard in which data is stored.

Format (television) Template of a program that contain program elements, stylistic signatures, editorial, talent and break information. Formats are currency and certain companies just develop formats. Formats are described in format bibles, which can be licensed. Example: a *Big Brother* license could cost more than A$20 million.

Frame The PAL system has 25 frames of video per second (fps), NTSC is 30 fps.

FTP File Transfer Protocol is a system for transferring files online.

Gimbal A motorised arm that keeps the smartphone steady while recording.

Headroom The amount of room in a frame of video between the top of a subject's head and the edge of frame.

Headline The title or description at the top of a news release, article or video, used to describe and attract attention.

HTML Hypertext Markup Language, the language used to mark up text files with links for use with browsers.

iMovie Edit software for Mac computer and iOS smart devices.

Intellectual property (IP) An asset that is the product of brain rather than brawn. Examples include patents, trademarks and copyrighted material.

Internet A worldwide system for linking smaller computer networks together via TCP/IP protocols.

Interstitial An intentionally intrusive 1–5-minute story or advertisement that loads between TV shows and Web pages.

JPEG Industry standard for image compression for photos, reducing them to a small percentage of their original file size.

Jump cut A transition between two shots which appears to "jump" due to the way the shots are framed in relation to each other.

Kinemaster Edit software for iOS and Android smart devices.

Lavalier (lapel) microphone A small microphone that can be clipped onto clothing.

Lead Another term for "Intro." The paragraphs that the presenter reads that lead into your tape item. Also called "the link."

LED Light-emitting Diode. A semiconductor which emits light.

Line Producer The key manager during daily operations of a feature or TV film or series.

Line-up Producer In news, bulletin producer who decides order of stories in the bulletin.

Link Another term for "Intro" that the presenter reads.

Listening shot Often called a noddy, this is a shot of someone listening to another person (interviewee) talking. Often used to insert over a jump cut.

Live cross The same as a live cross in radio, except it involves the talent or journalist being on screen. Involves having a crew and a Links Van.

Live read Where the presenter reads a script on an autocue.

Livestream Livestream is a video streaming platform.

Lower-third Refers to the bottom section of the TV screen when used for banners or the general location of name supers.

LumaFusion Edit software for iOS smart devices

Magazine format A program made up of varied segments on a variety of subjects or themes hosted by a presenter. Examples: gardening and cooking shows.

Matte The electronic keying of two scenes (laying in of a background image behind a foreground scene).

Medium close-up (MCU) A camera frame that is between a medium shot and a close-up, generally showing a person's head and shoulders and part of the chest. Usually a preferred interview shot.

Mojo Mobile journalist who uses smartphones and hybrid tools to develop, produce, edit and publish content and stories, often from location.

Montage The editing of a series of shots to tell a story.

Mid shot (MS) A camera frame between a close-up and a wide shot.

Multi-cam The use of two or more cameras simultaneously to shoot a scene from more than one angle.

Name supers The text that appears in the lower third of the screen to identify a person's name and title.

Narration The use of written or spoken commentary to convey a story point to an audience. It's a story glue that requires B roll.

NatSot Stands for Natural Sound on Tape. We don't use much tape these days but the term remains. This is the sound, usually recorded by the camera mic, laid down on Track 2 of the camera tape. It might be animal sounds from the zoo or parliament.

Net neutrality Essentially net neutrality suggests Internet service providers (ISPs) need to treat all Internet content equally.

Noddy An old-fashioned camera technique where the journalist (or the talent) are shot pretending to be listening intently and nodding.

Non-linear editing Computerised editing that allows for numerous audio and video tracks and for sections of content to be moved around the edit timeline almost instantaneously.

Off the shoulder Also known as "hand-held." This is where the camera operator takes the camera off the tripod so he can follow the action more closely.

Online Editor This editor does the final video compile and will tidy up all shots, insert final graphics, often do the grade and can even do a running audio mix.

Open question A question that asks *why* and requires more than a *yes* or *no* answer.

Opening titles See *credits.*

Picture lock-off The last edit of a program that has passed editorial scrutiny, which has had the picture and audio locked and is ready for an audio mix, a picture grade, graphics and delivery.

Piece to camera (PTC) Also known as the "stand-up." This is where the journalist speaks directly to camera for 10–20 seconds. It's used for a number of reasons: no pictures; ego; analysis; seguing the story from issue to issue.

Podcast The broadcast of audio content in a story form either dramatic, factual or entertainment. Podcasts are published on the Internet.

Post-production Also known as a compile edit, it happens after picture lock-off and includes music, graphics, track-lay, mix, credits.

Point of view (POV) shot A camera shot seen from or obtained from the position of a performer's perspective.

Pre-production Includes planning, research, script writing, developing taped segments to be dropped into a live production, hiring and rehearsing.

Pre-sale A financial indication by a broadcaster that they want your idea. It can unlock further funding.

Premier Pro Digital non-linear edit software. See also *Final Cut, Avid.*

Producer Oversees all aspects of video production for television, cable and online platforms.

Promo Refers to a video or audio segment that promotes the activity conducted by radio, TV or online Web TV programs.

QuickTime QuickTime is a multimedia framework developed by Apple Inc.

Resolution 640 × 360, 1280 × 720, 1920 × 1080 and even 6k. The higher the resolution, the more definition and the larger the file size.

Schedule Determines the budget and hence the format. A schedule includes line items from pre-production through to delivery of the program.

Screen direction (180 degree rule) An imaginary line called the axis connects the characters, and by keeping the camera on one side of this axis (within 180 degrees), the characters' eyeline and continuity is maintained.

Sequence A set of related events, movements, actions, dialogues, shots that follow each other in a particular narrative.

Shotgun microphone A directional microphone commonly used in run-and-gun news and documentary-type factual production that sits on top of the smartphone.

SMPTE timecode Society of Motion Picture and Television Engineers' system of giving each frame of video a number to allow indexing and control.

Streaming Video or audio content sent in compressed form over the Internet and displayed by the viewer in real time.

Stringer Also used in radio, this is a person who can be hired to fill in generally as a camera person or journalist.

Subtitles Text that appears to translate words spoken in a foreign language.

Synopsis A summary of the main point of your story or program usually written as a one liner, a paragraph and a page.

UPSOT Stands for "Up Sound on Tape." This is a studio or edit direction by the journalist or script writer. It means the vision editor, or director, should raise the background sound that's on the tape.

User-generated content (UGC) UGC is the term used to describe any form of media that was created by consumers or end-users of an online system or service and is publicly available via social media.

User-generated story (UGS) A collection of UGC edited in a narrative form to tell a video story.

Voice-over Words spoken by an off-camera narrator over the video.

Wipe An electronic effect that wipes up, down, left or right, from one still or video shot to another.

Wide shot (WS) A shot that shows a wide version of e.g. your presenter, journalist, or talent interacting on location.

Wireless microphone A microphone receiver and transmitter not connected by a cable.

INDEX